Pass It On

Pass It On

A Practical Approach to the Fears and Facts of Planning Your Estate

Barbara Shotwell

and

Nancy Randolph Greenway

HYPERION
New York

LIBRARY OF CONGRESS CATALOGING-IN-PUBLICATION DATA

Shotwell, Barbara
   Pass it on : a practical approach to the fears and facts of planning your estate / Barbara Shotwell and Nancy Randolph Greenway.—1st ed.
      p. cm.
   Includes index.
   ISBN 0-7868-6580-6 (hc)
      1. Estate planning—United States—Popular works.   2. Estate planning—Caricatures and cartoons.   3. Estate planning—Humor.
   I. Greenway, Nancy Randolph   II. Title.

KF750.Z9 S486 2000
346.7305'2—dc21

99-049481

Book design by Richard Oriolo

FIRST EDITION

10 9 8 7 6 5 4 3 2 1

Dedicated to the One I Love

To those who have gone ahead,
but left a wonderful legacy behind.

Mom, Dad, Toby, and Christy
Gibby, Jim, Mother, Jimmy Z., Judy, and Mrs. G.

Contents
Hit Parade

Acknowledgments   *For He's a Jolly Good Fellow*   xiii

Prologue: Recognizing the Need
Let's Face the Music and Dance

Ties That Bind   *American Pie*   7

Get Smart   *That'll Be the Day*   9

1: Getting Started
Think

Family Harmony   *Wouldn't It Be Love'r'ly?*   16

A Very Good Place to Start   *We've Only Just Begun*   18

Gathering the Facts   *Get Ready*   20

Making a List   *Checking It Twice*   20

Long-Term Needs   *Anticipation*   26

Family Discussions   *Yakety-Yak*   27

We Can Work It Out   *Send in the Clowns*   28

Let's Get Together   *Yeah, Yeah, Yeah*   32

Finding the Pros   *Shop Around*   36

Placing the Call   *Getting to Know You*   38

Setting Up a Team   *Come Together*   41

Contents

2: Essentials
If Ever I Would Leave You

The Will   *Where There's a Will, There's a Way*   46

   What Happens Without a Will   *Do the Mashed Potato*   48

   What Constitutes a Valid Will   *Ain't Nothin' Like the Real Thing*   49

   Appointments   *If You Want This Choice Position*   56

   Married Couples Making Wills   *Side by Side*   60

   Distributions Under a Will   *It Had to Be You*   62

   Special Instructions   *Listen to What the Man Said*   70

   Distributions Outside a Will   *Whatever Will Be, Will Be*   72

Other Essential Documents   *With a Little Help from My Friends*   73

   Power of Attorney   *I'll Be There*   74

   Health Care Power of Attorney   *Someone to Watch over Me*   77

   Living Will   *Let It Be*   77

Location of Documents   *Searchin'*   81

   Safe Deposit Boxes   *Behind Closed Doors*   82

Periodic Review and Update   *Turn Around, Look at Me*   83

Unified Transfer Tax   *Who's Afraid of the Big Bad Wolf?*   85

3: Trusts
Come Rain or Come Shine

Trust Basics   *Peaceful, Easy Feelin'*   88

   Revocable or Irrevocable   *Did You Ever Have to Make Up Your Mind?*   90

Helpful Tax Loopholes   *Here We Go Loop-de-loop!*   94

   Unlimited Marital Deduction   *You Make Me So Very Happy*   95

   Unified Tax Credit   *Money, Money*   95

Credit Shelter Trusts   *Gimme Shelter*   96

Marital Trusts   *Tea for Two*   98

Irrevocable Life Insurance Trusts   *You Bet Your Life*   103

Contents

Charitable Trusts:
CRATS, CRUTS, NIM-CRUTS, and CLTS   *Sweet Charity*   107

Generation-Skipping Trusts   *Teach Your Children Well*   111

Grantor-Retained Trusts   *Return to Sender*   112

    GRATs and GRUTs   *Half Heaven, Half Heartache*   113

    QPRT   *True GRIT*   115

A Trust by Any Other Name   *I Heard It Through the Grapevine*   116

4: Putting Your House in Order
Hold on, I'm Comin'

Gifts   *Hot Diggity (Dog Diggity Boom)*   119

    Completion of a Gift   *Got to Give It Up*   120

    Incomplete Gifts   *Oh, Dear, What Can the Matter Be*   121

    Deathbed Transfers   *In the Midnight Hour*   122

    Tax Advantages of Lifetime Gifts   *I'm into Something Good*   123

    Valuation of Lifetime Gifts   *Super-cali-fragil-istic-expiali-docious*   125

    Planned Giving   *When You Wish upon a Star*   127

    Gifts to Minors   *The Candy Man*   129

    Restricted Gifts   *Call Me Irresponsible*   133

Step-Up at Death   *The Morning After*   135

Entitlements   *A Little Bit Me, A Little Bit You*   137

    Property Titles   *From a Jack to a King*   137

    Property Rights   *Ticket to Ride*   139

Protecting Assets from Creditors   *The Way We Were*   142

Emergency Funds   *Pennies from Heaven*   146

Contents

5: Special Situations
That's Life

Divorce and Remarriage *Breaking Up Is Hard to Do* 150

  Pre- and Postnuptial Agreements *Fifty Ways to Leave Your Lover* 151

  Protecting the Family Estate *Show Me the Way to Go Home* 154

Elderly and Disabled *Help!* 158

  Government Programs *High Hopes* 160

  Long-Term Care Insurance *You'll Never Walk Alone* 163

Incompetence *Still Crazy After All These Years* 167

Singles and Widows *O Solo Mio* 170

Unmarried Partners *Sign of the Times* 174

  Unmarried Parents (All Parents, For That Matter) *Parent Trap* 181

  Childless Couples *Born Free* 186

6: Qualified Retirement Plans
When I'm Sixty-Four

Elements of a Qualified Retirement Plan

  She Works Hard for the Money 190

Types of Retirement Plans *I've Been Workin' on the Railroad* 192

Plan Distributions *Know When to Hold 'Em, Know When to Fold 'Em* 197

Beneficiary Designations *B-I-N-G-O* 201

7: Closely Held Businesses
Heigh Ho, Heigh Ho, It's Off to Work We Go

Continuing a Business *Jeopardy* 207

Types of Closely Held Businesses *Eight Days a Week* 208

  Sole Proprietor and Self-Employed *My Way* 208

  Family-Owned Business *We Are Family* 211

Contents

Partnership   *It Takes Two to Tango*   213

Family Limited Partnership   *It's a Family Affair*   213

Family Limited Liability Corporation   *That's the Way I Like It*   214

Corporations   *Risky Business*   215

Transfer or Sale of a Business   *Taking Care of Business*   217

Buy–Sell Agreements   *Hello Goodbye*   219

Private Annuity   *There's a Kind of Hush*   221

Installment Sale   *You've Really Got a Hold on Me*   222

Valuation   *The Price Is Right*   224

Valuation Methods   *Let's Make a Deal*   224

Freezing Techniques   *Time in a Bottle*   227

Special-Use Valuation   *Home on the Range*   229

Tax Deferral and Exclusion   *Take It to the Limit*   230

8: Final Arrangements
Happy Trails

Funeral and Burial Arrangements   *When the Saints Go Marching In*   235

Precatory Letter   *Gonna Sit Right Down and Write Myself a Letter*   239

Prepaid Funeral Plans   *Sounds of Silence*   241

Probate   *It's Too Late*   243

How Probate Works   *The Long and Winding Road*   243

Types of Probate   *Guess Things Happen That Way*   245

Who Assumes Responsibility for Probate?   *Big Shot*   247

Probate Costs   *Ain't That a Shame*   249

Is Probate All That Bad?   *It Ain't Necessarily So*   251

Settling the Estate   *After You've Gone*   252

Thanks for the Memories   *Twilight Time*   262

Contents

Big Scary Words (and Other Mysteries of Estate Planning Explained)

The Name Game   265

Index *A-B-C*   275

Without music, life would be a mistake.

— Friedrich Wilhelm Nietzche

Acknowledgments
For He's a Jolly Good Fellow

Countless family, friends, and associates deserve our thanks for their support, as well as the expertise and creativity they brought to the work.

We thank Gail Ross of the Gail Ross Literary Agency for understanding the urgency of the issues at hand and taking on our project. Thanks also to Howard Yoon at the Ross Agency for polish. Mary Ellen O'Neill at Hyperion recognized the unique character of our book from all the way at the other end of the baby boom. Her enthusiasm and commitment to the project made our work a pleasure.

Margaret Moore and John Shotwell—our family is smaller now in quantity, but never lacking in quality.

Barbara Kelley and Michael "Doc" Franey permitted no "bad heir days"—thanks for your tremendous sense of humor. Thanks also to "The" Lydia Chavez, who pointed us in the right direction all the way from Havana. We are grateful for the legal expertise of Karen Hansen and Glenn Kessel, and especially for their generous gift of time in reviewing the manuscript.

Thank you to the whole gang at PaineWebber, particularly personal messenger Connie Kopietz, and Dana Evans who is always a breath of fresh air. Special thanks to my associate Julie Schmiel for her hazardous duty in the tropics and her ongoing, invaluable assistance.

Bobi Murphy, Tom, John, and David Randolph, Margi Hacker, and Melissa Handa know all they have meant to the conception and writing of this book.

Thanks to T.F. Jackson III for sharing his amazing intellect; and to Nathan Guequierre, whose pen and perspective are truly inspirational. Valerie and Larry Thompson are ever true; and thanks to Lawrence Thompson, proofreader *extraordinaire*.

Dad, thank you for your wisdom, guidance, and the wonderful lake view. Mr. G., your inimitable spirit and kindness are examples to us all. Pamela Cunningham, Mercy! Laudie Greenway, Amen! And Betsy and Gibby, nothing happens without you.

Pass It On

Recognizing the Need
Let's Face the Music and Dance

What's Goin' On . . .

- The perils of poor planning
- Benefits of a good estate plan
- Taking responsibility
- The call to action

We all have to face the music sometime. What if the worst happens? The phone rings. It's bad news. Fonzie has gone to his great reward— for him it would mean fast cars, motorcycles, and plenty of women poured into leather, no doubt. Maybe not too bad for the Fonz, but his old friend Richie hangs up the phone in shock. He has absolutely no idea what to do. What would the Fonz want? Where should he be buried? Does he have a will, or life insurance? What does he own? And who on earth would know?

An estate plan, while perhaps not the most exciting of plans, is a necessity of life. Anyone with sense would choose to make a plan. To waltz in, smooth things over, snap his fingers, and make a graceful exit.

To build the meataphorical Bridge Over Troubled Waters and take comfort in the fact that the beat will go on. The Fonz, like most of us, wouldn't have it any other way.

This book is not about dying, but about living—and keeping one's perspective. Luckily, we have been able to keep ours through the losses of many who were near and dear. We write this book based on our experiences with those close to us who died sooner rather than later.

One of us lost a young husband who had a will and a well-planned estate, and left two small children. Each of us has lost a brother who had no will. In one case, the brother was single with a professional business of his own. In the other, the brother left a wife and two young children. One lost both parents after long illnesses; the other, a mother by tragic accident. In our close families, uncles, young cousins, and a niece have died long before their time.

We have been executor, custodian, and trustee; have dealt personally with wills, trusts, a sizable family business, distribution of family property, and retirement plans; have endured funerals, burials, and probate. And we have learned a great deal along the way.

Having been friends since college days, we stayed in touch over the years, occasionally lamenting our losses and rather extensive "careers" in coping with the various estates. Weren't we lucky to have the professional background to deal with the legalities and investment questions involved in administering an estate? we thought. And hadn't we learned the hard way not only how the process works, but how it could be made easier? The entire experience had, in fact, strengthened us. If only we could put it to good use. Thus, the idea for *Pass It On* was born.

Experience had also taught us that like any family gathering, even a meeting to discuss a will or a funeral is bound to have moments of levity. This is precisely the reason we have used humor in our book. A good belly laugh has a scientifically proven positive effect on health and general well-being. In time, one realizes that humor is a saving—and truly amazing—grace.

Recognizing the Need

Life does not cease to be funny when people die any more than it ceases to be serious when people laugh.
—George Bernard Shaw

Estate planning is not a dreadful task. It is neither as dull nor complicated as you might believe. It does, however, require initiative. We owe it to ourselves and those close to us to accept the inevitable. Some of us probably think we can control things beyond the grave, but think again.

Picture yourself in mid-1850s London. Smoke, fog, soot, and squinty-eyed characters dressed in black waiting around every corner. In Charles Dickens's aptly named novel, *Bleak House,* the entangled Jarndyce family battled over a large estate through hell, high water, decades, and generations.

The will that had been presented to the probate court was challenged from every corner, and the lawyers of Bleak House were little help. In fact, quite the contrary. Entirely too willing to continue pressing their suits and countersuits, they kept the family at each others' throats—and kept the meter running—until the valid will was finally discovered. Unfortunately, by then the entire estate was lost to lawyers' fees, and nothing at all was left for the heirs.

"What could be worse?" you might ask. Consider how Archie Bunker might have felt had he known his whole estate—primarily his favorite chair and his union card—had gone to the Meathead after Edith and Gloria were killed in a stampede at a Republican rally for Richard Nixon?

Or imagine the surprise of Dick and Jane's children upon discovering that their parents had left their very substantial estate in trust for their dog Spot (soon to be recognized by Willard Scott on his hundredth birthday).

Truth is stranger than fiction. The fate of your family, fame, or fortune depends on your making an estate plan. Where money and property are involved, families have lied, stolen, cheated, married, divorced, even murdered, among their own. Don't let this happen to you and your family!

HIS AND HERS
(WHEN HE DIES)

*　　*　　*

Naturally, none of us looks forward to the death of a parent, a favorite aunt or uncle, or anyone close to us. But how many can say, in all honesty, we have not dreamed of actually owning that cabin at the lake, getting our hands on the silver, or selling off the works and settling our debts, or sailing around the world on a whim?

Our parents, many of whom scraped through more than a few lean years, have much more to leave us than their parents left them. In particular, the baby boomers not only stand to inherit more than any previous generation—an estimated *$10,000,000,000,000 (that's ten trillion!) or more*—but with smaller families, we can live well and preserve more to pass on to *our* children.

Recognizing the Need

Saving is a very fine thing.
Especially when your parents have done it for you.
—Winston Churchill

Before we start shopping for yachts, we must cope with that ever-present, greedy relative, Uncle Sam, who stands ready to take a big chunk of what is rightfully ours! In some cases he'll clean us out completely and break up our families—not to mention what he can do to small family businesses and farms, which may soon go the way of the dinosaur.

A good estate plan includes a will and other essential documents, each designed to minimize the effect of estate taxes. Although not every estate actually pays tax, current federal rates are steep, ranging from 37 to 55 percent. In some cases, combined federal and state taxes on the estate, plus income taxes due during estate administration, can add up to more than 70 percent. Top it off with legal fees and there might not be much left for your family.

John D. Rockefeller, Sr., was apparently better at making money than holding on to it. Sixty-one percent of his $27 million estate was lost to settlement costs including taxes. Walt Disney's estate fared considerably better, losing less than a third of its $23 million value along the way.

What is the difference between a taxidermist and a tax collector?
A taxidermist takes only your skin.
—Mark Twain

While most of us are not concerned with millions, we are all well aware that we pay taxes all our lives. We're taxed on the money we earn, the money we spend, on some of what we keep, and the profit on anything we sell. Our taxes build the roads, and we are taxed on the automobiles and fuel we buy to use those roads. None of us likes the idea of paying taxes again on what we are lucky enough to have left when we die. The good news is, we don't have to.

"You know, the idea of taxation <u>with</u> representation doesn't appeal to me very much, either."

Planning—or not planning—your estate can have dramatic results. If you do nothing, you create unnecessary stress and work for your family, and line the pockets of Uncle Sam. You might end up holding a lifelong grudge because life isn't fair, being jealous of those who have more, or wallowing in self-pity and guilt because you have squandered your opportunities.

But if you act like a grown-up and make a plan, you win in every way.

Ties That Bind
American Pie

Let's skip ahead . . . *w-a-y ahead.* None of us wants to die, but we all will. Unfortunately, some sooner rather than later. If you want to keep your home, your savings, your investments, and your heirlooms in the family, make plans *now* while you have your wits about you, while your better judgment is not tainted by undue influence or (heaven forbid!) senility. Let's face it, we are not going to take it with us, and there is a lot more at stake than taxes.

In settling an estate, the circus of sibling rivalry and other family jealousies and tensions, certain to bring out the worst in everyone, can be most distressing. You may think you know your brother and your sweet little sister, but beware. The prospect of inheritance elicits unfamiliar strains in nearly everyone's character. It is important to strike a happy balance with everyone involved.

The original "Me first!" generation has taken for granted the stable influences of "old-fashioned" family harmony, which has served as a generational security blanket. We baby boomers think we can always have it our way simply because styles and markets have chased us with a vengeance all our lives. Even hamburgers have been sold to us because we can have them our way.

Then: Passing the driving test
Now: Passing the vision test

For some, the real boom of recent decades has been financial. As markets have soared, many baby boomers, now in middle age, have accumulated enough wealth to live comfortably, often very well.

Many have a comfortable home, a couple kids, a couple cars, and a couple jobs to stay afloat financially. Others have become new-age consumers with fancy homes, apartments in the city, cabins at the lake, or condos on the shore or in the desert; maybe a boat, a motorcycle to get through the midlife crisis, ski vacations, winter trips to the tropics, and on and on.

For a remarkable number of baby boomers and others, life is good, and for those lucky souls, an estate plan is critical to wealth preservation. But for *all* of us, even those of very modest means, a plan of some sort is necessary. For the sake of ourselves and our family's well-being, we ought to know what we have, what we need, and whether Uncle Sam is going to claim a share.

It is crucial not only to consider how to plan our own estates but also to recognize what we might inherit, and to discuss the situation with our parents. They may not be aware of desperate needs among their children and they would probably like to know if no one wants the silver tea set.

Parents, whose blood, sweat, and tears gave rise to well-to-do adult children, might rather spend what they have on themselves than preserve it for those who don't really need it. They'd feel better if they heard you say, out loud, "I don't really need it."

Parents might make gifts now not only to enjoy the giving, but to avoid taxes that will diminish their estates later. If they want to leave their property to you, they might as well preserve as much as possible. Perhaps they need a lawyer, or a better lawyer, a second opinion to confirm their plans, or just a bit of help locating pertinent documents. What they most certainly want and deserve is an offer of assistance, some honest information, and the privacy to make their own informed decisions.

Short sermon. It is important to be a decent child to your parents and a decent parent to your child, to be considerate of your relatives and friends who have special needs, who have done the unexpected or to whom the unexpected has been done. Respect and fairness in living preserve the most powerful legacy and probably a good deal of comfort in dying.

"Would you mind stepping out of the sixties, please?"

When not busy having it your way, or being decent, which rarely occur at the same time, take a minute to contemplate how you and your brother and sister are actually going to manage to "share" that family cabin. Who will take care of the house painting and the leaky roof? Who will choose the new canoe, and what if you don't even want a new canoe? Is it worth the trouble and expense if you can't have the cabin every Fourth of July? What if you want your money instead of a share in the cabin?

The way to get the most, keep the most, pass it on, and still have a happy family gathering every Thanksgiving is to think about it, talk about it with *everyone* involved, and plan it from every practical angle.

Get Smart
That'll Be the Day

Everyone needs a plan—perhaps not a fancy plan with trusts and tax schemes, but a basic "game" plan that will work for you and your family. Estate planning requires perspective and the advice of an expert; nevertheless, it can be accomplished quite easily and will prevent big disappointments and unwelcome surprises down the road. A thoughtful plan brings everyone concerned into the loop and helps keep the peace.

Little House, Big Trouble

After retiring from farming, Charles and Caroline Ingalls moved to Minneapolis to be closer to daughter Laura and her family. They spent long weekends and vacationed for most of the summer at the little house on the prairie with their children and grandchildren coming and going. When Charles died, the homestead was left to Caroline, who hoped she and the entire family would continue to treasure and enjoy the old place.

Laura took her family and her mother out to the little house whenever they could all get away. Mary, a working wife and mother, had moved to Seattle and came back to the little house every summer for vacation. Carrie had recently married Willy Oleson, who had taken over his folks' general store in Walnut Grove, and together they were able to keep a watchful eye on the property.

The Ingalls's youngest daughter, Grace, was in agriculture school in California and rarely had time to get back to the little house, though she looked forward to the day when she could turn it back into a working farm. Albert, the Ingalls's adopted son, was still working at the mill in town. Since Caroline had gone to the city, he thought he might just move back to the little house and make it his home. Well . . . that idea didn't go over very well, and there was no peace on the prairie for the next year or so.

Level-headed Laura huffed. She had been taking their mother out to the country nearly every other weekend, making routine repairs and paying for incidentals along the way. Albert not only wanted to move in, but he was pushing his mother to build a new barn for his stock cars. The girls thought the old barn was just fine and Mother should not have to lay out a lot of cash for Albert's benefit—and besides, they wanted a pool.

Then Grace announced that she was bringing her aggie pals up for the week of Mary's long-planned family vacation, and sweet, agreeable Mary blew up. There wasn't enough room for everyone and, furthermore, she had counted on having the place to herself for some much-needed family R & R. She said that was it—she would not be back east until Grace understood that family comes before friends. Everyone was mad and the pressure was on Mother, Carrie, and even Willy to take sides.

Caroline could see her family falling apart over the cherished little house that meant so much to all of them. They loved it to a fault, each feeling possessive and entitled, and Caroline could not bear it. She resolved to get her family back together no matter what and figured she'd simply sell the place to eliminate the problems.

Thankfully, Caroline did not make a rash decision, but called her lawyer before calling the real estate agent. She learned about trusts, family limited partnerships, life estates, and joint ownership, but mostly about the importance of addressing the sticky issues now. And the lawyer convinced Caroline that it was possible to work out a solution within the family and prevent the sale of the homestead.

Caroline invited everyone to the little house for Thanksgiving where the common-sense lawyer they all knew and trusted helped her present the options over pumpkin pie and hot apple cider. They talked it all over, all the concerns and gripes were aired, and Caroline made her decision—which did not immediately please everyone. But the deed was done. Mary, Laura, Carrie, Grace, and Albert would receive equal shares, and have equal rights and responsibilities.

The only person immediately thrilled was Caroline. She knew she had done what was fair and best for her family, as well as for her own peace of mind. And everyone now knew what to expect. No amount of pouting or pressuring or wrangling would change it. And so, over the years everyone adapted. Peace returned to the prairie and, except for predictable passing family disagreements, the little house, which could have been big trouble, was shared and enjoyed by the Ingalls's for generations.

Everyone should, at the least, have a will, a living will or health care power of attorney, and either a durable or springing power of attorney. Those with significant assets would be wise to consider a trust, insurance plan, or gift program to counter the effect of estate taxes. Specific situations, such as living with a disability, owning and working in a family business, or sharing finances with an unmarried partner, require custom-tailored solutions.

> *I thatched my roof when the sun was shining, and now*
> *I am not afraid of the storm.*
> —George F. Stivers

This friendly guide to passing it on walks through the essential elements of an estate plan, with a view toward the expanding wealth and diverse life situations of new-millennium America.

We do not intend to make light of a serious matter, but rather to throw in a little humor to ease the difficulty of getting the subject on the table. A lot of people are intimidated by the big, scary words and the legalities involved in planning an estate. But it could be even more frightening for your family to face a long and costly paper chase in settling your estate. Our purpose is to get past the fears and cut through the confusion often associated with planning and settling an estate.

- First things first. An estate plan begins by assessing personal and family situations. **Chapter One** dispenses a large dose of reality along with suggestions for getting started. Tips on making an inventory, identifying long-term needs, and initiating forthright discussions with those who matter are included.

- **Chapter Two** addresses the essentials of every estate plan: the will, powers of attorney, and the living will. The criteria for timely review and proper location of documents close the chapter.

- **Chapter Three** describes trusts, from basics to specialty trusts. Learn how to protect your family and property, and cut out Uncle Sam.

- The estate-planning potential of gifts and title to property are included in **Chapter Four**. Property and assets with certain forms of title are protected from creditors and could provide ready cash to those we leave behind.

- **Chapter Five** covers the not-so-uncommon lifestyles that need a little extra attention. Those who are divorced and remarried, as well as singles and widows, unmarried partners, single parents, and others have specific estate planning needs that are addressed step-by-step in this chapter.

- The complicated but very predictable elements of qualified retirement plans, like the 401(k) and IRA, are addressed in **Chapter Six**. Assets in these plans represent the largest— sometimes the only—nest egg of many Americans. Beneficiary designation and method of distribution have a tremendous impact on an estate plan.

- For others, the family business, explained in **Chapter Seven**, is the most important asset. Form of ownership and a plan to keep the business going are critical to the estate plan of every owner.

- The end is near. In **Chapter Eight**, funeral and burial, probate, and estate administration are explained in detail. No one looks forward to it, but knowing is half the battle. It's easier to cope with what we understand.

Explanations and descriptions provide general guidelines—meaning just that. Each circumstance is unique, requiring legal and financial expertise specific to state law, the property, and individuals involved.

This book is not designed as a legal treatise on estate planning or a do-it-yourself guide. The object of the exercise is to point out the pitfalls and some surprisingly simple solutions to familiar situations and problems. We encourage you to seek professional help and, perhaps most importantly, to have open and honest discussions with family members and loved ones to put your mind to rest long before you are laid to rest.

We want to help people become more comfortable with the issues of estate planning and get the subject on the table by giving it to them straight—and laughing a little as we go.

He laughs best who laughs last.
—Sir John Vanbrugh

1

Getting Started
Think

What's Goin' On...

- Evaluating your personal situation
- Anticipating long-term needs
- Starting the family discussion
- Finding the right pros
- Assembling your estate planning team

*It requires a great deal of boldness and a great deal of caution
to make a great fortune, and when you have got it,
it requires ten times as much wit to keep it.*
—Ralph Waldo Emerson

The most important—and toughest—part of planning your estate is simply to get started. Thankfully, the first item on the agenda is easy. All you have to do is think, follow your better judgment, and apply a healthy dose of common sense.

Begin by thinking about what you own. Next, remind yourself that This Is Your Life. Consider what you will need to provide for yourself, and those for whom you are responsible, for the rest of your life. Finally, think about what legacy and property you wish to leave behind, and to whom. You may be tempted to make a few notes, but stay in free form for the moment. Keeping track of your thoughts is the second step in the process.

When you stop to think, you will realize that you really *do* want to look after yourself, preserve your property to the best of your ability, provide for those you leave behind, and keep your family and closest companions together. And, like any sensible person, you want to pay the lowest possible taxes.

The thinking exercise is not necessarily compelling or pleasant, but it is critical. Once you get started, the process will begin to make sense and unfold quite naturally. If you find yourself procrastinating, do a reality check. Think about half your property going to taxes. Think about your family and loved ones falling apart because you left them out on a limb. Think about the forced sale of your family home or business. Motivate yourself. If you know the tune, hum along with Aretha, and Think.

> *Most people would die sooner than think; in fact, they do so.*
> —Bertrand Russell

Family Harmony
Wouldn't It Be Love'r'ly?

Attorneys report that the primary motivation behind most estate-planning inquiries is a strong personal desire to avoid anguish, disagreement, and disharmony in the family. No matter what the value of an estate—a modest retirement plan and family home, or millions invested in the market—family harmony is generally the first consideration.

Mentally review your group dynamics. If your family gets along, you've probably worked at it, and had some good luck. Do whatever you can to keep it that way. Family harmony is a precious commodity—an invaluable resource of personal strength, support, and comfort to each of us. If blessed with it, we usually take it for granted. Without it, families place blame, hold grudges, and hurt those they love most. Remember, every family has "baggage" and is at least a bit dysfunctional.

Consider potential problems. If you gave Jane a law school tuition loan, which she never repaid, do you want to make that up to Dick in

"This isn't a hasty decision. A lot of daydreaming went into it."

the will? You might think that what Dick never knows will not hurt him. Doubtful.

If you have transferred part of the family business to Dick, will Jane be furious if she doesn't get equal value under your will, even if she did marry a very successful banker? You bet. She is as much your child as Dick is, and feels equally entitled.

What if you remarried after their mother died and your new wife wants it all? Those who have remarried—or are in committed, unmarried relationships—face a variety of special considerations. And parents of minor children have critical obligations.

Planning an estate provides a golden opportunity to mend fences by bringing your family or other loved ones into the process. Old jealousies and grudges fade against a united effort for mutual benefit.

Each of us has unique concerns to address. Count on the fact that everyone in the family wants a piece of the action. Especially your good old Uncle Sam. There are many ways to diminish the effects of estate taxes, and every angle is worth consideration.

*　　*　　*

Fast forward. Picture your family together, deeply saddened by your departure, but not having the foggiest idea of how to take care of your affairs. They will do what they think you would want. And you wish you had talked with them about "things," don't you?

Life goes on. An estate plan does not die with you, but also lives on. The opportunity is yours—here and now—to make picking up the pieces after your departure a little less frightening for your family, and less costly in every way. Somewhere in the back of the mind that insists you are immortal, you have probably already thought about what you own and who should have it. It's time to act upon your thoughts.

A Very Good Place to Start

We've Only Just Begun

Starting at the beginning is always a good idea. A lot of us think anything to do with wills or estates must take place in the lawyer's office, but legal matters can be intimidating. Before going to a pro, even to ask questions, it is important to understand certain legal terms and the elements of an estate plan, and to do some legwork on your own. You also want to be able to understand everything the pro is saying. Throughout this book, and in the glossary at the back, legal terms are defined as straightforwardly as possible to help cut the confusion.

Seniors and others who might not be able to understand their lawyers—the same way we are all sometimes confused at the doctor's office—may need to ask their families and friends for help. No matter how confused you are (or become) by any estate planning issue, do not hesitate to ask questions. It is essential that you completely understand your situation and everything you are about to do.

Only You can truly understand the delicate issues surrounding the potential distribution of your own property. When meeting with your lawyer or other estate planning professional, you want to have a good idea of what you hope to accomplish.

Approaching your lawyer before adequately addressing your personal situation will cost time, money, and (more) gray hair. To begin the process of building an estate plan, your lawyer, investment advisor, accountant, or insurance agent will likely pose a few key questions. He or she will probably ask you to gather pertinent information about your assets—the value and title of real and personal property, such as your home, investments, insurance, and retirement plans, for example— before inviting you back to discuss your options.

Much of this preliminary work can be done on your own, avoiding an unnecessary and potentially expensive step in the process, and helping you get a handle on your unique situation.

Ideally, here's how it ought to go:

1. Think.
2. List your assets and gather the facts.
3. Hold a family meeting.
4. Think.
5. Locate your documents.
6. Seek professional help.
7. Think.
8. Hold another family meeting.
9. Think.
10. Make decisions and take action.
11. Go back to the pros to get the job done.
12. Keep thinking.

Whatever you do, don't stop thinking. Try not to get bogged down by all the possibilities, or the task will become overwhelming. It's not a full-time job, nor is it a project that should ever upset you. It's a bit like doing income taxes—a nagging personal assignment that can be completed in segments. Do as presidents do. Compartmentalize. As you go through this book, highlight material, write notes or questions in the columns, or turn down page corners. Do whatever it takes to remind yourself to ask the important questions, find the help you need, make decisions, and get the job done.

The brain is like a muscle. When we think well we feel good.
—Carl Sagan

Gathering the Facts
Get Ready

The practical work of making an estate plan starts with a general list of everything you own. Begin by setting aside a small block of time with a paper and pencil, alone if you like, or with your spouse, partner, significant other, children, or another who understands you and your situation well and, more importantly, whom you trust.

Some industrious souls already have inventories on computer programs or as part of old-fashioned budget plans. They're a step ahead for the moment, but must still address questions of title, value, and location for each property, and take action to protect those carefully recorded assets.

A spiral notebook is great for keeping your list and all your notes together. It's hard to lose or misplace bound pages.

Making a List
Checking It Twice

A useful format for the list is a chart with five or six columns. In the first column list the item. In the second, the item's value. In the third column, note how the item or property is titled or owned. Title is very important in determining how, or if, a property is passed along to co-owners or your heirs. The title of your home, real estate, business property, or anything with legal title, or which you co-own, ought to be noted in this column. In a fourth column record where the papers, deeds, and so forth, are located.

In the final column make personal notes about the property including the names of those to whom you consider giving or leaving the property. Write the family history or provenance of heirlooms and objects that have been in the family for a long time. Who owned the piece originally, where was it purchased or received, and what was the cost?

One very organized gentleman wrote information about each painting and piece of furniture on an index card and taped the card to the back of the paintings or inside drawers. If you own antiques or works of art, a detailed record will be very helpful both in placing a value on objects and distributing them to appropriate family members. Grandmother probably would have wanted her brooch to go to the granddaughter named for her.

Leave plenty of space for additions, changes, and questions, because as you progress you will want to jot down new thoughts and information.

Your list is a work in progress—an inventory worksheet. It does not have to be completed in one sitting, but if you take a break, be sure to make a date with yourself to get back to it, preferably within a couple of days. This is not hard work, just a little chore. And it won't take all day. Getting started is as easy as jotting down "house, car, boat, IRA, stock portfolio, silverware, diamond ring." Fill in the details as you go. If you have not already done so for insurance purposes, it might be wise to videotape or photograph your home, autos, boats, and items of personal or monetary value such as jewelry and silver. The visuals will jog your memory and assist in making a complete and accurate inventory.

It is a capital mistake to theorize before one has all the data.
—Arthur Conan Doyle

Inventory Worksheet

The first priority is to list your assets—everything you own of any value, monetary or sentimental. Include any and all property of significant value.

For **real estate**, make a note of where the property is located (particularly important if in another state), what portion you own, and how much you still owe on any mortgage. List who owns each property and how the title reads. (More about title and locating documents later.)

It is essential that your property is titled accurately, in keeping with your objectives and the law. Property owned by husband and wife, for example, may be subject to community property laws, or the rules of joint tenancy. State law often determines how property that is jointly held will be distributed, even if your will instructs otherwise.

When the time comes, a good professional, usually an estate planning lawyer, will ensure that title to your property is correct. The pro will know the law and any changes required to satisfy your wishes. The issues surrounding property title can be complicated, and it may take a little research to learn all the details, but for now, get what you do know down on paper.

If you personally own **business interests**, such as a family business, farm, or ranch, are self-employed, or are part owner of any closely held business assets, add these to the list. Follow the same format as with real property to describe your share of equity—partnership, family corporation—and exactly who has title to the property.

Add **financial investments**, such as stocks, bonds, and mutual funds, to the list. Using statements from various institutions and your own records, give your inventory a ballpark value for each of the various types of investment.

Retirement plans are considered financial investments. If you receive income benefits from a trust, the approximate income should be part of your inventory. You need not list a trust as an asset of your own unless it is revocable, like a living trust, and you control it. In that case, as explained in Chapter Three, living trust assets will be included in your estate for tax purposes, but they will still be distributed as prescribed.

Include **future interests**, such as insurance, trust distributions, and any funds or property you will or might receive in the future. This may seem a bit like counting the chickens before they're hatched, but if you know substantial property is coming to you, it should be considered in making your estate plan. In evaluating your property, don't overlook your liabilities. Personal and business debts, taxes, leases, in-

It's All in the Game

The inventory worksheet need not monopolize your time. A few minutes of thought will allow you to list and assess your properties and investments, perhaps pass probate, and collect $200 without taking a chance.

Item	Value	Title	Location of documents	Who should receive it
Real Estate				
Park Place Home	$320	JTWROS	safe	wife/ joint tenant
Atlantic Avenue Cottage	$100	one-half share, Tenant-in-common with brother JP	office	my share one-third each to wife, son Chip, daughter Dale
Business Interests				
Boardwalk Hotel	$2000	family corp. mortgage $1000, First National	bank	wife to receive 50%, Chip and Dale 25% each
Financial Investments				
B & O Railroad 100 shares	$1000	stock certificate held by broker	broker	Chip and Dale equally
Future Interest				
Family Trust at Monopoly Bank	($500 when Father dies)	residual beneficiary	bank	Chip and Dale equally
Personal Property				
railroad car	$50	bill of sale appraisal needed	desk?	donate to Community Chest
furs, jewels, cigars	$20	in safe at home	safe	after Luxury Tax distribute per precatory letter

stallment debt, and so forth, all affect the bottom line in determining your net worth.

Each of us has files of plans, policies, and accounts . . . somewhere. Some records are held by employers or financial institutions. Some are stuffed in the back of a drawer. This is a great opportunity to clean out the file cabinet. Before going to a pro, locate all your documents and pertinent information.

My Favorite Things

Listing your **personal and household items** is often the most fun and can be the most satisfying part of this process. Passing along personal treasures can be a real joy. You probably know who would like what. But you probably also have your own notions about who should receive what—especially the more sentimental items. If so, pencil it in now.

You might choose to make gifts now, while you are around to enjoy the giving. If the item has significant value, the gift will reduce the value of your estate for tax purposes. And if you make the gift now, your children won't have to fight over what mother said—and when—about her engagement ring, for example. It will be a done deal. The legal aspects and tax advantages of lifetime gifts are described in Chapter Four.

In some cases, it is most practical to leave personal items to a single trusted heir under the will, with the understanding that the items will be distributed to particular individuals. That understanding is usually based on wishes or instructions expressed in conversation or writing. For example, Snow White could leave her favorite things to Doc who, in turn, would distribute them to Happy, Sleepy, Sneezy, Grumpy, Bashful, and Dopey according to Snow White's personal instructions.

A personal list will generally not hold up in court on its own; however, a **precatory letter** (**preh**-ka-tory) containing instructions, written and signed, is usually considered legitimate. While not binding, the letter is honored by an executor whenever possible.

In a few states a precatory letter or a signed list could be considered a holographic will. And in some cases, lists that are signed and dated could be considered an addendum, or **codicil** (**cod**-uh-sill), to a will.

Unlike a will, which becomes part of the public record, a precatory letter is a private, personal statement. The letter might include who-gets-what instructions regarding items that more than one heir would like. Describe particular items, such as jewelry, and identify your intended recipient. If the letter is at all ambiguous or expresses any inkling of doubt, it will lose its effect. Funeral and burial preferences could also be declared in such a letter. To avoid misunderstanding, write a clear letter and refer to it in your will.

....

If you anticipate your kids fighting like cats and dogs over Granny's
china and silver, or mother's jewelry, clarify who gets what in a
precatory letter. Remember to include the men in distribution
of these items. They might like their wives or their children
to have something that belonged to grandmother.

....

If you have more than one residence, list the items from each residence separately—just to keep things straight. Property, real and otherwise, located in a different state from your permanent residence is subject to the laws of *that* state. A thorough list is the first step in determining how to properly title and locate assets to avoid problems.

Residuary Estate

There is a point of no return in making your inventory. You will know when you have reached it. Items of particular value and any property with written legal title should certainly be included. Personal and household property—anything movable, even a house trailer, a windmill, or a privy—not specifically bequeathed can be included in your will under a residuary clause, essentially a catch-all, and distributed as instructed. A **bequest,** or gift of personal property, is "bequeathed" or given under a will.

The inventory is a powerful tool, providing a general idea of the type of assets you own, your net worth, and how the distribution of some items is predetermined.

Long-Term Needs

Anticipation

Next, and *extremely* important, evaluate both your predictable and potential long-term needs, such as annual expenses, health care costs, and whatever it will take to continue to live and breathe, kick up your heels, travel, and do as you darn well please for the foreseeable future. Start a new list, on a new sheet of paper. It may sound juvenile at first, but we all know how hard it is to make decisions when all kinds of ideas are floating around in our heads. Little will be accomplished unless you put your needs down on paper—in real, let's-not-kid-ourselves dollars.

I have enough for the rest of my life unless I buy something.
—Jackie Mason

In exploring the future, it is necessary to play "What if?" What if you rent a condo in the desert every winter? What if you travel once a year for an extended period? What if your son never does get a job? What if you get hit by a car or have a stroke tomorrow, leaving you incapacitated, or worse? What if it happens to your wife, or unmarried partner? Examine all the possible complications of providing for yourself and those for whom you are responsible for the rest of your life. And be realistic. The best defense is a good offense. Hope for the best, but plan for the rest.

Gathering these facts and figures for long-term needs might take some doing. It involves thorough study of current and potential expenses and income. Use old checkbooks to budget future needs. Make a note of monthly expenses, such as rent and groceries; annual expenses, such as insurance and auto maintenance; potential capital expenses such as a new condo in the sunbelt; and extras such as travel and tango lessons.

Evaluate current life, health, and disability insurance, employee benefit packages, retirement plans, simple cost-of-living increases. What will you have to live on? What will the taxes be? And do you have adequate insurance?

As difficult as it might seem, consider the unthinkable, such as the expense of long-term care—a nursing home, hospice, or in-home medical care. General costs are quite easy to determine with the help of an insurance agent. (Tell him right off the bat you are not buying, but looking for general figures in evaluating your needs.)

Figure out what it would take to travel or retire to another community. Ask travel agents, real estate brokers, and moving companies about expenses. If appropriate, inquire about special opportunities and discounts available to seniors. Information is also available through local libraries and, like everything else, on the Internet.

Then: Moving to California because it's cool
Now: Moving to California because it's warm

The purpose of this book is to address the elements of an estate plan, not a retirement plan. Many investments and planning decisions affect both retirement and the distribution of your estate, and each ought to be designed to minimize taxes. Seek the advice of finance professionals to be sure you are making the most of your investments.

This is no time to be timid. This is your life, your future, your estate plan. As long as you're doing it, do a good job. Ask the tough questions. If you set the time aside and tackle the questions one at a time, you'll have what you need before you know it.

Family Discussions
Yakety-Yak

Admittedly, discussing the very personal thoughts and wishes regarding the end of our lives and rather private (*ahem*) money matters is an almost universally dreaded task. It's one thing to make an inventory and personal notes for our own use, but to discuss it all?! Just the thought of it makes us squirm.

Parents are not comfortable telling their children what they own, what they owe—what they're worth—and who they think should get what. Children are afraid to bring up the subject because they (for the most part) do not want to appear selfish or greedy. Everyone involved makes assumptions. Where second marriages, stepchildren, unmarried partners, and other common but "nontraditional" situations exist, a family discussion might be a can of worms. Yet these are the situations that most require honest communication. Remember, we are all afraid of opening old wounds and exposing raw nerves.

We Can Work It Out

Send in the Clowns

Not having the family discussion is almost always more harmful than having it. We can recover from hurt feelings, but what if a home, or business, or a big chunk of stock has to be sold to pay taxes—just because you were afraid to ask a question?

Most of us believe You Can't Always Get What You Want—maybe not even what you need—but there is no reason for Uncle Sam to come out smelling like a rose at the expense of your family. If you have learned the hard way that your family or friends made mistakes in drafting their wills or making financial plans, you have seen what can happen and know what it costs. Try not to repeat the mistake.

There are ways to begin successful conversations with parents, children, and anyone involved in estate planning issues. To get beyond the fear of making the first move, try looking at the situation from a viewpoint other than your own.

Parents of the baby boomers, Tom Brokaw's *Greatest Generation*, have seen just about everything. While they are generally not forthcoming with unsolicited personal information, it is practically impossible to surprise the older generation, except perhaps with the current cost of an automobile. (*"How can a car possibly cost that much? That's outrageous! Why, that's more than my first house cost!"*) Theirs is a realistic generation, which is more than can be said for many of the baby boomers—though at forty and fifty, we are showing signs of redemption.

Most people—even those who are not realists—are usually willing

"I get the 'boomer' part but I don't get the 'baby' part."

to discuss their estate planning concerns, private or otherwise, because they truly want to do the right thing. Each of us knows what we'd like to say or do, given the chance. For the most part older people do not want to be a burden, and younger people, though worried about invading the privacy of their elders, are genuinely willing to help. Planning an estate involves big, important issues. The only way to get the conversation started is to muster the courage. Here's how.

Be positive. Make the assumption that everyone who might be affected by your estate plan, or that of your parents, wants to do the right thing. Getting the subject on the table is good for everyone involved. Family discussions are almost always more fruitful than anticipated, and usually bring great satisfaction as well as a collective sigh of relief.

The key to successful family discussion is an approach that is conciliatory, not confrontational. For some, this is the trickiest work. Follow conventional wisdom. Think before you speak. Listen well, to everyone

Father Doesn't
Always Know Best

Jim and Margaret Anderson were proud of their children. "Kitten" grew up to be a serious student. After six years of medical school, financed through a series of scholarships and student loans, she became a successful brain surgeon in Chicago.

Bud pursued his love of cars and set up shop as an auto mechanic. Though not a big financial success, he is well-respected in the Springfield community, with a lovely wife and children.

Betty—acting more the "Princess" every year—dropped out of secretarial school to start her own acid rock band. Betty and the Bad Apples went on the road across small-town America. Jim was continually tapping into his pension and rushing to Western Union to bail her out of one crisis or another.

Jim and Margaret knew an estate plan was needed to make sure their modest estate went to the kids as they intended. They agreed that since Kitten had achieved financial success, nothing need go to her.

They wanted Bud to have a little extra for family vacations and planned to leave him $30,000.

The house and the balance of the pension plan would go to Betty, the lost soul who needed it most.

involved. Dwell on the subject. Make your decisions slowly and purposefully—in your own time.

Money is a touchy subject for every family. Many of us assume that if we bring it up we look greedy. But money is only one part of a meaningful estate plan. If you want to talk to your parents about their situations, ask about their health care, retirement plans, and the house. Find out what they want and need. Ask them if they have any problems, or fears. Are they comfortable and secure? Are they afraid they might end up alone? Help them review a few things they might have overlooked, and the costs associated with their plans.

Some parents may not want help from their children. But they will

Luckily for the Andersons, their estate planning lawyer was proactive, not reactive. He encouraged them to discuss their plan with the children—especially the decision to cut Kitten out. They figured she, more than anyone, would appreciate their thinking.

WRONG! Little Kitten threw a tantrum. She had worked hard to put herself through medical school and did not feel she should be penalized for her tenacity while Princess was rewarded for being a vagabond "musician." Even easy-going Bud was peeved.

Jim and Margaret, ever eager to do the right thing, organized a little family meeting, listened to the concerns of each of the kids, and decided to divide their estate equally among them.

At the prospect of an inheritance, Betty began planning a reunion tour for the Bad Apples, so Margaret and Jim decided to place her third in a protective trust. She couldn't get at the assets, but would receive benefits as needed.

Bud was thrilled to receive the family home as his share, and Kitten was pleased to be included at all.

The moral to the story? Father, Mother, and the proactive lawyer did know best. The family discussion saved the day. Betty was busted, Kitten had become the princess, and Bud ran all the way home.

appreciate an offer made in earnest. You know the old, "Don't worry, it's all taken care of" answer. If this is what you get, and you are pretty sure your folks haven't much of a plan, try (if the planets are aligned and the gods are smiling) blurting out the truth. Tell them you want to be sure that they will have what they need, and want to know if they are counting on you for anything. Let them know you are willing to help, of course.

If you are interested in anything they have—the piano, the trophy moose head, or great-grandmother's sugar bowl, tell them so. Believe it or not, they want to know. They also want to know if you are *not* interested in anything in particular, or for whatever reason are unable

"And don't go auctioning off my stuff."

to assist them in later years. They probably know by now on which family members they can rely.

Let's Get Together
Yeah, Yeah, Yeah

If you are unlikely to get your parents to talk about their plans, open the conversation by asking them to help you with yours. "We are writing our wills and making plans for the kids, and are hoping you might advise us based on the plans you have made." Invite them to dinner, tell them you want to talk, and ask for help. How did they make their decisions? What arrangements have they made for long-term care, or where do they keep their paperwork? You might just discover a few things you can do for them. And you will undoubtedly learn that they have thought about it, and will have some valuable advice.

Offer to help them review their plan if they have not done so for several years, or to serve as executor. Tell them you are concerned about

It's Showtime!

If you want to put on a "Really Big Shoe," get your act together. It might be a high-wire act, to be sure, and you may have to juggle at times. But with a couple of stars who can swivel their hips or shake their mops to bring in the audience, a few comedy routines, some good music to keep things light, and consideration of the notables in the "audience," you're ready.

A master of ceremonies, willing to play the gracious host even when he is bumbling about, and ill at ease, will be the Toast of the Town.

their big house. How will it be maintained if something happens to one or both of them? Ask what they expect or need from you.

If you are the parent or head of the clan, invite the appropriate family members or friends to a meeting. Tell them what it's about. Approach the meeting in a businesslike manner. Set a time limit and establish a few goals for the meeting. "Your father and I are making our plans for the future and we have a few questions for you. Does anyone want the house?" "If you're all interested, what are your suggestions for managing it?" "Who would rather have the money than the condo?"

Families are increasingly separated by geography. Bette has gone to L.A., James has moved to Martha's Vineyard, and Bill has taken on Washington, while Mother and Dad are still at home. Thankfully, e-mail and conference calls can accommodate a family "meeting" almost as effectively as a living room. Where all else fails, personal letters work just fine.

If you are thinking of cutting an heir out of the will, let that heir know your intentions and consider mentioning it at a family meeting. Straight talk often gets results. An individual who stands to be disinherited for certain reasons just might mend her ways. If unequal distributions have been discussed and accepted, make sure everyone understands that their decisions are binding, and a change of heart down the road will only cause huge problems.

If the discussion is likely to be stressful or argumentative, consider inviting your lawyer to explain the legalities. Those low, purposeful, disarmingly calm voices can cut tension like a knife. If you're serving refreshments, it's a good idea to put the issues on the table before the cocktails.

More than one meeting might be required. Consider making your first meeting an exploratory discussion and plan a second meeting to discuss options and decisions. If in the end your will is challenged, the meetings could serve as proof of your state of mind and verification of the instructions in your will. Those who accept certain distributions in the presence of others will be hard-pressed to argue to the contrary at a later date.

Refrain from inquiring about an individual family member's willingness to serve as executor, trustee, guardian, or agent until after at least the initial meeting, and after you have given the matter serious thought. When you have chosen your executor, trustee, and so forth—and each individual has accepted the responsibility—a family announcement is in order. Explain that you chose those suited to the job, that your choices had nothing to do with loving one person more than another. Keeping everyone informed forestalls jealousy and power struggles.

> *Coming together is a beginning; keeping together is progress;*
> *working together is success.*
> —Henry Ford

Any significant change in circumstances provides a valid reason to raise the subject of estate planning or suggest review of an existing will or plan. Moving, buying a house or other real property, marrying, divorcing, having a child or children, and changes in health, job status, or income are milestones marking new responsibilities that cannot be overlooked.

A very effective way to invoke solidarity in the family is to scare up the enemy—and there is only one: the tax man, our good old Uncle

Sam. The government will tax your property heavily if allowed. But you and your family can beat the enemy if you work together.

These strategies may seem silly, and some certainly are. But they work. The idea is simply to get the ball rolling. If that is all you accomplish, you will have improved your situation. Use a cartoon from this book, a family gag, or any line clever enough to break the ice. A series of casual conversations might lead up to an "appointment" to meet and discuss facts and figures. Take a deep breath and do whatever it takes.

Send in the Clowns—Really!

If all else fails, walk right up to your folks wearing a red nose à la Patch Adams and announce, "I'm here to talk about estate planning, and I'm not going to take off this red nose until you agree." Take along noses for them, if it might help. Hopefully, laughter will break the ice!

Wake Up Little Susie

Wives whose husbands don't share financial information need to get a handle on their own situations. One man, whose wife had stayed at home raising the children and having dinner ready at five o'clock on the dot, took his wife's Social Security check from her saying she hadn't earned it. This is unacceptable at any age or stage of life. After all, we go around only once.

Significant others often find themselves in the same boat, pouring personal finances into mutual accounts or projects that work more to one partner's benefit. Pay attention, oh liberated ones, and keep track of what is rightfully yours. Laws favor married couples and blood relatives over unmarried partners.

Heads up, husbands and gentlemen. This is a new millennium. Spouses, partners, and significant others are entitled to—and now have the legal means to procure—a fair share. Including spouses and partners at every turn is the only reasonable approach to a complete estate plan.

Families are funny (not the ha-ha kind) about revealing personal needs and desires. Tell them right out front that you care about keeping the family together and are determined to do what you can to make it so. Whatever you do, keep at it until it works.

Finding the Pros
Shop Around

When you have decided roughly what you want to accomplish, it's time to call in the professionals. You might need a team, or you might need only a lawyer and a financial advisor. If you already have a will, and it's still what you want, you might need only a living will (not actually a will—see Chapter Three) or a power of attorney, and a review and update of your life insurance or living trust. Any substantial change in your lifestyle or your assets requires rewriting or adding legally correct changes in a codicil to your will, as well as a review of other estate planning documents.

Finding the pros is not Mission Impossible, but a straightforward, methodical process. Choose only pros you know and trust to help you—not a pal or an acquaintance, perhaps not even a good friend. Getting to Know You—in the professional sense—means learning about the reputation and expertise of the person who will be instrumental in putting your estate plan in place. Good friends sometimes gloss over details, with, "I know just what you need," or "I'll take care of it. Don't worry about a thing."

All of us deal with attorneys and insurance people from time to time, but may not know The Right One. A little research will save a lot of time, money, and exasperation. In every case seek an individual with training and experience specific to estate planning, and settle for nothing less.

Think of someone you trust, who has had a good experience, whose assets are exceptionally well managed, or who might give you an entrée to a professional network. Ask friends, associates, your lawyer, or your broker for referrals. Steer clear of cronyism by accepting no fewer than three recommendations, and be sure to call them all.

If you are without leads, call the local or state professional associations or check the Internet or the Yellow Pages for referral services.

Always ask for three references. If you are not given three, try another referring agency.

Matchmaker, Matchmaker

Lawyers and accountants are usually the first line in an estate planning team. Many have specialized or have done extensive work in a specific field, such as family trusts, retirement plans, or estate tax. Experienced lawyers usually develop their own trusted networks of accounting, tax, and investment specialists, and vice versa. If you have a reliable lawyer or tax advisor, ask her or him for recommendations of other estate planning pros.

Stockbrokers and financial planners are increasingly expanding their services. As Internet trading has limited the demand for routine broker services, reputable brokerage firms are offering broader financial planning expertise including legal, tax, accounting, and insurance referrals. Many brokers are licensed insurance agents themselves.

Banks are in the business of preserving assets. Many have trust departments and personal asset departments specifically designed to assist their clients with estate planning and wealth preservation. A bank might be named as trustee or executor, especially if there is a long-standing relationship with the client's family.

Private investment advisory firms do it all. Experienced financial professionals manage assets, serve as trustees, and work closely with a handpicked network of lawyers and tax specialists. Ask friends and associates for recommendations of investment advisors. Be aware that many have a minimum investment requirement. In choosing a financial advisor of any type, consider investment performance as well as level of service and personal rapport.

Qualified **insurance agents** are a bit more difficult to locate. There are plenty of respectable name-brand insurance companies out there, including many that advertise estate planning expertise, but finding an experienced agent who will work with other members of your team to meet your needs is paramount.

Insurance agents sometimes get a bad rap because they're selling a product. But the variety and nature of insurance products make insurance agents aware of many estate planning opportunities. All professional referral services are selling a "product" of sorts—the services of their members.

Look for credentials. A CLU is a certified life underwriter; a ChFP is a Chartered Financial Planner. Certified Financial Planners (CFPs) offer expanded financial planning advice in conjunction with their primary professional expertise as insurance agent, stockbroker, and so forth.

In looking for a pro, you want to protect the fruits of your labors. Your family, your home, your property, and your life are at stake. This is no time to be shy. Make your initial inquiries by phone. Remember that trust and mutual understanding are not usually established in a phone call. Invest the time to find one with The Right Stuff. A good estate planning pro will usually offer a free, though brief, consultation. Take advantage of it.

Placing the Call

Getting to Know You

When you make your calls, be prepared with a written agenda or you will accomplish nothing. *Do not be intimidated.* You have every right to ask questions. You are the client. Ask about fees. Take notes. Even if you're talking to the old family retainer, stay the course. You are looking not only for a competent lawyer, but for one with the compassion to handle your family dynamics, and an individual who appreciates the value of family harmony. No matter how high the IQ or impressive the alma mater, a pro who is patronizing or is unwilling to deal with the smaller issues essential to your particular situation will not do.

With your priorities in mind, notes at hand, and a good attitude, you are ready to make the calls. Be direct and get the answers to your questions.

"I don't have time to talk about this now. Can't it wait until we're dead?"

Hello Central! Give Me No Man's Land

An accountant in the Washington D.C. area called the IRS about an estate tax issue. He says the IRS representative asked him: "Are you the decedent?"

—Tom Herman, "Tax Report," *The Wall Street Journal,* March 6, 1996, p. A1.

Use the following as a general guideline to get the phone conversation started:

■ I am looking for an experienced lawyer to help me make a will and consider a few other estate planning options. You were recommended to me by so-and-so. Do you have a few minutes to tell me about your estate planning training and experience?

■ How do you bill? Flat fee or hourly? What is included in the flat fee for a will? A living will? A power of attorney, including health care?

■ What is the estimated cost of creating a simple trust?

■ How long does it usually take you to prepare a basic estate plan?

■ How long to see an estate through probate?

■ Have you set up trusts before? A credit shelter, charitable, or generation-skipping trust?

■ Have you served as an executor, or trustee? Do you ever appoint yourself executor or trustee of wills or trusts you have written?

■ Are you reasonably accessible for appointments and telephone calls?

■ Will I be able to speak with you directly when I call?

■ Can we expect you to handle our wills, and so forth, personally? Will you turn the work over to an associate? If so, why?

■ Do you offer a free consultation?

Adapt the questions for calls to financial, insurance, or other professionals offering estate planning services. Be straightforward and, using a certain tone of voice or whatever persuasive talents you have at your disposal, let this person know he or she must be open and fair with you.

You might find a lawyer who can help you now *and* help your family after your death. Lawyers who draft wills sometimes serve as executors and keep wills in their offices so that they are readily available when the time comes. This full-circle relationship is not necessarily automatic, but it is often the case. Be careful of lawyers who appoint themselves trustee or executor without discussion—it verges on the unethical. Make decisions on these matters as you go along, but do not allow the lawyer to pressure you to use her services exclusively.

Anything you sign should state exactly and only what you wish. Be careful of standard, fill-in-the-blank forms. They are all the same, and therefore limited—and they are usually valid in only one state. Each situation is unique. If you have previously signed any forms or *executed* (put into legal effect) any estate planning documents, take them along to review when you meet with your lawyer. Most pros have, through experience, developed their own fairly standard forms with language that satisfies state law and has proven effective in probate court. With the technology of word processing, these forms serve as a solid foundation for creation of your personal documents.

As with everything else, in estate planning there is no such thing as a free lunch. Many lawyers who draft wills for a fee offer to throw in a health care power of attorney because it is a relatively simple document. Be sure the freebie is what you need. Ask, ask, and ask again if you are not certain about any little thing. There is no such thing as a stupid question. If you are made to feel so, you are talking to the wrong person.

Setting Up a Team
Come Together

One of the pros you select will become the quarterback of your team—usually your lawyer. He or she can oversee the development and implementation of your plan if you lack the expertise or interest to do so yourself. And you stay on as head coach.

You will not want or need to drop any of the pros who have helped you over the years, but they will all have to work together on this project. Each brings something to the party. Once you have chosen your team members, put them in touch with each other and let them go to work. Ask them to check in with you on a reasonably frequent basis. Even better, take the lead and keep in touch with *them*.

If you have an investment advisor or broker who holds your stocks or retirement plans, he will have advice based upon your investment history and will be involved in any title changes and beneficiary designations. *Beneficiaries* are those who are named—or designated—to receive benefits of a will, trust, insurance policy, retirement plan, or other legal arrangement. An accountant can determine the tax ramifications of an estate plan, but may need a lawyer and investment advisor to develop a complete plan and put it into action. A personal investment

---

We're for the Home Team, Rah, Rah, Rah!

Every member of a good team brings a certain expertise to the task at hand. Picture that lovable, crazy gang at the 4077th M.A.S.H. Unit.

When the call comes in, personal problems, adolescent antics, and dresses are left at the door. Everyone goes to work. The Colonel protects his team and keeps them focused while Hawkeye and Trapper John get to the heart of the matter. Hot Lips and Klinger tend to the details while Radar and Father Mulcahy provide critical support that makes the teamwork a success. Even in a state of constant crisis, humor is their constant companion, helping everybody cope with the unbearable.

On a winning team, everyone is there doing his or her best. A job well done is the only acceptable outcome.

---

advisor or CFP will have the expertise to complement or design certain elements of an estate plan—possibly develop the entire plan—but you will need a lawyer to draft the documents and legally transfer assets as required.

A lawyer does not do accounting and will hire an accountant (for a fee) to have work done for you. It might be extra work for you, but keeping the powers that be separate creates a little system of checks and balances. You may wish to avoid the extra expense of having one person hire or coordinate your team members. On the other hand, the expense may be incidental given the convenience, quality, and pace of the work.

To save time, you may just want to turn over the entire project to your lawyer. Do so only if you are confident that the person in charge will meet your objectives and see to all the details. If you are setting up a trust and will not serve as trustee, keep in mind that once you turn over your property you will be entirely dependent upon the trustee's integrity and financial know-how. Just one more reason to choose your pros wisely.

It's Now or Never . . .

- Be realistic in assessing your personal situation.

- Make a written inventory of your assets and estimate your long-term needs.

- Sing, dance, do whatever it takes to get the subject on the table and discuss it with everyone involved.

- Find and choose the best estate planning pros, as Sherlock Holmes would.

- Treat family harmony as your most prized possession and it will be your most valuable legacy.

2

Essentials

If Ever I Would Leave You

What's Goin' On . . .

- The will
- Power of attorney
- Health care power of attorney and the living will
- Safekeeping and periodic review of documents

Planning an estate is not an excellent adventure or a trip down the yellow brick road. You can't wing it or make it up as you go along. Consider what could be around the next bend in the road. There is precious little room for the impromptu.

Before going to your lawyer to have a will drafted, it's a good idea to understand the elements of the estate planning tools and documents you hope or plan to discuss. Naturally, we expect the pros to know the legal details, but it is important that we know what we're talking about, at least to a reasonable extent. Only with knowledge and confidence can we review what we are signing to ensure not only that it is accurate and complete, but also that each document accomplishes what we intend. Arm yourself for action.

This chapter describes the elements of a will, living will, and power of attorney, and the key persons involved in estate administration including executors, guardians, and custodians. The importance of secure but accessible storage of documents and the need for periodic and timely review of your plan conclude the chapter.

An estate plan is basically a custom-tailored collection of documents that establish how your property is held while you are alive and directs your property to be distributed in certain ways after you die. In order to be legally valid, each document must conform to the laws of the state in which you have established permanent residence, or domicile.

In our transient society, most states have now adopted the Uniform Probate Code which accepts a will that is valid in any state as an "international will." Most wills are therefore valid and legally enforceable from state to state. However, if you move and your legal domicile changes after you have executed (put into legal effect) your documents, it is generally a good idea to review and possibly revise your will to reflect the change.

Hopefully, you will already have thought about your goals, evaluated your property, cussed and discussed plans with your family. Understanding the most common documents—how each works and what each means—will help clarify your objectives, resulting in efficient, fruitful discussions with your chosen pros.

If you are quite confident about what you want to do, and have made an effort to find good professional help, getting started will be a relief. It will cost you and your family a great deal more—financially and otherwise—*not* to take care of this little task, which hangs over many of our heads like a black cloud. When you've finished, both the cloud and the little nagging guilt that accompanies it will be gone. Enough of a pep talk? Charge ahead.

Action is eloquence.
—William Shakespeare

The Will
Where There's a Will, There's a Way

We are about to give new meaning to the phrase *will power*. The most important document in a basic estate plan is the will. By law, every will must contain certain elements. Wills are as old as the hills and, until not too long ago, were just about all that was needed to transfer property at death. Historically, wills have been accepted in many forms, scribbled on scraps of paper, or simply told to trusted family members or friends.

As lifestyles have become less traditional, and wealth ever greater, wills have been *contested* (con-**test**-ed), or challenged, more frequently. The documents themselves sometimes raise questions because of poor or incomplete wording. And as more of us linger physically after our minds wander off, our intentions could quite understandably be open to debate. These days, with technology to keep us alive almost indefinitely and the tax man breathing down our necks, even simple estates often require more than a will. Yet the will remains the centerpiece of most estate plans.

Will—a dead giveaway.

It is important to have a will at every adult age. Older folks have usually acquired enough property to care about preserving it for heirs, but Generation X'ers and younger baby boomers are often cavalier, thinking that they do not own the type or amount of assets that require a will. Yet many draw hefty salaries straight out of college, which go toward glamorous—and expensive—purchases.

Young, single professionals have often accumulated larger estates than they realize. They may not care who gets their lava lamps, but the idea of giving up a big chunk of those yuppie earnings to Uncle Sam galls even the most carefree career person. It is worth making a will to ensure that your affairs are in order and your favorite things get into the right hands.

Young couples with minor children are often too busy to get around to making their wills, though without wills they unwittingly place their most precious treasures—their children—in peril. Even seniors who like their pets better than their children might not care to go to the trouble of making a will, but really must. Pet lovers often provide for their pets—don't laugh—by directing funds to a named (human) beneficiary in return for a promise to care for the pet for the rest of its life. Distributions directly to pets are not permitted. Without a will, the pet is out of luck.

"And to whom do you wish to leave the bulk of your estate, sir?"

What Happens Without a Will

Do the Mashed Potato

Those who die without a will die *intestate*. The property of a person who dies intestate is distributed according to state *laws of intestacy*. Big words for a simple concept resulting in distribution of property by the state to the nearest living relatives.

The laws of intestacy vary dramatically from state to state. In most instances, if an unmarried individual without children dies intestate, everything goes to the parents. If the parents are not living, everything goes to the nearest blood relative(s).

In some states, if a married person without children dies without a will, everything goes to the spouse. If a person is married *with* children, however, the intestacy laws of most states split an estate between a surviving spouse and children. But in a few states, the entire estate—100 percent—could go to the children. Distributions to nonrelatives, regardless of personal relationships, are highly unlikely.

Good Cause to Rebel

The original Rebel Without a Cause, *James Dean, died tragically in an auto accident at age 29, leaving no will. Under the laws of intestacy, everything—which did not seem like much at the time— went to Dean's father who had deserted the young boy after his mother had died.*

But after the image-making movie, Rebel, *was released, Dean's smoldering image of restless youth became an icon. Every movie house and poster store in the land displays and sells James Dean's image, and one generation of kids after another continues to buy it. The licensing fees turned out to be a gold mine, producing millions each year, but because Dean had not made a will, everything was payable to the unworthy father who had abandoned his son.*

What Constitutes a Valid Will

Ain't Nothin' Like the Real Thing

Everyone who needs a will (that's you) ought to know, at least generally, what is required to make the will legally acceptable. We begin by identifying the requirements of a valid will.

Legal age. Only those of legal age can make a valid will. Eighteen is legal in most states.

Sound mind. A person must be competent to make a will. The will must include a declaration of mental state ("... being of sound mind ...") indicating that you know what you're doing.

> *Lawyer reading a wise old man's will to the relatives:*
> *"And being of sound mind, I spent every dollar I had."*

Written. In most states, the will must be written. Oral and unwit-nessed, handwritten (holographic) wills, once widely recognized, are now accepted in a diminishing number of states.

Signed voluntarily. The will must be signed voluntarily, to demonstrate that you knew what you were signing and signed because you wanted to.

Witnessed. The voluntary signing of the will must be witnessed by at least two adults who then sign the will themselves to prove they were witnesses. Technically, witnesses must be available and competent to testify to such in probate court if necessary, though generally their signatures are considered self-proving *affidavits*— voluntary, sworn statements of fact which have legal validity. Some states require three witnesses.

....

Probate *is the legal process in which a will is "proven." In days of old, the court examined the will before deeming it authentic and emblazoning a seal authorizing distribution of an estate according to the terms of the will.*

These days, a will is "entered" into probate when the executor submits it to the probate court. The court issues Letters Testamentary, *a document authorizing the executor or personal representative to act upon the instructions of the will, paying debts, making distributions, and ultimately closing the business of an estate. See Chapter Eight for a full explanation of probate and the process of administering an estate.*

....

A probate court has the power to void any will that fails to meet even one requirement or raises questions about the intentions of the person who made the will. If there is no earlier will that is acceptable, the deceased (also called the *decedent*) could be declared intestate. Though not required by law, there are several other elements of a valid will.

....

Ouch!

The Johnson & Johnson family (of baby oil and Band-Aid fame) suffered through years of infamous litigation when grown children disinherited by their father challenged his will. The soundness of Mr.

Johnson's mind was questioned mostly because his loving-chambermaid-turned-loving-wife got almost everything.

The challengers said Johnson had been under duress and undue influence, was mentally incapacitated, and was a victim of fraud. Mrs. Johnson said hogwash. And the court said, just for the heck of it, let's see what Mr. Johnson's earlier wills contained. It turns out Johnson wrote a will practically every year, disinheriting whichever children were out of favor at the time. Everyone had been disinherited before.

Hot heads, hot air, and a hungry press caused a much-publicized fuss for quite a while, but in the end the family settled. Despite Mr. Johnson's will and his intentions—whatever they might have been—the challenge to the will resulted in the heirs' basically rewriting his will to suit themselves.

Domicile. A statement of domicile, or legal residence, establishes for the record which state laws govern an estate. If domicile is questioned, the probate court will examine indicators—driver's license and auto registrations, income tax returns, mailing address, proof of membership in local organizations, and legal documents such as an old will or a trust. They want to know where you really lived, not where you might have said you lived for tax reasons or whatever. If *community property* (property acquired by husband and wife during marriage and subject to specific laws in eight community property states) is at stake, domicile may be a critical factor.

If you own properties and reside part-time in several states, you should anticipate a problem regarding domicile. If for any reason you foresee a challenge, consider making a notarized affidavit or declaration of domicile to support the statement in your will. Some states, especially those with large part-time resident populations, have official Declaration of Domicile forms. Accurate personal documents and property titles support a statement of domicile and could be used to preempt a challenge by potential beneficiaries or the court. Discuss any concerns about domicile with your lawyer.

....

Boundary Hunters

The domicile of John Dorrance of the Campbell Soup family was so unclear that his sizable estate was ultimately taxed by both New Jersey and Pennsylvania, leaving his heirs a condensed estate.

All four states in which Edward Green, private citizen, owned property attempted to tax his substantial estate, resulting in a tax bill that exceeded the value of the estate. The courts ultimately ruled in the estate's favor, allowing only one state to collect the greenbacks.

Remember, an estate may be subject to state and federal, income and estate taxes, plus inheritance tax in some states.

....

Final. Make it perfectly clear that your will is your final will and testament, and clearly state your intent to dispose of your property under your will. *Testament* is legalese for statement of will.

Tell those involved that you have made a will, or a new will. Sometimes it is preferable to save old wills as proof of long-standing intentions should a new will be challenged. However, in most cases, particularly when a new will is substantially different from an earlier will, it is advisable to go on a search-and-destroy mission to eliminate all previous wills.

Executor. In your will, name an executor, called *personal representative* in some states, who—you've got it—executes your will according to its instruction. If no executor is appointed, or if the one appointed is unable or unwilling to serve, or if a person dies without a will, the court appoints an executor or estate administrator. For the sake of simplicity, we call them all executor.

The will gives the executor the specific powers needed to follow instructions and conclude the affairs of the estate—that is, to pay funeral expenses, pay "just" or "provable" debts, pay taxes, open and close accounts, and transfer property. If the estate involves a business, an executor might have to hire and fire employees, sign contracts, and so forth. While the estate is in probate, the executor has the whole world in his hands.

Serving as executor can be a tremendous burden. The appointment

YOUR GOOD
INTENTIONS
AT WORK

carries a *fiduciary duty* with the legal responsibility to follow the highest business and ethical standards. Depending on the size and nature of the estate, an executor could carry substantial responsibility and risk personal liability. In some cases, the job can be a nightmare!

At least as a precaution, give your executor the power to hire a lawyer. One never knows what legal snafus might occur. If you're quite sure your lawyer will participate in probate, introduce her to your executor. It'll make things easier for them when the time comes.

Choosing an executor is not a popularity contest. You want the best person for the job—a person who understands the task at hand, is willing and able to do it, and will perform efficiently. If you consider appointing more than one executor, choose individuals who will improve the work, not cause distractions or create conflicts.

Wives often choose husbands as executors, or vice versa, and parents choose their children. Some people appoint a trusted lawyer as executor to simplify the process. Others prefer to name a capable family member or friend as executor to save unnecessary legal expense. Whomever you choose, remember to ask if he or she will accept the job—especially if it's a big job. It could be years before the call to duty.

Consider the age of your chosen executor and ask if he is in it for the long term. Common courtesy, common sense.

Be sure to name a *successor* executor in case your first choice is unavailable when the time comes. If your executor is unable to serve and you have named no successor, the court will follow a list of priorities established by law to find a suitable executor. If a spouse or child is not available, a creditor of the deceased could be appointed.

If you are asked to serve as executor, trustee, or guardian, take the question seriously. Can you handle the job? Do you have the time? Are you comfortable with the responsibility vis-à-vis the family and beneficiaries involved? If necessary, ask to review the will to fully understand your role. It is generally considered an honor to be asked. Make sure you can—and want to—handle the job.

An *executor's fee* representing "reasonable compensation" is usually designated under a will. If the executor is also a beneficiary of the estate, the fee customarily is waived. For larger estates, a fee ceiling will encourage the executors to act expeditiously. To avoid income tax, an executor's fee is sometimes established as a bequest. When determining your executor's fees, remember that—no differently from anything else—you usually get what you pay for.

It is not legally required that a lawyer take an estate through the process; however, many executors prefer or need to use the services of a probate lawyer. Usually an executor and lawyer submit the will to the probate court together. An executor cannot act until and unless appointed by the probate court. Only after the will has been "entered" into probate and letters testamentary issued by the court is the executor empowered to act.

When the administration of the estate is complete—the distributions to heirs made, the trusts set up, the minors safe in the care of their guardians, the bills and taxes paid, and the dust settled—the executor or lawyer presents a statement of his work to the probate court, and the court officially closes the estate. It's all over.

*   *   *

Most state laws require executors to take out a *surety bond*—at the expense of the estate—in an amount that will protect your estate should the executor mishandle the assets or not perform his duties. It's a little insurance policy.

A premium is paid to a company that guarantees at least part of the value of the estate—usually the liquid assets—and the bond is issued. The actual amount of the bond is determined by the court. Any loss in value of the estate due to the nonperformance, negligence, or abuse of the executor is made up by the bond.

If your estate is fairly straightforward and you completely trust your executor, you can save a little money by declaring in your will that your executor is not required to post a bond. Absent such a statement, the bond is generally required.

A will includes statements and instructions of all variety. The language must be absolutely clear concerning the property and persons you intend to include, as well as those you intend to exclude—names, addresses, rationale for extraordinary instructions, and legal descriptions of property, if necessary.

Consider exactly how to leave property to your heirs. Some property may be titled in such a way that it is unaffected by your will, as in *Joint Tenancy with Right of Survivorship,* where the surviving owner gets it all. The potential for such an "automatic" transfer explains why title to your home and other real estate is extremely important. With imprecise or incomplete wording, your will might unintentionally exclude someone, or a group of people, you intended to include. Be sure your lawyer uses terms specific enough to avoid any confusion.

Statutory Wills

A few states allow statutory wills—free, fill-in-the-blank forms that are valid in the respective state when properly completed, signed, and witnessed. Whether you currently have a statutory will or are considering one, it is strongly recommended that you pay the minimal fee to have a lawyer review it. A simple, honest mistake could be very costly.

Changing a Will

Minor additions and amendments to a will are made in a properly executed *codicil* that becomes part of the original will. Substantial changes that alter your original intentions or affect legal requirements open the entire will to challenge, and therefore usually warrant making a new will.

Appointments
If You Want This Choice Position

The people you appoint or recommend in your will for certain responsibilities, including executor as explained above, could end up looking after your spouse, children, partner, or business. They ought to offer a good deal more than professional expertise.

Aim high. Choose only those who are completely trustworthy. And be sure to ask each appointee if he or she is willing to accept the job.

Trustee. If, in your will, you create a trust, you must also appoint a trustee to manage and distribute trust assets for the benefit of those you name (the beneficiaries). Trusts are created for all varieties of reasons, perhaps to provide for a certain individual(s), protect the estate from unnecessary taxes, or preserve property for future generations.

Choose a trustee who has the necessary experience and expertise, but also understands the purpose of your trust. If it is to protect and provide for an elderly spouse, a qualified family member or close friend who knows the spouse well would be a good choice. There is more information about trusts and trustees in Chapter Three.

Guardianships operate to benefit and protect those who are unable to care for themselves. Minor children, the legally incompetent or mentally ill, addicts, and senile elders all need protection. Some could need guardianships.

If you have *minor children*, you have a responsibility to name a guardian for them in your will. If something happens to you and/or your spouse and a guardian has not been named, the court will name one for you. This is not to be taken lightly. A guardian will do nothing less than raise your children.

Then: Being called into the principal's office
Now: Storming into the principal's office

If your children are old enough, you might want to ask how they feel about it. As hard as it may be for them to envision life without you, they will know, perhaps much to your surprise, whom they would choose, or choose not, to have as a guardian. Children are filled with jewels of information. Hello Muddah, Hello Faddah.

Be sure you understand how a guardianship works before making any decision. A *personal guardian* is responsible for the well-being—for food, clothing, shelter, health care, and so forth—of an individual, called a "ward." A *property guardian*, in some states called a guardian of the estate, manages financial affairs and property for the benefit of an incapacitated person or a minor.

In most cases, one person is appointed to do both jobs, avoiding potential conflict between guardians with different priorities. Because children under 18 are not permitted to own property, the law requires a property guardian to manage property for the benefit of a minor. Even if your minor children will inherit nothing under your will, a child could receive property from someone else.

It is a good idea either to name a property guardian or to give your chosen personal guardian the power to manage property for your child. Whenever possible, the court looks to the will of a parent in naming a guardian.

If your child is going to be raised in another home, look only to a guardian who will do what is best for the child. Choose an individual

"My daddy's rich and my ma is good-lookin', but I'm a mess."

with moral fiber and strength of character, and with values like yours. Don't give in to relatives who pressure you, and try not to rely on people who might let your child down. Be realistic. Think about what is most important to the child and choose a person who is most likely to provide it.

Somehow we automatically think of appointing a couple as guardians, to make a nice, "normal" home. If you choose the home of a couple for your child, give the legal responsibility to just one person. The appointment of an individual guardian is always better than a couple, in case the couple should separate for any reason.

Although you name the guardian of your choice in your will, the appointment is not automatic. Before officially appointing a guardian, the court makes a determination that he or she is properly qualified.

We have all heard about guardianship battles where grandparents fight their own families for custody of the grandchildren. When a second husband has raised children of your first marriage, the stepmother and birth mother are likely to fight over the children. These battles generally arise when no provision is made for guardianship. If you put the subject on the table and discuss it like grown-ups (possibly enlightened by the children), a consensus is bound to emerge.

The court will usually honor the choice of guardian expressed in a will. However, if you fail to name a guardian, if your recommendation is challenged or deemed unsuitable, the court will appoint a guardian at its discretion. This not only could be devastating for your children but will take extra time and money as the case works its way through the legal process.

It is very important to appoint a successor guardian in case your first choice is unable to serve. Remember to ask the person(s) you intend to name as guardian and successor if he or she agrees to accept the responsibility. If you want your children to have the best possible situation, be prepared to cross all the *t*'s and dot all the *i*'s.

Almost without exception, a property guardian is required to post a bond and make regular accounting reports to the court until the minor comes of age. Even if you are naming your rich sister who is a successful money manager as property guardian for your kids, the law requires that she post a bond and make the accounting reports.

Guardianship for an adult. The appointment of a guardian for an adult who is unable to manage his own affairs, or to protect and care for himself, is a totally different matter. In such a case, it is necessary to go to court to prove that the individual is legally incompetent. Responsibility for property of an incompetent is given to a *conservator*, rather than a property guardian. This type of guardianship cannot be created in a will, but is established in a thorough and very difficult legal process which often places family members at odds.

Guardianship for an incompetent is normally based on medical evaluation. Should a significant change in medical status or competence occur, the guardianship could be terminated by the court. Parents of mentally ill adult children know all too well the deep pain and personal conflict that guardianship battles entail. Adult guardianship or conservatorship does not usually arise in planning an estate but out of necessity. If you believe someone close to you requires the protection of a guardianship, get the help of a lawyer experienced in these matters. It could be critical in protecting your family and keeping the peace, as well as your peace of mind.

Custodianship. Under circumstances less restricted than a trust or guardianship, property may be held for the benefit of a minor in the name of a custodian. Property may be left to a child under a will only if directed to a custodianship.

The most important element of every custodianship is the naming of at least one successor custodian. If you are custodian for your child, but did not name a successor when opening the account, include the name(s) of a successor custodian(s) in your will.

Otherwise, the court will insist on appointing a property guardian for the minor, with bond and accounting requirements. In the worst case, if Desi dies before Ricky comes of age, and no successor custodian has been named, Lucy would have to become a court-appointed property guardian for her own child. Absurd, but true. The law goes to extremes to protect children.

Married Couples Making Wills
Side by Side

Married couples have distinct tax advantages, but also face dilemmas in creating their wills. Both the marital assets and the personal interests of each spouse—which could involve children of previous marriages—are protected best if each spouse has a separate will. No two wills are identical, but they can be mutually beneficial. Properly drafted separate wills for married persons include *simultaneous death clauses*. Thus, if both spouses die at once and it is impossible to determine who died first, one spouse is declared first-to-die, leaving everything to the other. The provision prevents double probate and imposition of the laws of intestacy.

> *I want there to be one man who will regret my death.*
> —Heinrich Heine (Bequeathing his entire estate to his wife, on the condition that she get married again)

Some couples who share everything else might want to make a *joint will*. Sweet thought, but not a great idea. Should the couple die in the same accident, one spouse will be determined by the will, or by law, to have died first. The second-to-die then effectively has no will, and the estate becomes subject to laws of intestacy.

Envision your family having to straighten this out in probate court and you will realize the money saved in making just one will is definitely not worth it. Just to confuse things, the joint will is sometimes called a mutual will, but is not to be confused with mutual wills described below.

With separate but equal *joint and mutual wills*, each spouse leaves all property to the other, and under identical terms each will stipulates that the survivor will leave specific property to named children, relatives, or other heirs. These mirror-image wills are sometimes called "I Love You" wills. Some married couples make an actual contract, possibly in the form of a pre- or postnuptial agreement, leaving property to certain beneficiaries under their wills. The contract overrules previous wills and any subsequent will to the contrary.

But, be careful. Mutual wills or a nuptial agreement could be considered a *contract to make a will*—essentially a deal cut between husband and wife—and usually excludes the couple from the benefit of the *Unlimited Marital Deduction*, which permits spouses to transfer property to each other tax free.

And if joint property is valued above the *Applicable Credit Amount* of the unified tax credit ($675,000 in the year 2000), estate taxes will take a heavy toll when the surviving spouse dies. Tax rules and trusts specific to marital property are explained in Chapter Three.

Statutory Spousal Shares

In some states, spouses are entitled to certain property or a statutory share of the *marital estate* comprising property acquired during marriage, regardless of what the will of a deceased spouse says. Fifty percent is the standard statutory share in most community-property states, and increasingly in others. In some states, a surviving spouse may keep the family home by law. Elsewhere, a statutory allowance is given to a first spouse, but not to a second or third. It is not possible to completely disinherit a spouse under a will in any state.

In many states, a spouse substantially left out of a will may *elect against the will.* Anyone can challenge a will, but only a spouse can elect against a will to claim a statutory share.

Some states permit probate courts to create an *augmented estate,* drawing into the estate properties that the deceased spouse transferred out of his estate, perhaps to intentionally bypass the surviving spouse. This unusual action affects only assets in which the deceased retained significant interest or control.

Distributions Under a Will
It Had to Be You

All My Children

In describing and providing for children, there are several options. Consider exactly who are your "children." Do you want the term *children* to include natural-born children and adopted children, or stepchildren, or children of different marriages or relationships?

Issue. Natural-born children are known legally as "issue." Adoption makes a parent fully, legally responsible for a child, but the adopted child is not issue.

Descendants include adopted children and issue as well as *their* descendants. As values and cultures shift, bend, and mutate, the specific language used to describe children is increasingly open to challenge and, therefore, critical. When you draft legal documents, be precise. It is best to name names and to explicitly identify a *class*, or group, of children or heirs.

Pretermitted child. If you are a parent planning—or could be surprised—to have more children, it is advisable to expressly include children born after your will is written on equal footing with those living at the time you write your will. The future-born bundle of joy is called a "pretermitted child," and in most states is included in a will with other children by law.

Where a will is contested, or the status of a child is unclear, the courts usually look to the laws of intestacy to determine the "order of descendancy"—establishing which family members get what property and in what sequence. Under these rules, adopted children usually have the same rights as natural children, and half-brothers and sisters are usually treated as full siblings.

Most states treat illegitimate children the same as legitimate children with regard to the mother. But the father is recognized only if he eventually marries the mother and is legally recognized as the father of the child. Unless otherwise specified in the will, the share of an illegitimate child will be determined by the laws of intestacy in your state.

The same order of descendancy is true if you are an aunt leaving everything to your nieces and nephews, with the intention to include others who might be born into that same class of heirs in the future. However, it is wise to make a codicil to your will to provide specifically for additional children, rather than rely on state law to determine distribution.

Let's face it, distribution of property is the single most important, and potentially most troublesome, aspect of a will. Everyone wants to know "What's in it for me?" and "How much does everybody else get?" Envy, ego, pride, and all the emotions that can unhinge a family rise to the surface.

When making a will, decide how your property is to be divided or

"OF COURSE I LOVE THEM... I'M THEIR BENEFICIARY."

shared among your heirs, and state it clearly. You probably have different distributions in mind for children, or classes of heirs, and individuals, as well as the beneficiaries of any trust created under your will. Choose a method of distribution appropriate to each particular situation.

What If Your Heir Dare Die?

The specific language used in a will determines what happens in case a beneficiary of your will dies before you do. If you are leaving a bequest to an individual, or to be divided among a class of heirs, your will should declare whether property will be distributed *per stirpes* (**stir**-peas) or *per capita.*

Per stirpes distribution preserves assets for the named beneficiaries and their descendants. If a beneficiary dies before you do, his descendants receive his share. Let's say you state in your will that you are leaving property to your four children, in equal shares *per stirpes.* Should a child predecease you, his one-fourth share will go to his children. The property will bypass his wife, protecting it from being lost to your grandchildren because of remarriage or improper use and abuse. If the widow is property guardian or custodian for her children, she manages the children's property for *their* benefit, not her own.

Per capita distributions are divided equally among named beneficiaries, or a class of beneficiaries as identified in the will. Ordinarily, if a *per capita* beneficiary dies before you do, her share will *lapse* and be divided equally among the remaining heirs in the class.

In the majority of states, however, anti-lapse statutes have now been passed, automatically transferring the "lapsed" share intended for a descendant—and only a descendant—on to *his* descendants. The law prevents a person from excluding, unintentionally or otherwise, descendants—possibly his own grandchildren!

If you have not designated distribution specifically as *per stirpes* or *per capita,* and a beneficiary of your will predeceases you, his share could lapse and revert to the residuary estate. In the worst case, the share of a beneficiary who predeceased you could end up being distributed according to the laws of intestacy in your state—as if you had not written a will for that portion of your property at all. Everything depends on the exact wording of your will. Cover all the bases.

Types of Distribution

Bequests. Wills customarily include specific bequests of personal property. Some people leave cash or personal items to close friends or

Bonanza!

Pa Cartwright wanted his three sons to share equally in the Bonanza empire he had scratched out of the Nevada hills. His will stated that his three sons—Adam, Hoss, and Little Joe—or their descendents who survived them, were to receive the property in his estate—the ranch and everything else he owned—in equal shares per stirpes. By the time Pa died, the Cartwrights had suffered many personal tragedies.

Adam had died while pouting in Paris, leaving a French widow, but no children. Hoss had married and had eight children of his own before adopting three orphaned neighbor children, but had died in a roping accident. Little Joe worked the ranch and was a content and confirmed bachelor.

Because Adam left no descendants, and the property was to be distributed per stirpes, the estate was divided equally between the two remaining interests, Hoss's natural and adopted children (all were his descendants), and Little Joe. Hoss's half was divided equally among his eleven children. Hoss's widow received nothing. Little Joe received the other half of the Bonanza.

Had Pa left his property per capita, and there was no anti-lapse statute to protect Hoss's children, Little Joe would have gotten the whole Bonanza.

those with special associations—the old fly rod to the grandson as a souvenir of that first fishing trip, the engagement diamond to the second son for his future bride, cash to the boy who loyally mowed the lawn, or the piano to the child who only once said she loved it. If the bequests are many and small—and not cash—they are more appropriate for a precatory letter than a will.

All gifts and bequests made under a will, including those mentioned in a precatory letter, are included in the estate for estate tax purposes. Depending on your situation, it could be to your advantage to make tax-free gifts during your lifetime under the Annual Exclusion rather than wait to distribute property under your will. Annual gifts of

$10,000 or less are excluded from Unified Transfer Tax (formerly the Unified Gift and Estate Tax). The elements and effects of lifetime gifts are described in Chapter Four.

Nurse! Nurse!

In his will, and therefore in the public record, FDR left a bequest for the care of his private nurse/paramour, affectionately known as Missy. The gesture appeared very gracious at first glance, but the funds for Missy were paid from wife Eleanor's trust.

Residuary estate. Your residuary estate, as it is called, consists of what remains after all specific bequests and transfers have been made. It is distributed as the will instructs—possibly divided equally among certain named heirs, or given to one individual. In a simpler estate, you may want to designate a *trustworthy* individual to receive the residuary estate and, in turn, deliver the property odds and ends according to your precatory letter or verbal instruction, or his best judgement.

Pour-over will. Under a pour-over clause in a will, property from an estate literally "pours over" into either a preexisting trust such as a living trust, or a trust created by the will. Entire estates can pour over into trust. Or a residual estate can pour over, tying up loose ends of an estate quickly, rather than lingering in probate while small distributions are parceled out. The business of the estate is thus concluded in one cleansing sweep, rather than piecemeal. A will with a pour-over clause is sometimes called a pour-over will.

Property that pours over goes through probate, into the hands of the appointed trustee, and on to beneficiaries as named in the trust document. Except where the Unlimited Marital Deduction and unified tax credit apply, assets pouring over into trust will be part of the estate for tax purposes.

* * *

Trusts. Certain situations require creative thinking. You might want to create a trust under your will to protect assets from future taxes, or to provide for someone with specific needs, no matter what the tax implications. A trust created by a will is called a *testamentary trust.*

If, for example, one of your children (possibly an adult) or a parent is disabled or incompetent, or relies on you for income or other financial support, consider creating a trust for her protection under your will. At the same time, if equal distribution is a concern, make certain that she is not also included with your other children in a class of heirs who may receive property outright.

The trust needs a trustee to manage assets and make distributions. The trustee could be instructed to pay certain expenses such as food, clothing, shelter, or medical treatment, or make other distributions.

Another part of creating a trust is choosing the *remaindermen,* those who get what's left after the interest of the primary trust beneficiary expires. When creating a trust, you decide who is to receive the assets of the trust, or continuing benefits, when the elder or disabled beneficiary dies or is no longer in need. Various trust types, their benefits, and tax effects are described in Chapter Three.

A **life estate** can also be created in a will. Property is bequeathed to a named individual for his lifetime, usually in the form of a deed. That deed also states who is to receive the *remainder* (remaining) interest in the property when the life estate ends.

For example, you might give your son a life estate in your fishing cabin, to use and enjoy for his lifetime. He has full use of the property until he dies, at which time it vests in (is completely and legally transferred to) another or others you have named. Upon your son's death, the cabin would pass directly to his children, your grandchildren. Everybody's happy, especially when the fish are biting, and you keep it all in the family.

An *in terrorem* **clause** is used to make a distribution under your will conditional—to threaten, give "terror" or fair warning of the condition (i.e., "You will be disinherited if you challenge my will"). For example, the will could permit distribution to an adult child as long as the child remains drug free for two years, or doesn't gamble. It's a last-ditch (literally) attempt to get someone to shape up. In this case, the responsibility of the executor can be very personal—be sure to choose someone who is up to the task. An *in terrorem* clause provides an incentive for personal improvement as well as a means to prevent inherited assets from being squandered.

Equal Distribution

In your will you may leave specific property to specific individuals, with the intention that the inheritance among a certain group or class of these individuals—your children, for example—be equal. Let's say you write your will, intending to provide an equal share to each of your three children. You leave the condo to Moe, the house to Larry, and the farm to Curly, providing an equal share to each of your three children. If property values change dramatically between the time you write your will and the time you die, Moe could end up with a gold mine, and Curly with a money pit, or vice versa.

To preserve your intention to provide equally for certain heirs, your will could include instructions to prevent significant changes in property value from resulting in unequal distributions. Your executor can obtain appraisals of the respective properties and can direct your heirs who receive greater value to pay the difference to those receiving lesser value, possibly from other assets left to them under your will.

You may give property to a category or class, such as "to my children," "to my nieces and nephews," or "to members of my slo-pitch baseball team, the Speed Demons, in Sacramento, California, provided I am a member of the team at the time of my death." This language includes those who are born to or join that class in the future, despite the fact that they are not specifically named in your will.

Many parents make personal loans to their adult children to help them make a down payment on a house or get them through difficult times. The outstanding balance on such a loan is often forgiven upon the death of the parent, and could unintentionally result in unequal benefits to other children. If you want to equalize distributions, but are unable to settle an outstanding personal loan before your death, instruct your executor, in your will, to take the forgiven debt into consideration in equalizing distributions.

If property is to be distributed equally among a class of heirs, be sure to use the word "equally." In making a will, *you* decide who is to get what. Your lawyer translates your decisions into explicit, legally correct terms.

Special Instructions
Listen to What the Man Said

Funeral and burial arrangements are sometimes included in a will, though many wills are found only after it's too late. A separate precatory letter is usually more successful. If you express your desires for funeral plans in your will or in a letter, make sure the right people know about it so they can do as you wish before The Party's Over.

One woman left a letter choosing the hymns for the church, the reading at the cemetery, and—in her case—the party, the caterer, and her dress for the funeral. It no doubt gave her great pleasure to envision the whole affair, and it made things quite simple for her family—to say nothing of the chuckles it provided all around.

If you intend to be an organ donor, or leave your body to science, say so in a precatory letter, register with the appropriate agency, and make your intentions known.

> *He left his body to science, and science is contesting the will.*
> —David Frost

Disinheritance. If you intend to exclude or disinherit a person, spell it out in your will. A ne'er-do-well whom you believe does not deserve anything, or a well-to-do child whom you believe might not need anything, could nevertheless expect to be included in your will. Name the person excluded and state your reason for a decision that could be questioned. If you intend to exclude a child or heir apparent in favor of others of the same or similar status—a class of heirs, such as siblings—it's probably smart to run it by the one to be left out. It is costly, in more ways than one, to have your family suffer through the legal battles of a contested will.

If you want him to mourn, you had best leave him nothing.
—Martial

Take precautions to avoid a lawsuit or challenge by the person you disinherit. Explain your decision to appropriate family, friends, and beneficiaries. Support your will with a personal letter or a videotaped statement explaining your rationale. If you believe it could be necessary to prove you were competent to make the decision, ask a psychiatrist to confirm your sound mental state at the time you make the decision, and go in for a physical exam to provide medical records as further evidence of your health status.

Without sufficient proof of sound mind or with evidence of undue influence, certain provisions of a will, or the entire document, could be voided. In some cases it is advisable to leave a tiny bequest rather then disinherit a person entirely. The intent of the bequest is more difficult to challenge.

On the other hand, if someone close to you is out of control or under improper influence, and is making or changing his will, consult a lawyer. In extreme circumstances, courts have the power to protect people from their own incompetence. Under extreme circumstances, a court could establish a conservatorship to impose responsible management of property for the benefit of a living individual as well as respective heirs.

Any unreasonable favoritism could open your will to challenge. If family harmony is as important to you as it is to most of us, make an effort to clear the air by having the difficult conversations before making any decisions. The prodigal son may not necessarily be the most deserving, and, for that matter, may not want anything at the expense of his brothers or sisters. Or a wealthy doctor who worked her way through med school may not think it's fair to be penalized for her success.

Games People Play

Family dynamics are one of life's great mysteries. Even if
Professor Plum spends every afternoon in the library with
Colonel Mustard, he probably has no intention of leaving the manor
house to anyone but his favorite niece and nephew, Miss Scarlett
and Mr. Green.

If, however, the natty professor had the slightest clue that his
heirs were plotting to kill him by hitting him over the head with a
candlestick in the pantry, and to turn the estate into a mystery
theatre, he would delightedly play the investigator. Once he exposed
the dastardly derring-do, he would surely disinherit his niece and
nephew, and name his trusted friend Colonel Mustard sole
beneficiary of his will.

Distributions Outside a Will
Whatever Will Be, Will Be

Most retirement plans, life insurance, annuities, trusts, and joint
tenancies—often representing substantial financial interests—are distributed outside of probate. Any property with beneficiary designations
or right of survivorship bypasses the probate process and therefore need
not be addressed in a will. It could, however, be subject to estate tax.

If equal distribution of all your assets is desired, be sure to review
your designated beneficiaries—and what each will receive—before de-
ciding who receives distributions under your will. It is important to
name successor or contingent beneficiaries for all nonprobate assets to
prevent them from going through probate by default.

In making a will, a good estate planning lawyer works with you on
a practical level. The process is give and take. He listens, you listen.
Both of you might want to discuss issues with tax, insurance, and investment specialists. Developing an effective plan almost always takes
more than one or two meetings or conversations to resolve. But if you

have realistically addressed your long-term needs, have thought about how to distribute your property, and are familiar with the basics of an estate plan, your meetings will be productive.

Should you go to your lawyer to draft your will and he in turn gives you 20 pages of legalese, or a document you do not understand, which he asks you to sign, don't sign it. Sign only what you fully understand—what is crystal clear to you. Ask to have *everything* explained. Don't let your lawyer—or any of your advisors—pat you on the head and tell you it's all right, this is just the way it's done. Remember, you're paying for his services. If your lawyer is not willing to listen to you and answer every question regarding your will or any other aspect of your estate plan, find a better lawyer.

People do weird and wonderful things in their wills. It's part of life to think about your legacy. Make the most of it. Generosity of both spirit and wealth create the most endearing—and enduring—legacy.

Other Essential Documents
With a Little Help from My Friends

A will takes effect only upon death. But of course, we don't know how life will play out. We could very well end up needing help while we're alive—perhaps with a simple thing, like writing a check. It is hard to admit that one day we might become incapacitated. Those things only happen to others, right? But what if the unthinkable happens?

Who will make life and death decisions for you if you are not conscious? Will your business continue if you are incapacitated? Who will pay household and personal bills—to keep the heat or air conditioning running—if you are in the hospital? My wife will do it, you say, or my partner, or doctor, or daughter. All logical candidates. But these individuals may not know what you would want or, more importantly, may not have the legal right to make any decisions or sign any checks.

We have all heard of a power of attorney, living will, and health care directive. Each takes legal steps to protect your personal interests while you are alive—in end-of-life or threatening situations where you are unable to carry out responsibilities on your own. If you cannot make your wishes known, or make responsible decisions, these documents make your intentions clear.

The following sections address many options for giving someone else permission, if necessary, to make important decisions for you and manage your affairs. Exactly opposite a will, these tools are valid only as long as you are alive. Any transfer of authority ends upon your death. Like any other estate planning document, each should be custom-made for you, and every appointment requires a successor. We begin with the most comprehensive and conclude with the most limited.

Power of Attorney

I'll Be There

A *power of attorney,* signed by you, gives a person whom you trust the power to manage your affairs and make important decisions for you—to act in your place—in case you become physically or mentally impaired. The power must be signed and notarized, and should include an affidavit explaining any unusual circumstances. A person with your power of attorney is known as your *agent,* or *attorney-in-fact.*

Power of attorney is all about responsibility. None of us knows what fate has in store. If you run your own small pet store today and are disabled tomorrow, what happens to your business? If you linger in a coma with no hope of recovery, do you want your family to suffer the strain and pay medical bills to keep you breathing indefinitely?

Each of us has undoubtedly given these eventualities some thought. However, if we have not signed a power of attorney—durable, springing, or limited—we are not facing facts. Be sure your power of attorney makes clear your intentions, takes effect when you choose, and yields all the powers necessary to take care of you and your responsibilities.

Powers of attorney are created in different forms for different purposes:

Durable power of attorney is unquestionably the most comprehensive. From the day you sign on the dotted line, it establishes and

continues the authority of another person—your agent—to act on your behalf, throughout your incapacity and otherwise. The durable power of attorney is generally used for businesses where ongoing management and operations are essential. It remains in effect until either you cancel it, you die, or it expires at a time specified in the document. Unless the power is restricted in the document, an agent with a durable power of attorney has unqualified power in handling your affairs.

Springing power of attorney takes effect only under circumstances prescribed by *you*, for example when you become medically incapacitated. The springing power could arise once, occasionally, or frequently. Likewise, the springing power ends when you regain your abilities and sensibilities.

A person requiring continuing debilitating medical treatments might not want his business dealings interrupted by his treatment cycle. A springing power of attorney could permit his agent to run things during treatments. The springing power of attorney is also a good choice for unmarried partners, newlyweds, or associates who own separate assets. Should the need arise, the legal authority of their partners is clear.

Some states do not permit a springing power of attorney; therefore, it may be necessary to execute a durable power of attorney but reserve it until needed.

Hail to the Chief's Agent

When President Reagan went under general anesthesia for surgery, his presidential powers were transferred to Vice President Bush for those few hours under the Thirty-second Amendment, much like a springing power of attorney.

Limited power of attorney is just that. It is limited by its own terms. You give power to a certain someone, for a certain task, for a certain time. For example, if you are buying a home but are not able to be present to sign documents at the closing, a limited power of attorney empowers your agent to sign the papers for you. The power ends when the closing is complete.

For the elderly who can no longer read or write well enough to manage their checking accounts and pay bills, but understand perfectly what they are doing and why, a limited power of attorney allows another person, perhaps a daughter, son, or personal secretary, to make deposits, sign checks, and keep the household running.

Thankfully, because the law fiercely protects individual property rights, a power of attorney imposes a *fiduciary duty*. An agent handling property and finances on behalf of another is legally bound to act in good faith and follow the highest business standards.

With a power of attorney, the potential for abuse is obvious, providing a persuasive argument for choosing your agent wisely and perhaps early, while you can look right into the eyes of the person you are considering. Eventually, we all have to place our trust, if not our lives, in the hands of others. Think about it now. You can always change your mind, and meanwhile, you will have a working plan in place.

Health Care Power of Attorney
Someone to Watch over Me

A health care power of attorney appoints a person to act on your behalf and make judgments about your medical treatment. This important document pertains to your mind, body, and well-being. It is usually separate from the durable, springing, or limited power of attorney, which directs property and business management to another. A health care power of attorney is sometimes called a *health care directive* or *health care proxy*.

Many estate planning lawyers consider a health care power of attorney so important that they throw it in with a will, free of charge. Obviously it's not that complicated a document or they wouldn't be giving it away. But be sure you and your lawyer are speaking the same language when you decide to give someone else the authority to make health care decisions as the need arises.

Living Will
Let It Be

A living will is not actually a will, but a limited, legally enforceable set of instructions, in effect while you are alive. In the case of a terminal illness, or a medical emergency or condition from which there is no hope of recovery, a living will declares your personal wishes to be resuscitated, treated, put on life support, and if and when to "pull the plug"—or not. Whether you have a serious, potentially life-threatening condition, are terminally ill, or simply want to protect yourself and your family from emotional and legal wrangling in case of an emergency or in your old age, the living will makes your wishes clear.

A living will requires a statement of your intentions, your signa-

And Away We Go . . .

*I*t was no honeymoon when Ed Norton slipped in a sewer tunnel and nearly drowned. Just as his whole life passed before him, he was dragged from the sludge by none other than his buddy Ralph Kramden, who had heard screams from the bus stop and rushed to the rescue.

Norton lay in his hospital bed for days, too weak and confused to do anything. His wife, Trixie, meanwhile was unable to cash Norton's paycheck and could not pay the rent and other bills. Ralph and Alice cleaned out their life savings from the peanut butter jar to help Trixie.

When Norton came to his senses, he admitted he had not thought he would ever put Trixie in such a predicament. After much huffing, puffing, and bluffing, Norton and Ralph signed springing powers of attorney giving each other the right and responsibility to look after things if either ever got into trouble again. Not ready to relinquish manly duties to their wives unless absolutely necessary, they begrudgingly named Alice and Trixie successors.

Next day Ralph was playing his travelin' music a little too loud when he plowed his bus into a truck of city sewer workers. This time he and Norton both ended up in the hospital, seeing stars for days. With complete legal authority, Alice and Trixie paid the bills and hit the shops. They bought yellow polka-dot bikinis and headed for Coney Island. When Ralph and Norton awoke, there sat the girls, relaxed, tanned, and lovely, looking like dreams. How sweet it is.

ture, and, in most cases, two witnesses, and is limited to the specific circumstances it describes. Most states have statutory forms which are available, ready-made.

In the few states where right-to-die laws have been passed, they remain subject to legal controversy. If you want a living will, we suggest making your own, with the advice of your lawyer and, if circumstances warrant, your doctor. Like any other legal document, a living will should address your individual needs.

*"I'd just like to know why, if you trust me so much,
you've named your daughter to pull your plug."*

Though certainly better than nothing, a living will, even when
properly executed, may be of no consequence among emergency room
staff, or even friends and children, who might not know that it exists.
Hospital staff are obligated by the Hippocratic oath to resuscitate. That's
their job. By the time your spouse, partner, or child arrives to state your
wishes, you could be on life support. If you make a living will, and
particularly if you are ill or at risk, be sure to tell your family and friends
about it.

*If I am ever stuck on a respirator or a life support system, I definitely
want to be unplugged—but not til I get down to a size 8.*

—Henriette Mantel

The Night of the Living Will

As a mystery writer, Jessica knew all too well about unlikely endings. She had a living will and was not the least bit timid about recommending that everyone have one. Her dear friends Dr. Seth Hazlitt and Sheriff Tupper took her advice and signed living wills, but her unpredictable nephew Grady thought living wills were just for old people.

The residents of Cabot Cove were distraught when Seth suffered a massive stroke that left him helpless and hopeless, breathing on his own but with no chance of recovery. His colleagues and the hospital staff were told about his living will, and when he suffered another stroke, his do-not-resuscitate wishes were honored. After a long, productive life, the good doctor died a dignified death. Without a living will, he might have been placed on life support indefinitely, straining both his finances and his family, who did not want him to suffer.

Grady went from the funeral to the lawyer's office to sign his own living will. Jessica was right. Everyone can be a mystery writer and write his own ending.

Unmarried Partners

Unmarried partners, including same-sex couples, often face distressing family conflict when health care documents and/or cohabitation agreements are not properly executed. Without authority, the one who knows you best and cares most about you may be unable to have any influence on your medical treatment.

Many individuals, including those with AIDS or other terminal illnesses, may prefer to have their partners—not their families—make medical decisions for them. In the absence of a legal document to the contrary, hospitals follow the law, which allows only blood relatives to make health care decisions. A health care power of attorney can give your partner the legal authority to make medical decisions on your behalf.

Crisis situations are delicate and difficult at best, though everyone with any sense usually ends up wanting the same thing—the best care for the patient. Unfortunately, when facing an emergency, sense is sometimes hard to marshal. To avoid conflict, protect yourself and your partner by getting the necessary papers in order ASAP.

See Chapter Five for more about important estate planning issues facing unmarried and same-sex partners.

A single document can include different powers of attorney—a business associate to make your business decisions, your son to write your checks, your husband to make medical decisions. A living will is usually separate. Be sure to name a *successor* for each appointment.

Ask your lawyer what will work best for you, and how complicated (and expensive) it might be if you have a change of heart or circumstance. Frankly, thanks to word processing, changing a name or even a descriptive line to two in any legal document is very simple. Revision of even a long document should cost no more than a nominal fee for signing and notarizing.

Location of Documents
Searchin'

An important part of a complete estate plan is a list, perhaps the inventory worksheet, of your assets indicating the location of relevant documents, legal and otherwise. At the very least, write down where you think everything *might* be found. At best, create a file, in a private, secure place—a shoebox if necessary—of the materials you have gathered, and make a list of those items not in your possession.

Some important papers are necessarily held by others, such as stock certificates and mortgages. Insurance policies, agreements for retirement plans, judgments, and deeds are usually held by the owner— you—and need to be stored in a secure but accessible location. The back of the desk drawer will not do.

If, for example, the deed to the house is held by the bank because of a mortgage, write that down on your list of assets, with the name of the bank, the phone number, and your contact. If you have copies of the papers, add them to your file. You need not have all the documents in your possession, but knowing their location is essential. It is best if someone you trust also knows the location of your records.

Safe Deposit Boxes
Behind Closed Doors

Many of us keep bank safe deposit boxes for important documents. By law, a lockbox in your name can be opened by an official request for a will search. However, in a few states, a safe deposit box in the name of the deceased cannot be opened except by authority of the probate court. And if you can't get into probate without the will . . . well, it could be a real pickle.

Better than storing your original will in a safe deposit box, keep it in a fireproof safe at home, or give it to your lawyer for safekeeping. Make copies and distribute them to your spouse, partner, or adult child. You don't have to give away your secrets. If you would like to have your will read at a family gathering after the funeral, give a copy of the will to someone who can make it happen.

If you have written a precatory letter expressing your desired funeral and burial arrangements, put it in a sealed envelope and give it to someone who will be involved in making the plans. Tell her it's about your funeral and ask her to read it after you die. Tell her, until then it's For Your Eyes Only.

Emergency funds. Like a will locked in a safe deposit box, cash left in your personal checking account might not be available to pay family bills without permission of the probate court. This will not do. Make sure your family or partner will have access to emergency cash or income of some sort until distributions from the estate begin. See Chapter Four.

Periodic Review and Update
Turn Around, Look at Me

One certainty in life is that things change. Even after all your hard work, difficult choices, and final decisions, your estate plan needs to be reviewed periodically—every five years or so. Of course, any significant personal or financial change requires an immediate and complete review of all estate planning documents.

Major lifestyle changes such as marriage, divorce, remarriage, a birth or death require thorough reconsideration of an estate plan in its entirety. You don't have to reinvent the wheel, but may want to reevaluate your assets to be sure your planned distributions remain fair and continue to represent your intentions.

If equal distribution is important, update your list of assets and rethink your bequests. As family situations change, you might want to add, remove, or change the beneficiaries named in your will, or designated in retirement plans, insurance policies, and living trusts. If necessary, change the appointment of an executor, trustee, guardian, or successor who is no longer able to handle the responsibility.

Tax issues are an ongoing concern, subject to changes in both the law and personal circumstances. Your accountant will make quick work of crunching updated numbers for an estate plan that she helped put together—just another good reason for choosing pros who know your estate and know their stuff.

Minor additions or changes that do not substantially alter the will are made by codicil, an addendum to the will. This amounts to an extra page, prepared in the proper language, signed and witnessed, and attached to your original will.

However, if an important aspect of your will is to be changed—addition or removal of a significant beneficiary, or creation of a new trust, for example—your lawyer will undoubtedly recommend executing an entirely new will. In the age of computers, rewriting a will is not a major undertaking and should not cost as much as the original. If any significant change is required, a new will is strongly recommended.

I get the distinct feeling that Dad's
changed his will again.

You might want to add a bequest to a charity. You might want to
disinherit your nephew. You might not want to change a thing. But if
you review your will every so often, you will sleep better knowing your
plan is still a good one.

Well done is better than well said.

—Benjamin Franklin

Wipe Out
Unified Transfer Tax Table

For taxable gifts and estates above	Rate
$ 675,000	37%
750,000	39
1,000,000	41
1,250,000	43
1,500,000	45
2,000,000	49
2,500,000	53
3,000,000	55

Unified Transfer Tax
Who's Afraid of the Big Bad Wolf?

Before going any further, it is important to understand how taxes apply to gifts and estates. In 1976, federal gift tax and estate tax were combined under the umbrella of a unified gift and estate tax, recently renamed the *Unified Transfer Tax* (catchy name, isn't it?).

Because of the changes in the law, there is a bit of a problem with semantics, even among the professionals. The term Unified Transfer Tax applies to both gifts and estates, thus it is commonly called "gift tax" in reference to lifetime gifts and "estate tax" in reference to estates. *Death tax* is an older term that also means estate tax. In either case, it is also called the "unified tax," for short. But it's all the same tax. We use the terms interchangeably, and you will find that most estate planning professionals do the same.

The unified tax is applied to the cumulative value of taxable lifetime gifts *and* estate transfers at a progressive tax rate of 37 percent to 55 percent—the greater the value, the higher the tax rate. A very few states impose an additional, though much more modest, inheritance tax.

In planning an estate, it is essential to be aware of three key regulations that can be used to tremendous tax advantage.

The *Unlimited Marital Deduction* allows unlimited, tax-free transfers, in life and death, between husband and wife.

The *Unified Transfer Tax* permits every individual to pass along a certain amount of gifts and estate assets, tax free. The *Applicable Credit Amount* refers to the actual tax savings; and the *Applicable Exclusion Amount* refers to the amount of gifts and estate assets that are permitted to be transferred free of the tax. Just as the Unified Transfer Tax is usually called the "unified tax," so is the Applicable Credit Amount commonly referred to as the "unified tax credit," as it has been for many years. And the Applicable Exclusion is also known as the "unified credit equivalent."

The *Annual Exclusion* is an entirely different exclusion from the unified tax credit. Under this regulation, every person is allowed to make as many gifts of $10,000 to as many people as he likes, every year, year after year, tax free. Gifts under that amount are excluded from the unified tax. Annual gifts over that amount must be reported on gift tax returns and are charged against the unified credit equivalent.

Combined gifts and estate transfers that exceed the Applicable Exclusion Amount are taxed at progressive Unified Transfer Tax rates.

....

Throw the Bums Out!

Whoever voted to use the word exclusion for both the Annual Exclusion and the Applicable Exclusion Amount—which are very different—ought to be EXCLUDED from writing and voting on any more tax regulations! These regulations are tough to understand even without confusing the terms.

....

A good estate plan takes full advantage of these loopholes to preserve assets through trusts and lifetime gifts. Specific application of the regulations is discussed in Chapter Three, particularly with regard to credit shelter and marital trusts; and Chapter Four, related to lifetime gifts.

It's Now or Never . . .

- Everyone needs a will. Period.

- Sign a power of attorney giving an individual of your choice the authority to act on your behalf should you become incapacitated. Not something we like to think about, but a possibility nevertheless.

- Provide clear instructions for end-of-life or medical emergencies by making a living will or health care directive.

- Parents can—and must—protect their minor children by naming guardians in their wills.

- Choose your executor wisely. He will have your whole world in his hands.

- Update or make a new will if you change your partner, do-si-do, or make any major lifestyle change.

- Keep your will and all personal legal documents in a safe, accessible location. Inquiring minds need not know, but those you trust ought to know where to find your papers.

- Take the time to understand the way gift and estate tax works—and look for loopholes.

3

Trusts
Come Rain or Come Shine

What's Goin' On . . .

- Basic forms of trust
- Tax benefits of trusts
- Credit shelter trusts and marital trusts
- Irrevocable life insurance trusts
- Charitable trusts
- Generation-skipping and grantor-retained trusts
- Other familiar trust types

Trust Basics
Peaceful, Easy Feelin'

Although trusts have traditionally been associated with great wealth, great wealth isn't what it used to be. As the stock market has steadily climbed and individual assets increased, the financial tools once available only to the very wealthy have become useful to a great many. Remember that *trillions*! will be left to the baby boomers by their parents.

The essentials of a trust are straightforward. You, as grantor, place property in a separate account, a trust, to be managed by someone of your choice, a trustee, for the benefit of a specific person or persons (or charity)—the beneficiary(ies).

Co-trustees may be named to balance power and expertise. In the *trust instrument,* the document containing the terms of the trust, successor trustees are named to take over if an original trustee becomes unable to serve.

Beneficiaries for whose immediate benefit the trust is created are known as *primary beneficiaries,* sometimes *income beneficiaries.* Those who receive what's left, or what remains of the trust assets, or *corpus,* after the primary beneficiary has died or the term of benefits ends, are known as the *remainder beneficiaries* or *remaindermen.*

The reason that property is put in trust determines what form a trust takes, how long it will last, who will manage it, and for whose benefit. It can be costly to set up a trust—make sure the savings outweigh the expense.

Trusts are named to match their objectives. We stick to traditional terms as close to everyday English as possible. Special trusts to meet specific needs are addressed in the following sections. First, let's review the basics. Trusts can be living or testamentary *and* revocable or irrevocable:

Living trust. Created while one is alive. That makes sense, doesn't it? Also called *inter vivos* trust, from Latin—meaning among the living.

Testamentary trust. Created when one dies, according to his or her will.

Revocable trust. May be revoked or amended at any time by the grantor.

Irrevocable trust. May not be revoked or amended. Set in stone whether you like it or not. Testamentary trusts are, by definition, irrevocable.

The type of trust you choose depends on your individual objectives. Those envious of trust fund babies might consider their parents remarkably generous, but trusts have very practical purposes. Most are designed to avoid taxes with the incidental perk of starting a nest egg for someone—more than likely someone who would inherit the property anyway.

Remember, when putting property in trust, you must reregister your assets in the name of the trust, or you have accomplished nothing.

"One thing we do share with you—we both live on capital accumulated by others."

Revocable or Irrevocable

Did You Ever Have to Make Up Your Mind?

In a *revocable* trust you effectively retain control of the assets through your right to revoke or modify the trust at any time. The most familiar revocable trust is the *living trust*. There is a benefit in creating a revocable trust, but saving taxes is *not* it. As long as you can change any aspect of the trust, you are considered in control and are taxed as usual, dead or alive. The IRS will tax you on income you receive from the trust and will include the trust assets in your estate when you die.

The major advantage of a revocable trust is that, upon your death, it will be continued or distributed for the benefit of those you have named without the delay and expense of going through probate. The assets will not be tied up while the court fits your will into its docket.

Thus, the primary objective of a revocable trust is to establish terms for distribution. Some people place nearly everything they own in a living trust and name themselves trustees. Nothing really changes except that the property in trust avoids probate.

If the grantor, perhaps you, becomes disabled and can no longer serve as trustee, the trust will continue under the named successor trustee. If another person is entirely dependent upon the income stream of certain assets, keeping those assets out of probate could be critical. It might be a good idea to place out-of-state property in trust to avoid probate in more than one state. In most cases it is simply convenient to create a trust that will pass outside probate, while reserving the right to change your mind.

If you choose to create a living trust, consider your costs. Ask your lawyer for an estimate of probate expense—which will be higher if you have property in more than one state—and compare that to the cost of setting up and maintaining a trust. Beware that your lawyer may not be totally unbiased in this assessment. His revenue will be affected by your decision.

In an *irrevocable trust,* the grantor gives up any and all control of assets placed in trust. The trust is a separate tax entity, paying its own income taxes at trust rates. However—and this is the big advantage of an irrevocable trust—the trust is no longer part of the estate of the grantor and therefore is not subject to any estate tax.

As grantor, you set up a trust as you like. You may elect to receive the income or not; to have it distributed to your children, your grandchildren, your disabled sister, a charity, or your hair designer. You will be taxed only for the income you receive. Other beneficiaries will be responsible for tax on their income.

Distributions may be made in any way and at any time the grantor chooses. Depending on the objective of the trust, the trustee may be required to follow strict guidelines in making income distributions only as specifically needed. Or, the trustee may have broad discretion including the right to invade the principal of the trust if necessary.

In any case, an irrevocable trust must terminate on a given date—which could be upon the death of the beneficiary—when assets will pass, estate-tax free, to named beneficiaries outside of probate. The grantor chooses how long the trust will last, the "trust term," but must stay within the *rule against perpetuities.* It can't last forever.

Don't Leave It to Beaver

Now an elderly multimillionaire, Ward Cleaver can ensure continuing financial assistance for his family by placing a portion of his assets in a revocable living trust. He doesn't actually give the money away, and the trust income pays his usual expenses—i.e., the high cost of his wife June's nursing home care, rent for Wally who lost everything as business partner of that conniving Eddie Haskell, and tuition for the grandkids, Little Beav and Junella. The way this trust is set up, Ward could cut off Wally on a whim, or pull all his assets out of trust at any time.

Because Ward can change it at any time, he is considered to "control" it. Consequently, Ward pays the taxes on the income. The only advantage of this trust is that it continues to support June and the gang without interruption when Ward dies. Probate court does not interfere with property held in trust, and benefits continue to be distributed as directed.

The trust assets will, however, be taxed as part of Ward's estate when he dies because he retained that control. What Ward leaves to Beaver will be diminished by estate taxes.

Once you have made your decision and an irrevocable trust is in place, it's a done deal. You have given up control of those assets and cannot revoke or modify the trust, having passed, as Gene Pitney said, the "last chance to turn around."

Naturally, you have to be able to do without the money or property you place in an irrevocable trust. And it is, of course, critical to consider the tax effects of creating a trust. Transferring assets into an irrevocable trust could result in a gift tax liability. Transferring funds out of an IRA into a trust also could trigger a significant income tax liability. And jointly owned assets might have to be divided into individual ownership before transfer to a trust.

Keep in mind that avoiding taxes might not be as important as

Leave It to Beaver

If June dies just as Wally is in the money again—never mind that it's in another get-rich-quick scheme with Eddie—Ward Cleaver might decide to leave everything to the Beav, a respected teacher and solid family man. Beaver could use the income because, as a teacher, he will never make a fortune. Ward doesn't need it all and promises "NEVER!" to bail out Wally again.

If Ward keeps everything, giving Beaver the occasional tax-exempt gift, the estate will be taxed at a high rate, diminishing what Ward leaves to Beaver. However, if Ward puts what he no longer needs in an irrevocable trust, naming a trustee (not Wally and certainly not Eddie Haskell!) and establishing distribution parameters, he is giving up those assets and any control over them, and the trust will pass to Beaver outside of Ward's will. The Beav will pay tax on whatever income he receives, but the trust assets will not be taxed as part of Ward's estate. Ward leaves a lot more to Beaver.

allowing for the unexpected. Just how much you put into trust, what form that trust will take, and how cost-effective it is to create and administer a trust depend on your individual circumstances.

With an understanding of the trust concept as well as your needs and long-term objectives, you are ready for the next step. The following sections include general information to help you identify the attributes of certain forms of trust and begin to formulate your plan. A lawyer specializing in trusts and estates will be able to clarify your options and draft required legal documents to create a trust just for you.

A Word about Trust Fund Babies
Million Dollar Babies, or Should They Get a Job?

Trust fund babies are typically the beneficiaries of sums of money put in trust for them when they were young. Over the years, with wise investment by a responsible trustee, the assets grow and the income increases until just about the time one of these kids finishes grad school and is ready to get a job. He suddenly realizes he has enough income to live without working, maybe take a year or two off before beginning the big career.

This story seems familiar. The budding, educated adventurer decides to be a ski bum or travel for a year. Twenty years later, the "kid" is still skiing, or selling refrigerators in Peru—not a bum, but nowhere near the career track once planned and often not all that happy.

Generous, well-intentioned parents who provide security for the future sometimes unwittingly pave the way to destinations unknown, surely unforeseen, often resulting in disappointment—their own and their child's. Some parents tie strings to the trust benefits (age restrictions, education parameters, for example), limit the income, or provide for invasion of the trust assets only for specific purposes.

Despite the stereotype, trust fund babies are not bad people, and not all of them go astray. Like all of us, trust fund babies just try to make the most of what they have. The Fortune 500 includes at least a few trust fund babies who used their trust assets wisely, in some cases as seed money to start their own companies.

Helpful Tax Loopholes
Here We Go Loop-de-loop!

The Unified Transfer Tax is applied to all property in an estate with a few important exceptions. The exceptions provide opportunities—loopholes—to preserve income for your family and assets for future generations through trusts. Let's review the relevant regulations and how they work in some very useful trusts.

Unlimited Marital Deduction

You Make Me So Very Happy

It may be old-fashioned, but estate tax—Unified Transfer Tax—regulations favor married couples. All property passing from one spouse to another by reason of gift *or* death is exempt from the unified tax under the *Unlimited Marital Deduction*. When one spouse dies, the surviving spouse can inherit *everything* without paying any estate taxes.

If the only objective of a married couple is to provide for each other, this is ideal. However, if husband and wife hope to provide for each other *and* leave something to their children or others, they could create a trust either while they are alive or under their individual wills to continue to protect marital property from estate tax.

Unified Tax Credit

Money, Money

Under another favorable federal tax regulation, every individual is allowed to pass along a certain amount of gifts and inheritance free of the unified tax.

The *Applicable Credit Amount* is a dollar-for-dollar credit against Unified Transfer Tax due. Estate taxes saved by the credit are approximately $200,000.

The *Applicable Exclusion Amount* is the equivalent value of an individual estate that is exempt from the tax under the rule—$675,000 in the year 2000. The applicable exclusion will increase on a sliding scale to a maximum of $1 million in the year 2006.

These terms were renamed in 1999. The applicable credit was formerly called the "unified credit," and the applicable exclusion was the "credit equivalent." You will find reference materials with the old terms and might hear lawyers, accountants, and other estate planning pros using them. Remember that the rule has not changed—only the name has been changed.

Similar in name, but entirely different from the applicable exclusion amount, the *Annual Exclusion* allows an individual to make tax-exempt gifts of up to $10,000 each year to as many individuals as he or she wishes. Any gifts *below* the annual exclusion are not taxable and are not counted against the applicable exclusion amount. Any gifts *above* that amount must be reported on gift tax returns and are applied toward the applicable exclusion of the donor. See Chapter Four for more about gifts and the unified tax.

Count Me Out

It's no surprise that Washington has set up the sliding scale to raise the Applicable Credit Amount *and* Applicable Exclusion Amount *in election years when politicians running for reelection can take personal credit for it. There are no changes in the years 2001 and 2003 when—you've got it!—there are no elections. When questioned by constituents, congressmen answered, "The Devil Made Me Do It."*

Unified Transfer Tax Applicable Exclusion Amounts

1999	$650,000	2003	$ 700,000
2000	675,000	2004	850,000
2001	675,000	2005	950,000
2002	700,000	2006	1,000,000

Credit Shelter Trusts
Gimme Shelter

In order to preserve the unified tax credit of both spouses, a married couple is advised to create a *credit shelter trust,* sometimes called a "by-pass trust." Each spouse provides in his or her will that the trust will be created when the first spouse dies.

The trust is funded—tax free—with assets up to the amount of

Lucky Laverne

*et's say Laverne wins $1 million in the lottery. She leaves Shirley
their little house now worth $500,000, gives the Fonz $200,000
with instructions to buy a hog of a Harley for his retirement, and
leaves Squiggy a designer wardrobe to the tune of $100,000. That's
$800,000, plus the $400,000 in her money market account, which is
to be divided equally among her named heirs. Of the $1.2 million,
$675,000 is exempt from estate taxes under the* **Applicable
Exclusion Amount.** *Laverne's estate will pay taxes on $525,000.*

*Had Laverne snagged the Fonz and married him, she could
leave everything to him free of estate taxes under the* **Unlimited
Marital Deduction,** *but when he dies, the entire estate will be
subject to estate taxes. And the greater the value of the taxable
estate, the higher the rate.*

the Applicable Exclusion Amount ($675,000 in the year 2000). The
value of any taxable gifts made during your lifetime is charged against
the applicable exclusion first. Then, any balance of the Applicable Exclusion Amount in the estate is eligible for a credit shelter trust. For
example, if Amos has given Andy taxable lifetime gifts of $100,000, only
$575,000 of Amos's estate is eligible for a credit shelter trust.

The surviving spouse is often named sole income beneficiary of a
credit shelter trust, but any person could be named. Under terms established in the trust document, income benefits are paid for an established period of time. The trustee is usually given discretion to invade
trust principal if additional payments are required.

In choosing a trustee or co-trustees, consider the purpose of the
trust. A family member who has a good understanding of finances as
well as the personal needs of the income beneficiaries makes a good
trustee for a credit shelter trust.

When the trust terminates, assets are distributed to remainder
beneficiaries, again tax free. Even if trust assets have quadrupled in
value, they will not be subject to estate tax upon distribution to the
remaindermen.

> WARNING: *If you and your spouse have assets of more than $1.35 million (year 2000 figure) and do not have a credit shelter trust planned, you might as well sit down and write a check to the IRS for $200,000. That money is gone!*

Without a credit shelter trust, a surviving spouse could inherit marital assets without tax penalty, but difficulty arises when she dies. Her estate, now representing her assets *and* those she inherited from her spouse, will be diminished by estate tax—most likely at a higher rate because of the combined value of marital assets.

Credit shelter trusts are appropriate for almost any estate, but especially where marital assets exceed the Applicable Exclusion Amount. Upon closer examination, the perceived savings of transferring everything to a spouse under the Unlimited Marital Deduction may not result in actual tax savings to the marital estate. A little math exercise with your lawyer or accountant will compare the potential estate tax savings with the expense of creating and administering a trust.

Even with a credit shelter trust, a surviving spouse who does no further estate planning exposes her estate to the disadvantages of probate and estate tax. Probate is not inexpensive, especially if a lawyer is hired in the process. Privacy is compromised by the public record, and the paperwork and delay are a pain in the neck at the least. On top of that, Uncle Sam will push right in front of those you care about to collect his share!

Marital Trusts
Tea for Two

Marital deduction trust. Under a provision in the wills of both spouses, a marital deduction trust is created when the first spouse dies. Assets of a married couple may be joined in trust for the benefit of the surviving spouse, with no tax penalty under the Unlimited Marital Deduction.

The trust gives the surviving spouse a general *power of appointment* allowing complete access and authority to do as she pleases with any and all of the trust assets. In case the surviving spouse becomes disabled, a trustee or successor trustee is in place to continue trust benefits. When the surviving spouse dies, trust assets are counted as part of her estate for tax purposes and are distributed according to instruction. The marital deduction trust is also called a *power of appointment trust.*

The Wizardry of Ozzie

*zzie—husband, father, and putterer extraordinaire—is on his
way out and wants to leave everything to Harriet. She's still in
the kitchen wearing an apron, nearly ninety and ailing, and hasn't
the foggiest idea what's going on. And she needs income and security
for the rest of her life. No one is quite sure if Ozzie ever went to
work—he was never actually seen doing anything productive—but
let's say he managed to live well and accumulate a sizable estate.*

Under his will, Ozzie could create a credit shelter trust.
*The trust takes advantage of Ozzie's unified tax credit and pays
income to Harriet for life. Sons Ricky and David make good co-
trustees because they know their mother's personal needs better than
a banker would.*

*Property representing the Applicable Exclusion Amount passes
from Ozzie's estate to the trust tax free. And trust assets are
ultimately distributed to the boys, tax free.*

*At Harriet's death, her own estate is also entitled to the
unified tax credit. The combined marital estate of Ozzie and Harriet
takes advantage of the tax credits to which both are entitled.*

One can only imagine how a general power of appointment could
quickly become counterproductive. If, for example, your intended heirs,
or the remaindermen of the trust, are the children of your first and
second marriages, but your third wife has general power of appointment
over trust assets, your children may never get a nickel.

Those who seek asset protection, or prefer *not* to empower their
spouses (don't ask, don't tell) regarding the future distribution of property, should consider a form of irrevocable trust.

QTIP trust. The QTIP is a marital trust designed to provide for
a surviving spouse but direct trust assets to others, possibly the children.
The irrevocable QTIP—Qualified Terminable Interest Property—trust
is sometimes created while the grantor is alive, sometimes as part of a

If Ozzie's estate is given to Harriet outright, or is placed in a marital deduction trust, the estate passes tax free to Harriet under the Unlimited Marital Deduction. But look out, Harriet has complete control under the marital deduction trust, and at age 100 could give it all away to the newspaper boy or her nurse. Ricky and David can do nothing to prevent it.

Many married couples choose to create both types of trust, transferring everything out of the estate of the first spouse to die, tax free. The credit shelter trust preserves the unified tax credit. And the marital deduction trust gives everything else to the spouse to do with as she pleases. It may not be the perfect estate plan, but it may be the best one for a particular situation.

The marital deduction trust also has estate tax consequences quite different from those of the credit shelter trust. All trust assets are under Harriet's control and therefore considered to be owned by her. When Harriet dies, her estate includes her own assets as well as those she received from Ozzie's estate, but only one tax credit is available. What Harriet hasn't given away, the tax man could take away, at least partially. What would a good husband and father like Ozzie want for his family?

pre- or postnuptial agreement guaranteeing benefits between spouses. The idea is to ensure that the wife, possibly the trophy wife, lives well but the kids still get their inheritance.

In an exception to IRS rules, the QTIP qualifies for the unlimited marital deduction despite the fact that benefits to the spouse are limited. The difference between the marital deduction trust and the QTIP is the surviving spouse's control—it's unlimited in the marital deduction trust, restricted in the QTIP. The important difference between the QTIP and the credit shelter trust is that when the QTIP ends at the death of the spouse beneficiary, trust assets are considered part of the estate of that spouse and are taxed as such.

* * *

Qualified domestic trust—QDOT. In accordance with long-standing policy, the Unlimited Marital Deduction is *not* available to U.S. citizens transferring property to noncitizen spouses. A recent exception to the rule presents a valuable estate planning opportunity. If, under a will, the estate of a citizen spouse is left to an irrevocable *Qualified Domestic Trust—QDOT—*for the benefit of a noncitizen spouse, the estate may take full advantage of the Unlimited Marital Deduction.

A noncitizen surviving spouse may now receive the benefit of marital assets, estate tax free, if requirements are met. The trust must have at least one U.S. citizen trustee. Benefits are limited to income and "hardship" payments. And the trust must hold back assets sufficient to cover estate taxes should they become due if the trust fails for any reason.

As globalization increases and the world becomes ever smaller, marriages between citizens and noncitizens are more frequent. The QDOT both preserves the marital estate and protects the assets of U.S. citizens.

Marital trusts—all trusts for that matter—may be designed to suit all variety of circumstances, too numerous to describe. The idea is to provide for the surviving spouse *and* capitalize on the unified tax credit by removing, to the extent it is practical, the applicable exclusion amount from the marital estate. For extended families, a combination of trusts may be necessary to take care of everyone and take advantage of every tax benefit.

In addition to escaping probate, property held safely in an irrevocable trust is protected from the potential lapses in good judgment that old age might bring. And Uncle Sam is left empty-handed in the bargain. Very satisfying.

Irrevocable Life Insurance Trusts
You Bet Your Life

Life insurance is well known as a tool for wealth replacement. Insurance proceeds often replace assets used to pay estate taxes and creditors or to fund charitable contributions. Benefits could also provide for relatives, business associates, or those who are acutely dependent upon an income stream.

An *irrevocable life insurance trust—ILIT* (say "eyelet," not to be confused with *Chantilly lace*)—takes the policy out of your ownership, providing a clever safeguard against potential estate tax losses and an excellent vehicle to provide generously for your chosen beneficiaries.

Ownership of the policy is key. Life insurance owned by you is considered part of your estate and treated as such. Upon your death, insurance proceeds are distributed without going through probate, but are subject to estate taxes, though the person(s) who receives the proceeds incurs no income tax liability. A pretty good setup, but you can do better with a change in policy ownership, or an ILIT.

An insurance policy on *your* life, owned and controlled by *another* person or a trust, escapes income tax, probate, *and* estate tax. The policy is not considered part of the estate of the insured person; therefore, it is not subject to estate tax.

To create an ILIT, place funds in an irrevocable trust and direct your trustee to purchase a life insurance policy. Or create the trust and make an annual cash gift to enable the trustee to pay the premiums for a policy on your life. The trustee could be your intended beneficiary—perhaps your son or grandson.

These cash gifts may be tax free if they are within the annual gift exclusion, and as long as they do not violate the *Crummey power*—so named because the Crummey family initiated the lawsuit resulting in the ruling.

The gifts may be intended for, but not restricted to, payment of insurance premiums. A restricted gift is considered a future interest, and not a gift at all. Under the rule, the donee must have the "power"

"We cannot write a life policy for your husband, Mrs. Blaine, because he is already dead. In insurance terms, that is considered a preëxisting condition."

to use a gift as he likes, even if it means withdrawing the gift from a trust—and that option must be available, at least for a specified period of time.

It's Crummey and S'wonderful, all at the same time.

Transferring a life insurance policy. It's Easier Said Than Done. If you transfer your life insurance policy to an ILIT, the law requires that three years pass before the transfer is legally valid.

The *contemplation-of-death rule* imposes the assumption that the transfer of a life insurance policy within three years of death would not have been made unless the owner of the policy knew she was going to die. The law voids the "deathbed" transfer on the presumption that it is more of a last-ditch effort to avoid probate and death taxes than the completion of an intended, irrevocable transfer. As of 1977, most other gifts and transfers are no longer subject to the old three-year limitation.

Beneficiaries. When creating an ILIT—and only then—you may instruct your trustee to name whomever you choose to be the beneficiary. If you retain any element of control, such as the power to change beneficiaries or have access to cash value of the policy, you are still considered the owner. Proceeds will be counted as part of your estate and be subject to estate taxes.

Married couples often own second-to-die life insurance policies to provide untaxed assets for heirs. An ILIT can do the same. If you have a new partner or significant other, you could make everybody happy by making your partner the beneficiary of life insurance and leaving the family home to the family. Or vice versa.

An ILIT also provides invaluable and inviolable protection for minor children. Upon the death of the parent, funds are immediately available to sustain the lives of the children without interruption. A trustee is already in place to manage funds until the children are of legal age, avoiding the appointment of a guardian who must otherwise present annual accounting to the court.

In other instances life insurance in trust or owned by another can protect very important assets. Benefits could pay off a home mortgage or enable your business partners to buy out your share, leaving the business to the partners while providing cash value to your heirs. Benefits protected by an insurance policy could compensate for estate taxes on family farms or businesses, preventing their unnecessary sale— and, not incidentally, the demise of agrarian and small-business communities.

An ILIT is also an excellent vehicle to use in conjunction with a charitable remainder trust. Heirs receive insurance proceeds in place of the assets donated to charity.

In settling an estate with ILIT proceeds, a little tax technicality

After Three Years, Frasier May Leave the Building

Frasier is listening to the advice of others for a change, and is making an estate plan. He has decided to remove the life insurance policy he has owned for many years from his rather grandiose estate. The policy is for the benefit of young Frederick, now sporting a bow tie and boater as he swaggers through the Ivy League back east—nothing but the best, of course.

Frasier could create an ILIT and transfer the life insurance policy he already owns into trust with Frederick as beneficiary. If Frasier dies within three years of the transfer, he will have achieved absolutely nothing and insurance proceeds will be treated—and taxed—as part of his estate. Hardly appropriate for someone of his intelligence.

A more suitable idea might be to take the cash value of his existing policy and place it in the ILIT for the trust to purchase and own insurance on Frasier's life. In this case there is no three-year waiting period.

In either case, there are two other legalities to consider. First, Frederick must have the right to exercise his "Crummey power" before the gift is considered complete. Second, if the cash value of the policy or the gift exceeds the annual gift exclusion, the transfer could also trigger a gift tax liability. Good intentions poor result.

But if all goes well, as it surely must—that is, if Frasier transfers a policy and lives the three years, and makes a complete gift—master Frederick will receive the proceeds tax free to use as he chooses. Well done, my good man. Ta-ta.

must be observed. Even though the trust may be designed to replace assets used to pay estate taxes, regulations do not permit proceeds from the trust to be used to pay estate taxes *directly*. Insurance payments to the trust must be exchanged for assets from the estate before they can be used to pay estate taxes. A little administrative detail that is usually worth the trouble.

*   *   *

Like other trusts, an ILIT is not appropriate for every situation. It may be less expensive to simply have another trustworthy person own a life insurance policy than to go to the expense of creating a life insurance trust. Without the protection of a trust, however, the cash value of an individually owned policy is accessible not only to the owner but also to creditors, including divorce settlements. Furthermore, the policy owner can change the beneficiaries at his discretion. Your life insurance could vanish into thin air.

Charitable Trusts:
CRATS, CRUTS, NIM-CRUTS, and CLTs
Sweet Charity

Don't panic. These are just a lot of intimidating acronyms for different types of charitable remainder and charitable lead trusts, a set of simple ideas that allows you to:

- donate to your favorite charity
- save income and estate taxes
- retain—and often increase—your income

It's a WIN-WIN-WIN!

The great tax gods have deigned that giving is good and have made it highly beneficial to everyone involved. Choose a form of charitable trust to meet your specific income and tax needs. In all cases, your property is placed with a trustee who manages the assets and income according to your direction. In some cases, the charity might serve as trustee, saving trustee fees. To achieve maximum tax benefits, charitable trusts must be irrevocable.

*   *   *

In a **charitable remainder trust (CRT)** the trustee provides income to you or your chosen noncharitable beneficiary (your spouse, a disabled relative, for example) for a given period of time. At the end of that time or when the last named beneficiary dies, the remainder—what's left in the trust—goes to the charity outright. The donor takes an income tax deduction for the remainder interest at the time assets are transferred into trust.

CRTs are a great option for those who have no children or are otherwise providing for them, perhaps through an ILIT. Or for those who are rah-rah for their alma maters, want a big building or new wing named after themselves, or simply can and want to do something for the greater good. All smart charities send out brochures periodically, asking if they can help you with your estate plan. They're talking CRTs.

CRTs take many forms:

CRAT—charitable remainder annuity trust. Pays a *fixed amount* each year representing not less than a 5 percent return on the initial fair market value of trust assets. Once established, no additions may be made to the trust.

CRUT—charitable remainder unitrust. Pays annual income representing a *fixed percentage* of trust assets, not less than 5 percent even if it requires selling assets. Payments are variable because the trust can be added to and is revalued each year.

NIM-CRUT. Pays only *net distributable income.* The trustee is not forced to use principal assets or to liquidate assets which might incur capital gains tax, but can make up payments to meet percentage requirements at a future date.

A *charitable gift annuity* and *pooled-income trust* are not charitable trusts, but private agreements between a donor and charity. The donor makes a gift to a charity in return for annual income for life.

CRTs save taxes three ways. First, the grantor pays no tax on appreciated assets.

"Dad, the dean has gone over your financial statement, and he doesn't think you're working up to your full potential."

Second, the asset is removed from the estate of the grantor, saving estate taxes.

Third, the grantor receives an income tax deduction calculated on the value of the assets, the ages of income beneficiaries, and the rate of distribution. Any deduction not used in the first year can be carried forward for five.

> *This is a peculiar country. A fool can make money—not only can, but does—but it takes real brains to give it away wisely.*
>
> —Will Rogers

A **charitable lead trust (CLT)** is essentially the reverse of the CRT. Assets are placed in trust with the income going to the charity for a specified period of time. The remainder then passes to whomever you have named—back to you (the grantor) or to your designated ben-

Move 'em Up, Head 'em Out

A fter movin' on up through the hard-earned success of their cleaning stores, Louise and George Jefferson's wealth continued to grow as they rode the bull market of the 1990s. Louise managed to talk George into creating a trust for son Lionel, but she wanted to do more—to share their good fortune with others, to give back some of what they had gained.

Age had done nothing to mellow George, however. He was as headstrong and cantankerous as ever and would not give away what he might need for himself—not to mention what Louise might need.

But Mama Jefferson had taught her children well. If they wanted George to listen to their plan, they had to stand up to him. There was only one thing to do—call for backup.

When Florence arrived, she took her battle station at the door, planted her hands on her hips, and ordered George to stop strutting, sit down, and stay there. It took all they had, but Lionel and Louise talked as they circled George, and stated their case. After much finger shaking, George became convinced that everyone with humble beginnings like his own deserved a chance to move on up.

The Jeffersons created a charitable remainder trust to provide income to themselves for life, and provide remaining trust assets to support urban neighborhood enterprise. George grumbled plenty about how the trust might benefit some people he might not consider suitable. But he got his income and an income tax deduction, and the trust assets were removed from his estate. George even had to admit it was for a good cause—especially if a brilliant and handsome young entrepreneur like himself should come along.

eficiaries. This type of charitable trust obviously requires that the grantor be able to do without the income.

The income tax deduction takes place each year as trust income is paid to the charity. The trust ends on a specific date, which could coincidentally be your date of death, and assets pass to your chosen beneficiaries. The trust bypasses probate, but it could be subject to estate taxes.

When the CLT ends, if assets are returned to you they are, of course, treated as part of your estate and taxed as such. But you receive the annual benefit of a charitable deduction while you are alive, and your children still get the goods.

The National Charities Information Bureau offers guidelines for charitable giving. Your donation is tax deductible only if the charity receiving it is *qualified* under federal tax regulations. Before turning over one red cent, study the operation of your favorite charity. And appoint only a trustee or administrator experienced in charitable trusts.

Whatever the motive for generosity, even Uncle Sam approves and, in the case of charitable trusts, let's us have our cake and eat it too. It's enough to make even the greediest among us think philanthropist for a moment.

Generation-Skipping Trusts
Teach Your Children Well

Parents should leave children "enough money so they would feel they could do anything, but not so much that they could do nothing."
—Warren Buffett

The idea behind a *generation-skipping trust* is clear from its name. Property is placed in trust providing income to one generation and leaving the trust assets to the next. This type of trust is also called a "dynasty trust" because it amasses wealth for future generations.

A trust created to provide income for grandchildren could skip two or more generations before final distribution is made and, most importantly, before any estate taxes are incurred. Sounds like a good deal, doesn't it? In 1990, the government realized it was too good a deal.

Recognizing that generation-skipping trusts allowed wealth, particularly great wealth, to escape estate tax generation after generation, the government imposed restrictions. Now there is a lifetime exemption per person, permitting a maximum of $1 million to be put into generation-skipping trusts tax free. A special generation-skipping tax is imposed on any amount over the exemption, at an astounding rate of 50 percent.

Under the 1990 regulations, no matter how large the trust becomes, it will not be subject to estate tax when final distributions of the trust assets are made. In defining generations, family lineage is followed and a minimum of 12.5 years is assumed between generations. For unrelated persons, 25 years is the measure for each generation.

Because the life of a generation-skipping trust spans generations, it is generally administered by more than one trustee. Appointing a bank or financial institution as one of the trustees guarantees continuity even as individual trustees change over the years. As with every trust, appointment of successor trustees is prescribed in the trust instrument.

Grantor-Retained Trusts
Return to Sender

In this specialized form of trust, a grantor places property in trust but keeps income or other benefits of the property, while miraculously achieving the estate tax benefits of an irrevocable trust. It's very tricky, but highly effective if properly designed.

Here's how it works. You as grantor transfer property into trust, reserving a certain benefit—income or use of property—for yourself for a certain number of years.

The property you place in trust is considered a future gift, or future interest, and is subject to gift tax. At the time the trust is created, the value of the taxable gift is reduced by the value of benefits reserved for the grantor—the retained interest.

The taxable value of the gift is reported, but taxes are due only on amounts in excess of the Applicable Exclusion Amount. Sorry, a future gift does not qualify for the $10,000 annual gift exclusion.

Stock, real estate, and any other highly appreciating assets make ideal properties for a grantor-retained interest trust because the trust

"Omigod—that's your dirty little secret? That you have a trust fund?"

removes the value of the gift, as well as future appreciation, from the estate of the grantor.

GRATs and GRUTs

Half Heaven, Half Heartache

In most grantor-retained trusts, the grantor places property in trust for a period of time during which he receives income from the trust. At the end of the specified time, the trust ends, the grantor's income stops, and the trust assets are distributed to the remaindermen, estate-tax free.

The trust may be used to transfer personal property or a family business interest to a chosen family member or desirable successor. In any case, it is an effective way to remove property *and* future appreciation from an estate at a low tax cost. As you might imagine, strict rules govern trusts offering such a great benefit to the taxpayer.

Striking a balance between requirements and benefits in this sophisticated trust is almost an art. The true benefit to the grantor is determined by a formula that, in turn, establishes the taxable value of the gift. A grantor-retained trust is required to preserve certain levels of trust assets while meeting income payment requirements. The period of time over which the grantor receives benefits, usually a certain number of years, is therefore a critical factor. If income distribution rules are broken, the entire transfer is subject to the unified tax.

There are two grantor-retained income trust forms:

GRAT—grantor-retained annuity trust. Pays a *fixed amount* of annual income for a specified number of years.

GRUT—grantor-retained unitrust. Pays a *fixed percentage* of the value of trust assets annually. Income increases as assets grow, providing a hedge against inflation.

Like all things almost too good to be true, there's a big catch to the estate tax benefit of a GRAT or GRUT. The grantor (you) must *outlive* the trust. Only when the term of the trust ends, and your income benefit ends—when the trust goes to your remaindermen—does the law view the gift as truly made. This is when the property officially leaves your estate and is no longer subject to estate taxes.

Should you die before the term ends, the trust works like a living trust. It is considered part of your estate for estate tax purposes, but is distributed in keeping with the terms of the trust.

For married couples, there is another option: When creating a GRAT or GRUT, specify that if you die before the term ends, it will become a QTIP trust for your spouse. The spouse thus retains the interest in your place. The transfer avoids estate taxes under the Unlimited Marital Deduction, but still directs the assets to named remaindermen.

As an alternative to a grantor-retained trust, property may be sold to children or others in return for annuity payments for life. The arrangement removes the asset from the estate and spreads out the tax consequence of the sale, while affording the buyer an extended payment plan without the high-wire balancing act required under a grantor-retained trust. Private annuities used in transferring family business property are explained in Chapter Seven.

Hi-Ho Silver—Away!

*L*et's *say the Lone Ranger transfers ownership of Silver, his stalwart steed—and valuable business asset—to a grantor-retained trust, naming Tonto as remainder beneficiary and retaining the right to ride the handsome horse for the next ten years. If the Lone Ranger lives beyond the ten years, Tonto gets Silver and the Lone Ranger gets a tax break on the transfer because Silver's taxable value is reduced by the Lone Ranger's use of him during the term of the trust.*

If, however, the Lone Ranger does not outlive the ten-year trust terms, Silver will go to Tonto, but the Lone Ranger's estate will be liable for estate tax on Silver's full value. Who was *that masked man, anyway?*

QPRT
True GRIT

In 1990, grantor-retained income trusts (GRITs) with no established obligation for income payments were effectively eliminated. Now, only the GRAT and GRUT forms, with structured income obligations, may be used for transfers to *descendants*. The GRIT is restricted to transfers of a personal residence or tangible property such as a valuable painting. If used for a residence, as is most common, it is called a *QPRT—qualified personal residence trust.*

A QPRT basically allows you to continue to live in your home after you have put it in trust for your children or other designated person(s). You give it away, but get to stay. The QPRT form may also be used to transfer certain tangible property such as a valuable painting. Your children could own the Picasso, but it hangs over *your* mantelpiece.

As with a GRAT or GRUT, you have to outlive the term of the

trust, or the house or painting will be considered part of your estate. And if you live in the house or keep the painting beyond the term of the trust, you will have to pay rent to the new owners, your remaindermen. Also subject to strict rules, a QPRT may hold only the qualified property as its major asset. It cannot be used as a catchall for personal property.

Tax, investment, and legal advice is crucial in setting up a GRAT, GRUT, QPRT, or private annuity to meet requirements. If the trust is properly executed, you will have your income and your heirs will have their inheritance, all at a low tax cost.

A Trust by Any Other Name
I Heard It Through the Grapevine

Over the years, trusts have been given all sorts of names, some reflecting the purpose of the trust, some the distribution. The result is a conglomeration of trust names that can confound even the experts. A quick review of the more common trust names helps cut the confusion.

A and B trusts are traditional terms still used by some pros:

The *A trust* is a marital deduction trust, possibly a QTIP. It benefits the surviving spouse, and is also known as a *power of appointment trust* or *spousal trust*.

The *B trust* is the credit shelter trust, usually created to take advantage of the unified tax credit for the benefit of the family. It is also called a *bypass trust* and sometimes a *family trust*.

Trusts designed to protect family assets or family members, whether using the tax credit or not, are also sometimes called *family trusts*, even when they are generation-skipping trusts. These trusts are hands-off to the in-laws, the outlaws, and other riffraff.

A *protective trust* is generally designed to protect an individual, perhaps a disabled or elderly family member.

A *spendthrift trust* protects a beneficiary from his own vices. Trust distributions are permitted only for specific purposes, such as food and shelter, not for mad money or to settle gambling debts.

A *sprinkling trust* is named for the method of distribution. At the discretions of the trustee, trust distributions are sprinkled to beneficiaries as needed.

You get the idea. A trust can be designed to suit your personal situation. Make sure the expense of creating a trust also suits you. The average cost of setting up a revocable living trust for one person is $1,000–$1,500; for a married couple, $2,500–$5,000. A will with a simple credit shelter trust costs about $1,500–$3,000, the same as an ILIT. There is much to consider, and in most cases much to be gained from a trust.

It's Now or Never . . .

- A well-planned marital estate includes a credit shelter trust that saves an estate of $1.3 million about *$200,000* in taxes!

- Parents with children of several marriages are wise to protect their families with separate trusts.

- Consider creating a life insurance trust by transferring an existing policy or funding a trust for premium payments.

- Give and you shall receive. Set up a charitable trust to get a big, fat tax break.

- If you want to keep property in the hands of your family and out of the hands of Uncle Sam, a trust can do it all.

- Be sure to compare the cost of setting up a trust with the real advantages.

Don't put your trust in money; put your money in trust.
—Oliver Wendell Holmes

4

Putting Your House in Order
Hold On, I'm Comin'

What's Goin' On...

- Gifts as estate planning tools
- How a gift is valued and taxed
- Lifetime gifts versus bequests of an estate
- Property titles and property rights
- Protection from creditors
- Emergency funds for survivors

A thorough estate plan is fine tuned to take advantage of everyday events. Matters we take for granted, like owning property and making gifts, can have a dramatic effect on an estate plan—especially if the property involved represents a substantial portion of an estate. Even with your essential documents in place, unattended details such as completion of gifts, transfer of title, or change of a designated beneficiary could foil your plan.

The many and somewhat convoluted options and tax benefits of gifts, property title, and property rights as well as several options for protection of family assets from creditors are reviewed in this chapter. Take the broad view in determining how these factors will figure into your estate plan, and let the pros tackle the technicalities. But remember, these finishing touches make the difference between a good estate plan and a great one. Go for great.

Don't be afraid to give up the good to go for the great.
—Kenny Rogers

Gifts
Hot Diggity (Dog Diggity Boom)

Lifetime gifts are an important part of almost every estate plan. There are tremendous tax advantages to making significant gifts while you are alive. Most of us like to give as well as to receive, and some people are unquestionably more generous than others. But make no mistake about it, there is a very practical side to giving away property. The tax benefits are powerful enough to turn even the Scrooges among us into generous spirits. And the most generous reap the greatest rewards.

If you have a certain gift in mind for a special someone, give it while you are alive, not only to make sure your gift is received, but to enjoy the giving. You see the expression, you share the sentiment. Making a gift now, rather than under your will, also guarantees that the right person will receive the gift as you intend.

Just about everybody likes to receive gifts. But the sheer pleasure of giving is one of the great joys of life.

Here's the short course on gifts. Estate, capital gains, and income tax can all be affected by lifetime gifts.

Whatever you give away is no longer part of your estate. The gift thus reduces the value of the donor's estate. The lower the value of the estate, the lower the estate taxes.

If you give away property that is likely to appreciate in value in the future, you unload a possible capital gains tax burden *and* give a gift that keeps on giving.

If the gift is income producing, there is icing on the cake. The donor has removed the assets as well as the income from his estate. And if the donee is in a lower income tax bracket than the donor, income produced by the gifted property is taxed at the donee's lower rate.

Completion of a Gift
Got to Give It Up

Gifts require more than good intentions to be effective in the eyes of the law. A gift is a complete transfer of the use, possession, and control of property. That means it belongs to someone else—no strings attached.

Donor: makes the gift
Donee: receives the gift

Like a lot of things that sound perfectly simple, a gift has certain legal elements:

Donor's intention. The donor must intend to make the gift. If you take Dad's MG when he's suffering from Alzheimer's and he doesn't know about it, it's not a gift.

Delivery. The gift must be delivered. An actual transfer of the property must take place. The title to the MG must be changed to show your name.

Possession. And the gift must be in your possession or control. With a big smile, accept the keys and the title to the MG, say thank you very much, and drive away. It's yours.

A gift is a *present interest,* not a future interest. If you have "given" the old MG to your grandson but are keeping it for him until he's 16, it's not a gift until he's 16, the MG is registered in his name, and he drives it away. As long as it's in your name and in your garage, it belongs to you and will be considered part of your estate no matter what your intentions.

"And the Haves, you might say, are divided into the Gives and Give Nots."

Incomplete Gifts

Oh, Dear, What Can the Matter Be

Certain gifts are by their very nature incomplete:

A *retained life interest,* in which property is transferred but the transferor holds back some benefit for herself, is not a gift. If you create a QPRT to give away your home but still live there, the transfer is a future interest, and not a complete gift. If, however, you deed the home to another person, it is a complete gift whether you continue to live there or not.

A gift that takes effect upon your death gives away nothing during your lifetime and is considered a bequest, or *testamentary gift,* distributed under your will. It will be treated as part of your estate and will be subject to estate tax.

A *revocable transfer* in which the donor retains the right to change any aspect of a transfer is not a gift. If your mother-in-law gave you a beautiful diamond brooch but reserves the right to take it back, she can not only take it back but give it to someone else! It's never really yours and the brooch is not a gift after all. In this case, diamonds might not be a girl's best friend.

A *general power of appointment*, giving another person the right to control or change any aspect of a property, is usually considered a gift. In this case the donor is effectively giving up control of the property, and the transfer is subject to gift tax. But a donor who "gives" something away while retaining a power of appointment over the property has not made a complete gift.

A *life insurance policy transferred within three years of death* is not considered a complete transfer. Proceeds are counted as part of the donor's estate. Transfer of the policy into the name of another person or a trust must take place more than three years before death to remove the policy from the estate of the insured owner.

Deathbed Transfers
In the Midnight Hour

Under current law, gifts may be made right up until the moment of death if all elements of the gift are proven. Even if you are *non compos mentis* (out of it), a person acting as your agent under a power of attorney may continue to make gifts on your behalf if specifically authorized to do so.

Under the old contemplation-of-death rule, pre-1977, any gift made within three years of death was considered invalid. Thankfully, the current rule is more in keeping with the lightning speed of life on the information highway. Beep-beep.

"Hey, Gramps, is 'deathbed' one word or two?"

Tax Advantages of Lifetime Gifts

I'm into Something Good

When all is said and done, taxes could diminish the overall benefit of a gift, to both donor and donee. The donor is primarily responsible for the tax, but if for some reason the donor does not pay gift taxes due, the tables are turned and the donee becomes responsible for the tax. Some gift.

Making gifts while you are alive has valuable tax benefits:

The **Annual Exclusion** allows an individual to make as many annual gifts of $10,000 to as many individuals as she likes without incurring any gift tax. You can reduce the value of your estate, make gifts to heirs who would receive the property anyway, and *pay no taxes* on the gifts. Spouses who agree to a "split gift" are

Music to His Ears

When Jack Benny was told by his estate planning lawyer that he could afford to, and should, make annual tax-free gifts to reduce the size of his estate, he could not believe his ears. "Give? GIVE? You want me to give something away?" And then that look— the one with the arms folded, head turned to give the full effect of a wilted smile which amounted to nothing more than lips pulled tightly across gritted teeth.

Renowned as a tightwad, Jack had his own personal guard for his vault and would take no pleasure in giving anything away. But he tried. He gave Rochester $5,000 on the condition that he buy a new car. But this was not a gift. Rochester was the chauffeur—the new car was for Benny, not Rochester.

Jack said he gave his treasured violin to the conservatory. But in fact he made the bequest in his will and kept the instrument at home to play and enjoy until he died. This was not a gift because Jack did not hand over the instrument. It was not a lifetime gift, but a testamentary gift which would take effect only at death.

A real gift would be earplugs for wife Mary, Rochester, and the neighbors who would have to go on listening to Benny's violin music.

allowed a combined Annual Exclusion of $20,000. Thus, parents can make annual tax-free gifts of $20,000 to each of their children—or anyone for that matter.

As of 1999, the Annual Exclusion is indexed for inflation. However, the exclusion will actually increase only in $1,000 increments. Sounds like a committee worked on the plan, doesn't it?

Any gifts above the amount of the Annual Exclusion must be reported on gift tax returns filed no later than April 15 in the year after the gift was made. Gift taxes may not be due at the time of filing, but the value of the gift is applied to the Applicable Exclusion Amount.

In addition to the Annual Exclusion, every U.S. citizen is allowed a credit against the Unified Transfer Tax for combined lifetime gifts and estate transfers. The **Applicable Exclusion Amount** is $675,000 in the year 2000, but it is scheduled to increase on a sliding scale through the year 2006, when it tops out at $1 million. Only transfers that exceed the exclusion amount are subject to the United Transfer Tax.

The **Unlimited Marital Deduction** is available only to married couples. Spouses are permitted to make gifts and transfer properties of any value to each other at absolutely *no tax cost*. The deduction applies to lifetime gifts as well as estate transfers.

Lifetime gifts between spouses are therefore of little tax benefit. If the couple files a joint income tax return, it doesn't matter which spouse receives income. And if spouses file separately, the tax rates are higher, washing away any perceived benefit of shifted income.

Under the Unlimited Marital Deduction, any property from the estate of the first spouse to die passes to the surviving spouse tax free. When the surviving spouse dies, however, the accumulated assets of both spouses are subject to that whopping, progressive Unified Transfer Tax. Spouses have the unique opportunity to preserve the credit amount to which both are entitled—and save about $200,000 in estate taxes—by creating a credit shelter trust under the will of the first to die. The trust is a straightforward arrangement in which the ends definitely justify the means. See Chapter Three.

Valuation of Lifetime Gifts
Super-cali-fragil-istic-expiali-docious

It's not fair, but a lifetime gift is valued one way for the donor and another way for the donee. For purposes of the Annual Exclusion and the unified gift and estate tax, a *donor* gives a lifetime gift at *fair market value*, or the average of the high and low price of the gift on the date it is made. Establishing a value may be as simple as looking in the newspaper, or as complicated and costly as obtaining a professional appraisal. The fair market value of a gift must be $10,000 or less to qualify for the annual gift exclusion. Gifts whose value exceeds excluded amounts are reported on annual gift tax returns.

A *donee* receives a gift at the *cost basis* of the donor regardless of fair market value. If and when the donee sells his gift, the capital gains tax is based on the donor's original cost basis.

Be careful to give gifts that suit everyone's purposes. Weigh the tax benefits of removing an asset from the estate against the potential capital gains tax burden placed on your donee.

Cost Basis Versus Stepped-Up Basis

If a gift of stock, received at the donor's cost basis of $1, is later sold for $100 a share, the donee is responsible for tax on the full $99 capital gain.

On the other hand, when a bequest is made under a will, it is given a stepped-up basis at death. The share with a cost basis of $1 is received by the beneficiary of a will at a stepped-up basis. Let's say the stock was worth $95 on date of death. If the beneficiary later sells the share for $100, only a $5 capital gain is taxed.

Low-basis gifts from portfolios of appreciated assets are often made purposely in an effort to reduce the size of an estate and transfer capital gains to donees in a lower bracket. However, with long-term capital gains tax rates of 20 percent for all but those in the lowest income bracket, making a gift of a low-basis stock usually shifts rather than reduces the tax burden. To achieve a capital gains tax advantage for the beneficiaries of her will, a donor in her golden years should consider withholding low-basis lifetime gifts in favor of estate transfers with a stepped-up basis.

On the other hand, when appreciated assets are taxed as part of an estate, the tax rate is higher because of the higher value of the estate. The estate might pay more taxes than necessary, and your family might receive less than if you had made lifetime gifts. A little number crunching will indicate whether lifetime gifts or bequests under the will offer the best tax advantage.

Some are tempted to undervalue lifetime gifts to exploit both the Annual Exclusion and unified tax credit. Beware of the IRS. There is a three-year statute of limitations for reevaluation of a gift, but in some cases, courts have permitted reevaluation much later, for estate tax purposes. Don't try giving away a Van Gogh as an unremarkable Dutch oil painting of little value.

Planned Giving

When You Wish upon a Star

The words *planned giving* are usually associated with charitable giving. However, the tax benefits of giving are hardly limited to charitable deductions.

If you can do without the money, a pattern of annual gifts to your intended heirs benefits just about everyone except Uncle Sam. You have the pleasure of making the gift. Your children or other donees receive a valuable gift that will almost certainly appreciate. A systematic program of gift giving can, over the years, significantly reduce the value of an estate, diminishing the effect of estate taxes and preserving the bulk of the estate for the beneficiaries of a will.

Partial Gifts

A partial gift is a transfer of less than full value of a property. If, for example, you want to shift ownership of a business to your partner, daughter, or whomever, you can do it in partial gifts that slowly but surely transfer defined shares of the business, tax free, by keeping each gift within the Annual Exclusion.

Medical, Educational, and Charitable Gifts

Medical and educational payments on behalf of someone else—someone for whom you are not legally responsible—are technically considered gifts but are exempt from tax. Payment must be made directly to the medical provider or school.

Eight Is More Than Enough

If over the course of ten years, widower Tom Bradford made an annual gift of $10,000 a year to each of his eight children, the value of his estate would be reduced by $800,000. But Tom remarried, and his annual gifts were eligible for the spousal combination. With gifts of $20,000 per year, Tom and bride Abby could now follow a gift-giving program that would remove $1.6 million from the marital estate over ten years.

If Tom and Abby could truly afford to make the gifts, they will have significantly reduced their marital estate. The amount of the gifts, as well all the future appreciation, is passed along, tax free.

Assuming the gifts totaling $1.6 million earn 7½ percent per year, their value would more than double over ten years. At a Unified Transfer Tax rate of 37–55 percent, the potential tax savings amounts to hundreds of thousands of dollars. And those eight children will have more than enough.

We are all well aware that medical costs and tuition are forever increasing, straining many a family budget. Grandparents, this tax loophole presents a great opportunity to remove funds from your estate, tax free, and give a meaningful gift to your grandchild. Medical and educational gifts are separate from the Annual Exclusion.

Charitable gifts made during your lifetime do not fall under the Annual Exclusion or unified tax credit, but are deductible from taxable gross income in the year the gift was made, with some limitations. Likewise, charitable bequests made by an estate are included as part of the estate for tax purposes, but are deductible from estate taxes or final income taxes paid by the estate.

In some cases, a donor transfers assets to a qualified charity in exchange for a commitment by the charity to pay back to the donor a specific amount of income annually, for life. A *charitable gift annuity* is a private agreement between the charity and the individual donor. Some charitable organizations pool gifts in income-producing trusts—*Pooled Income Trusts (PITs)*—with donors receiving pro rata income benefits. For example, if the contribution represents one-fifth of trust assets, the donor will receive one-fifth of the income. The deductible value of the charitable gift is, in this case, reduced by income benefits to the donor.

As government dollars allotted to not-for-profit organizations shrink, private gifts to charities are encouraged by individual tax benefits. There is a real advantage to using your Annual Exclusions and your unified tax credit now. Get more bang for the buck with a plan for lifetime gifts.

Gifts to Minors

The Candy Man

In many families, it is customary to make gifts of cash or stock—remember savings bonds?—to children, particularly on special occasions. Children, grandchildren, stepchildren, nieces, nephews, and special friends—or their parents—often open greeting cards with "a little something" tucked inside.

Extra money comes in handy when raising a child. Regular gifts build a nest egg for a child and remove the value of gifts from the estate of the donor. The donor saves future taxes. And if the child is going to get the money or property anyway, a gift-giving program makes sense all the way around.

A child who is a minor is not permitted to receive a gift outright. You can't just hand a kid a big check. If your great-uncle gives a savings bond or a check, or 50 shares of stock, to your new baby, the best place for it is a custodial account.

A gift is not complete unless it is immediately used or available to be used for the benefit of the minor. A gift may be *intended* for a certain use, but *not restricted* to such use. When Popeye puts $10,000 in trust for Sweet Pea, with benefits restricted to the purchase of spinach, the gift has no present value to the child. It is not a gift until it is spent for the spinach and Sweet Pea's biceps are bulging.

Custodianship

Under the Uniform Transfers to Minors Act (UTMA) and the Uniform Gifts to Minors Act (UGMA), an adult may accept a gift on behalf of a minor. Each state subscribes to elements of UTMA or UGMA consistent with its own property laws. Your financial and estate planning advisors will be familiar with the requirements and limitations of a custodial account in your state.

Under UGMA, a minor is a person under 18 years of age. But most states have adopted UTMA, which clings to the more historic 21-year milestone and generally permits a broader range of property holdings. A minor coming of age is said to "reach his or her majority."

Plan ahead: It wasn't raining when Noah built the ark.
—Richard Cushing

To create a custodianship, an adult simply opens a custodial account with a financial institution, such as a bank or broker, naming the custodian and successor custodian. The gift of cash, check, securities, or other property is deposited, and income and principal become immediately available for the child's benefit.

A custodian has a fiduciary responsibility to manage, protect, and preserve the custodial property according to a high standard. Unlike property guardianship, there is no involvement of a court—no bond or periodic accounting—in custodianship.

The title to custodial property will read, for example: Sheriff Andy Taylor, custodian for Opie Taylor, UTMA North Carolina. The signature for every endorsement, every transaction in the custodial account, must read that same way. Andy has to write out the whole thing every time he makes a deposit or withdrawal.

When Opie turns 21, the property in the custodial account is his. Period. No more custodian. He will have to change the title on all the assets from the custodial account to his own name. Andy is no longer involved. Everything is owned outright by Opie.

A youngster who has received money or stock for 21 years will have accumulated a substantial amount of property, and that could be a problem. With a large account at his disposal, Opie could find plenty of trouble without even looking, even in Mayberry.

The importance of naming a *successor custodian* cannot be overstated. If a custodian dies or is incapacitated and a successor has not officially been named, a court is likely to intervene to protect the minor's interest. The court will appoint a property guardian with specific powers and accounting responsibilities. A guardianship is a more restricted, cumbersome, and costly form of management than custodianship, though it will continue to operate to the exclusive benefit of the minor.

Tax effects. Custodianship is not without tax consequences. Until the minor reaches the age of 14, the first $700 of custodial income is a deduction for the child and the next $700 is taxed at the rate of the child. Any income over $1,400 is taxed at the rate of the parent. If custodial income is high and the parent is in a high income tax bracket, taxes could reduce the value of the custodial account. After age 14, a minor falls into his own income tax bracket. Income taxes are paid separately on behalf of the minor, almost certainly at a lower, more favorable rate.

A parent who serves as custodian has complete control of the account. Consequently if the custodian/parent dies while the child is a minor, the custodial property is counted as part of the parent's estate for estate tax purposes.

To keep custodial property out of the estate of a parent, consider naming a close friend or relative, rather than a parent, as custodian. The parent can continue to receive custodial income for the benefit of the child, and income over $1,400 is still taxable at the parent's rate. However, with control of the property removed, the account will not be considered part of the parent's estate. The separation of power and benefits also prevents the property from being considered part of the custodian's estate.

A parent who places funds in a custodial account with the intent to remove them at a later date has not made a complete gift in the eyes of the law. If, for example, custodial funds are dipped into for general household support, the funds are not a gift to the child. The custodial account is a sham.

If a custodial account accumulates assets of significant value whether by gift or growth of investments, and income taxes become unreasonable, it's time to reconsider the pros and cons of custodianship. In the long run, the assets might be more beneficial to the minor if held in trust.

As a separate entity, a trust pays taxes at its own progressive rate rather than the parent's rate. And if the trust benefits only the minor, it will not be considered part of the parent's estate, even if the parent serves as trustee. It's a matter of simple arithmetic to determine if a custodianship is beneficial or counterproductive.

Trusts for the Benefit of Minors

Creation of an irrevocable trust for the benefit of a minor could be a very effective way to protect a child's interest and preserve assets— especially in combination with gift giving. Contributions to a trust are, of course, subject to gift tax if above the Annual Exclusion.

An irrevocable trust is a separate entity that cannot be modified or revoked. Management of the investments or property in the trust, as well as distributions of income and principal, is the responsibility of a trustee who must follow the specific instructions of the trust document. Trust income is taxed at its own rate.

Because the trust is a separate entity, it is not considered part of the estate of the parent. However, if a parent serves as trustee and could be perceived to benefit from the trust in any way, the trust could be deemed in the control of the parent. Thus, the trust *could* be considered part of the parent's estate. It is a better idea to appoint another individual (not the other parent) or a financial institution as trustee. A trust offers the estate planning combination we like best. More for your heirs, less for Uncle Sam.

Restricted Gifts

Call Me Irresponsible

"Gift" Loans

An old estate planning trick is the gift loan. You know, the parents make a loan of $100,000 to help the son buy the house. The parents forgive $10,000 each year under the Annual Exclusion and collect no interest. All the while, the son lives in the house with the full benefit of the full $100,000.

Our laws do not recognize no-interest and below-market loans, but treat them as gifts. The uncollected interest is considered both income to the donor/lender and a gift to the donee/borrower. The donor could be liable for income *and* gift tax on the "gifted" interest. Gift tax might not be due now, but the value of the gift is applied toward the unified tax credit.

An acceptable gift loan involves legitimate interest paid at the going rate and annual amounts of the loan balance forgiven under the Annual Exclusion. The son pays the interest and deducts it as allowable from his taxable income. The parents declare the interest they receive as income. Legitimate, less costly, and the parents still help the son buy his house.

If one or both parents die before a legitimate loan is forgiven in full, the balance of the loan, plus unpaid interest, reverts to the estate of the parent. The loan balance is usually settled as a transfer of the estate, but could result in unequal distributions to their heirs. Be sure to clarify your intentions about equal distribution in your will, and if appropriate, refer specifically to outstanding family loans. Consult your estate planning lawyer and investment advisor before making a gift loan.

Nonresidents' Gifts

Gifts made by U.S. citizens living abroad have limited tax advantages. Nonresident citizens are permitted to take advantage of the gift and estate exclusions and credits *only* with regard to property *located within the United States*. An American doctor working in China cannot make annual gifts of Tang dynasty porcelain to his daughter under the annual gift exclusion.

*"Son, you're all grown up now. You owe me two
hundred and fourteen thousand dollars."*

Gifts to Noncitizen Spouses

The Unlimited Marital Deduction is *not* available to noncitizen spouses. To compensate, the annual gift exclusion for gifts to noncitizen spouses is $101,000. The idea is to keep Romeo from inheriting all of Miss America's property and taking it back to the Motherland. Although this concept is somewhat outdated by the global economy, it represents an honorable attempt to preserve America's wealth for its own citizens.

*   *   *

A final word about gifts. The affluent usually follow lifetime gift-giving programs to reduce the size of their estates and the impact of future estate taxes. The rest of us have to be very careful not to give away too much and to make sure we have enough for ourselves. We'll need plenty if we live to be 110. Giving it away may be gratifying for the moment, but if your children have to turn around and use your gift to pay your expenses, the true benefit of the gift will be lost.

Step-Up at Death

The Morning After

The tax basis of a lifetime gift is considerably different from that of a testamentary gift (a bequest or transfer made under your will). *Cost basis* is the fair market value of a property—what it costs—when acquired. Generally, when a property is transferred or sold, any appreciation over the cost basis is subject to capital gains tax.

Gifts made while a donor is alive are transferred at the cost basis of the donor. If and when the donee sells, he will be responsible for capital gains tax on any and all increase in value over the cost basis of the donor.

Property in an estate, however, is given a *stepped-up basis* of fair market value determined either on *date of death* or the *alternate valuation date* six months later. The executor chooses the date that is most advantageous for tax purposes.

The bad news is that the estate is taxed—if it is taxable—at the stepped-up basis. Capital gains of the property in the estate are effectively taxed at the higher estate tax rates. Not too bad for Uncle Sam.

But the good news is that property is also distributed from the estate at the stepped-up value, reducing the potential capital gains tax liability of the heirs. A beneficiary who sells is liable for capital gains tax only on the increase over the stepped-up basis.

But this good news for heirs may be too much for Uncle to bear. The step-up provision is being reexamined by his people in Washington.

Walton's Wood Stock

Pa, John-Boy, and Jim-Bob took the family lumber business public in 1940. Their shares of Walton's Wood (WOOD) had a low cost basis of $2 per share.

Living in fear that a depression might come again, Pa sold his shares early on and stuffed his mattress with the dollars he received in profits. He didn't care what taxes he had to pay; he wanted the cash on hand.

Pa's profits are subject to capital gains tax. His WOOD stock with a cost basis of $2 sold for $50, resulting in a capital gain of $48 per share. At current rates, that $48 is subject to capital gains tax at a rate of 20 percent. Capital gains taxes are due annually, along with other income taxes.

John-Boy and Jim-Bob began giving WOOD stock to their children during the economic boom of the 1980s. Their children received the gifts at the original cost basis of $2 per share, even if the market price was $200 on the day the gift was made.

Jim-Bob managed to give nearly his entire estate to his 12 children. When he died, the estate qualified for the unified tax credit and no estate taxes were due. But when his children sold the WOOD stock, they paid tax on all the capital gains over the $2 cost basis.

Feeling terribly responsible, as always, and wanting to keep the business in the family, John-Boy kept control of the business by holding on to most of his stock until it was distributed under his will to his grandchildren, Esther Tina and Zeb (named after his grandparents). The basis of shares remaining in John-Boy's estate were stepped up at his death.

Let's say the price, or fair market value, for a share of WOOD on John-Boy's date of death is $250. Esther and Zeb receive the shares at the stepped-up basis of $250 each. If and when they sell the WOOD stock, their capital gains will amount only to the difference between the stepped-up basis and the price at which they sell the shares.

It sounds like a better deal than it is. Even though the

*grandchildren will pay no capital gains tax on the $248 increase,
John-Boy's estate will have been taxed at the stepped-up basis. A
quick comparison of estate tax rates of 37–55 percent and the capital
gains tax rate of 20 percent indicates that Uncle Sam, rather than
the immediate family, gets the best deal. The moral to the story? It
may be smarter to sleep on a lumpy mattress than sit on WOOD
stock.*

Entitlements
A Little Bit Me, A Little Bit You

Property Titles
From a Jack to a King

In days of old, ownership of land was conveyed by the crown, by
royal title, such as Duke, Marquis, Earl, or Baron of this-or-that. Title
and ownership were passed from generation to generation.

The U.S. Constitution does not recognize royal titles, and ownership of property takes many forms. Title to property establishes who
owns what, and sometimes determines under what circumstances property may be sold, or distributed at death.

Fee Simple, Joint Tenancy, and *Tenancy-in-Common* are the basic
forms of property title, each with special characteristics and effects. All
properties in your estate, from checking accounts to real estate, must be
titled to meet your objectives.

A gift, sale, or transfer of any type is complete only when title is
transferred. Transferring title is one instance in which a paper trail is
desirable. If you buy a house, the deed must be free and clear, and
registered in your name. If you buy a car but the seller does not sign
the title on the back transferring it to you, you will be unable to register
the car in your name. Until the car is registered in your name, the sale
has technically not taken place. Handing over a stock certificate to your
grandson is not a transfer. Only reregistering the stock certificate in the

name of your grandson, or that of his custodian, makes the transfer complete.

If you have a joint checking account with no restrictions, the other signator could have the right to everything in the account. That's okay if you share the account with your spouse, but not okay if the other signator is an employee who has account privileges for administrative purposes.

An estate plan begins with an inventory worksheet listing all your property. Be sure to make a note of how the title on each asset reads, and, if necessary, ask your lawyer to explain the title and its effect. A good lawyer will automatically review all titles for accuracy and will reregister titles and deeds as required.

Let's review basic property titles:

Fee Simple is the ancient legal term for absolute ownership of a property. If you own your house in your own name, have no mortgage or liens on it, you own it in Fee Simple. Property owned outright is distributed under your will.

Co-ownership of property takes many forms:

In a **Joint Tenancy with Right of Survivorship**, each "tenant" owns an equal, undivided share in the property. There is no limit to the number of owners who may be joint tenants.

The Right of Survivorship means that when one owner dies, the surviving owners hold equal undivided shares of the property. The last surviving joint tenant is left owning the entire property, all by herself.

The most important effect of Joint Tenancy with Right of Survivorship (there's really not an easier way to say it) is that it bypasses a will, overcoming any distribution terms in the will of an individual joint tenant. Bypassing probate may be of particular importance to unmarried and same-sex couples who co-own their home. They usually don't want family interfering with distribution of their property. In a Joint Tenancy with Right of Survivorship, the family doesn't have the opportunity to interfere.

Under a Joint Tenancy with Right of Survivorship, no owner has complete control of the property, and none can give away or sell his share without the consent of the other joint tenants. However, if the property is the primary asset in the estate of a co-owner, it may have to be sold to raise money to pay creditors or estate taxes.

Similarly, if your children are your joint tenants, the property could be subject to *their* creditors. If you and your spouse are joint tenants, and you die "simultaneously," the joint tenancy loses its effect and the property is subject to probate.

Tenancy-by-Entirety is another form of joint tenancy permitted between husband and wife in just a few states. The property is owned equally and wholly by each spouse. Despite the fact that such a description defies all logic, the title prevents one spouse from disposing of his or her share in the property without the consent of the other spouse. The surviving spouse, through Right of Survivorship, takes full ownership of the entire property.

Tenancy-in-Common is joint ownership with *no* Right of Survivorship. In this case, the title reads that the co-owners own the property "equally as Tenants-in-Common." Each co-owner owns a separate share in the property, and each may give away, sell, or otherwise transfer his share *without* the consent of the other Tenants-in-Common.

Tenants-in-Common are advised to obtain mutual, written rights of first refusal on any transfers by co-owners.

Even though most joint ownership is now assumed by law to be Joint Tenancy with Right of Survivorship, to avoid confusion make sure your deeds and documents include those precise words. Otherwise it could be assumed that co-owners are Tenants-in-Common.

It is not a good idea to use a Joint Tenancy with Right of Survivorship in place of a will, even if the property is the largest asset in an estate. Without a will, all other property, including personal belongings, will be subject to state laws of intestacy.

Home Is Where the Bart Is

Marge and Homer Simpson bought their home as Joint Tenants with Right of Survivorship. No matter who died first, the surviving spouse would own the home outright—no probate, no taxes, no fuss. Homer couldn't sell the house without Marge's approval and vice versa. He was furious when he secretly tried to sell his share of the house to pay for a surprise anniversary trip to Sunny Siberia, as the pamphlet read. Their title prevented his selling without Marge's approval. He thought asking would ruin the surprise, and he cried himself to sleep wondering what he could do to change his luck.

One day, a moment of self proclaimed (and mistaken) brilliance came over Homer. He told Marge that it would be better for them if they changed their title to Tenants-in-Common. He figured there was not much of a difference. (That way he'd be free to sell his share of the house without Marge ever knowing, and he could still live at home with her, because she'd still own "half" the house.) They changed the title; Homer sold his "half," cashed in, and booked cheapo tickets for a dogsled tour of Siberia. Homer was so pleased with himself he could not stop humming.

Bart was the first to see the moving van and the new half-owner pull around the corner and watched in horror as it stopped, opened its huge doors, and began to disgorge Liberace-style furniture. Bart burst into the house with the news, Marge blew her beehive, and Homer hung his head and confessed that he only wanted to treat her to a second honeymoon in Siberia next January. "D-oh!"

"Aren't you adorable!" Marge warbled. But now what?

As usual, Lisa came up with a whiz-bang solution. She played her saxophone, Bart bellowed, Homer howled, and Marge sobbed, until the Liberace look-alike swept up his candelabra, gladly took his money back, and huffed back to Las Vegas. Right after Marge had her hair done, she dragged Homer right back to the lawyer's office where they reinstated their Joint Tenancy with Right of Survivorship.

Property Rights
Ticket to Ride

Community property is not about title, but about *entitlement* between spouses. Community property laws govern the division of property between spouses in Arizona, California, Idaho, Louisiana, Nevada, New Mexico, Texas, and Washington. Other states have adopted similar legal provisions.

Any property acquired during a marriage is deemed community property, with each spouse owning one-half. In divorce, each spouse can argue his or her case, but the property will generally be divided right down the middle. Similarly, in case of death, a surviving spouse in community property states is usually entitled to a statutory share of a marital estate, regardless of the provisions of a will.

Community property is not a universally admired policy. A spouse who earns all the income, buys the house, and starts a new business while her mate stays at home to hire a staff to cook and clean while he plays golf all day may not think community property laws are fair. But the law is intended to recognize and reward the contributions that both spouses make to a marriage equally. Each brings something to the party, so to speak.

You might think you can avoid community property laws by moving to another state before divorcing. Not possible. By law, property acquired by couples in a community property state retains the half-and-half status whatever the domicile of the couple.

On the other hand, gifts and inheritance, even if received after marriage, remain the separate property of each spouse, unless the property is used as a marital asset. An inheritance used as collateral for a mortgage on a new home for the happy couple, for example, has become a marital asset and is subject to community property law.

Payment-on-death. Ownership and access to a checking account or securities account are established when the account is opened. A signator is required to select the type of account, identify the owner(s) of the account, and elect an option for distribution at death. Somewhere in the fine print, the account agreement or signature card presents options that determine rights of survivorship and payment-on-death provisions.

If a joint account with Right of Survivorship is chosen, the surviving owner of the account takes all. If *payment-on-death* is authorized, the death of an owner triggers payment of the account assets to the surviving owner(s) or the beneficiary named on the card. The old Totten Trust is the precursor of the payment-on-death provision, essentially turning over the account to a named beneficiary independent of probate.

A payment-on-death option provides critical, ready cash to a family in mourning, but not yet in probate. If the account holds substantial assets, payment-on-death could distribute a significant portion of an estate outside probate. If the named beneficiary of the account is a minor, outright payment is not permitted. The account will be transferred only to a custodian, property guardian, or trust for the benefit of the minor.

If you do not know how your account is titled (and who can remember exactly?), call your bank or broker and ask for a copy of your signature card or account agreement. Read the fine print and consider your options. Make the necessary changes. If you are not sure what to do, ask your lawyer before making any change.

Power of appointment is basically a property right. It does not convey title, but control. A power of appointment can be created much like a power of attorney, to share control with another person. Or it could be conveyed to a business partner, the beneficiary of a trust, and so forth. A power of appointment, granted by written statement and properly notarized, could trigger a gift tax liability.

A *general* power of appointment conveys total freedom and flexibility. A person holding the power has unqualified control of the property. He can "appoint" the property as he chooses, changing any aspect of it, spending as much of it as he likes, making gifts and specifying where the property is to go upon his death.

The law equates a general power to ownership, and counts the property in question as part of the estate of the person holding the power.

A *limited*, or *special*, power of appointment prescribes specific purposes for which income and assets may be used, restraining the person holding the power from devaluing or spending down the property or draining a trust. Because a limited power of appointment does not convey control, the property involved is not considered part of the estate of the person holding the power.

Protecting Assets from Creditors
The Way We Were

Asset protection is an important concern for many families. Giving the beach house or the family business to your grown children may be a great idea, but if the kids take over, is the house or business subject to the creditors—possibly a divorce court—of each one? Could the financial obligations of one become a problem for all? Without adequate legal protection, they sure could.

Estate planning devices can protect family property under almost any circumstance. Keeping an asset in the family sometimes requires removing assets from a personal estate. If irrevocably transferred, the assets escape estate taxes as well as creditors' claims. After all, a creditor cannot claim a right to property not owned by the debtor.

Courts do not tolerate fraud, however, and will void any transfer designed exclusively to protect assets from existing creditors.

> *We can't cross a bridge until we come to it; but I always like to lay down a pontoon ahead of time.*
> —Bernard M. Baruch

Contracts. Between couples, the best protection for nonmarital assets is a written agreement between spouses—the pre- or postnuptial agreement. A contract between unmarried partners serves exactly the same purpose. The couple agrees to a division of property in case of divorce or death, and separate property ownership keeps one spouse's creditors from the other's door. Marital or shared assets are, nevertheless, subject to the creditors of both spouses. In this case, what you don't know *could* hurt you. See Chapter Five for more about nuptial agreements.

Contracts among co-owners of property or business interests—even if family members—similarly establish terms for orderly transfer or sale.

Trusts. An irrevocable trust is particularly effective in keeping family property in the family as well as protecting assets from creditors of the grantor and individual beneficiaries. The trust owns the property, possibly a vacation home, valuable artwork, or funds intended for wealth accumulation, and preserves it for the remainder beneficiaries.

Trust benefits are restricted until the trust terminates and assets are distributed to remainderman, perhaps two generations away with a generation-skipping, or dynasty, trust. The trust escapes estate taxes over the generations, and creditors cannot get at legitimate trust assets.

An irrevocable life insurance trust—ILIT—also removes insurance proceeds from the estate of the insured, keeping them out of the reach of creditors and Uncle Sam.

A living trust offers absolutely no protection from creditors. For all practical—and legal—purposes, the grantor is considered to be the owner of trust assets.

Beware of foreign trusts. There is significant expense in creating and administering overseas trusts as well as significant risk of losing control of the assets. And U.S. courts have the power to scrutinize such trusts to confirm that they are not created to defraud creditors.

Family limited partnerships. The protection of family and small business assets is addressed in Chapter Seven; however, one particular form of business protection is also effective for family asset protection. The beach house, the family business, or any family asset can be protected from creditors under a properly structured family limited partnership (FLP).

Typically, husband and wife are general partners, holding all the control and power, but responsible for management and liable for losses. The children are limited partners with no say and no liability.

In terms of asset protection, a creditor's claim or order may be charged not against the partnership assets, but only against distribu-

tions. The *critical provision* in an FLP agreement gives the general partners complete discretion in making distributions. And if the general
partners, at their discretion, make no distributions, nothing comes of
the claim. A creditor cannot force distributions. The limited partner's
creditors, including an ex-spouse with a divorce order, are out of luck.

For estate tax protection, the general partners make partial gifts of
their partnership interests to the limited partners over the years. If the
gifts stay within the Annual Exclusion, ownership of the assets or property can slowly but surely be transferred to the children. The estates of the
parents/general partners benefit from the reduced value of their gifts.

Birds of a Feather
Flock Together

A family limited partnership *is a great way to structure the
business of the rock-n-rollin' Partridge Family, where minor
children are both a business asset and a potential liability.*

*Mother Shirley as general partner has all the control and all the
responsibility, as she and her children tour nationally and
internationally during school vacations. The kids are limited partners,
but their shares and their income are held in custodianship by good old
Reuben, their faithful manager, until they come of age.*

*As the kids grow older, they make the usual show biz blunders.
Heartthrob Keith falls for groupies, marrying and divorcing twice
before age 25. Beautiful Laurie starts a side business marketing her
own line of eye makeup. But the makeup looks good only with blue
eyes, and the business fails miserably. Naturally, Keith's ex-wives and
Laurie's creditors go after the family business, but they get nowhere.*

*The FLP is out of the reach of creditors of limited partners.
Distributions to partners are accessible to creditors, but the partnership
assets are protected. Keith and Laurie's partnership income is all that
suffers from their misadventures.*

*When all the kids grow up, Shirley can make annual gifts of
partial shares in the business, slowly but surely transferring the
business, and its control, as she finally admits that she no longer digs
rock and roll music.*

Furthermore, income and appreciation of the assets, if any, shift to the children/limited partners. By agreement, the general partners are usually permitted to resign in order to become limited partners, but may be removed only by a supermajority.

A limited partner's interest cannot be transferred without permission of the other partners, but it may be transferred into a living trust to ensure succession. Furthermore, a fractional partnership interest is not very marketable. Between lack of marketable value and protection from creditors, the FLP keeps it All in the Family.

Be sure to weigh the potential risk against the expense of the protection you have in mind. Setting up even a simple FLP can cost between $2,500 and $5,000.

Emergency Funds
Pennies from Heaven

If you know your spouse, partner, or children will never stop worrying about finances, talk about it, and figure out what action will allay the fear. If special medical care or household help will be required in your absence, make sure insurance proceeds or other funds will be immediately available. Also make sure that someone will come forward to help the one you leave behind.

A properly titled checking or financial account will pay at death, directly to a named beneficiary. Cash accounts must be held in certain ways to ensure liquidity upon your death.

If you have a joint checking account with a spouse or partner, don't assume the joint owner of the account will have access to the funds after you die. Read the fine print on the account signature card and look for the words *right of survivorship* and *payment-on-death,* meaning the survivor takes all and takes it right away. If it's your wife, she'll have access to liquid assets and can buy groceries and pay her bills. If it's a partner, he won't have to cope with pesky relatives and probate to access his own joint account. Some joint accounts do not have a right of survivorship. Make the necessary changes to ensure your account serves your purposes.

"No, it's my husband that's expired. Is his credit card still good?"

Life insurance benefits, though independent of probate, take a reasonable number of business days to process. A death certificate will need to be filed with the insurance company, along with a few other forms, no doubt. Insurance payment may not be immediate, but it is certain to be downright speedy compared to distributions from an estate in probate.

Distributions from an estate can begin only when an executor knows that estate assets will cover liabilities and taxes. Because estate taxes are due nine months from date of death, and no one but a fool pays taxes early, final distributions from an estate are likely to take months.

If you have not previously created a trust and your estate is complicated, probate could go on for months or years before distributions are made. If your family is dependent upon income, consider placing at least some assets in trust to avoid probate. Trust distributions are uninterrupted by death, providing immediate and continuing benefits to named beneficiaries.

It may sound crass, but if your spouse or partner is dying, it is a good idea to have cash on hand. If an account is not properly titled, if a joint account balance is low, or if probate is delayed, you could run short at a very difficult time.

*   *   *

There is no need for a cash flow emergency at death. A simple provision on a bank or securities account, or a trust, offers financial stability at a time when it is most needed. In preparing an estate plan or anticipating the death of someone close to you, do your best to take the steps necessary to balance emotional and practical matters.

It's Now or Never . . .

- Gifts made during your lifetime reduce the size of your taxable estate and transfer property exactly as you choose— not to mention the sheer pleasure of the giving.

- Pay close attention to property title. For joint owners, title often determines distribution at the death of an owner, regardless of what his will says.

- Set up legal protection to keep family property in the family just in case creditors, unforeseen divorcées, and the like come knocking.

- Sweat the small stuff. Attention to detail puts your estate plan to work.

Special Situations

That's Life

What's Goin' On ...

- Divorce and remarriage
- The elderly and disabled
- Singles and widows
- Unmarried partners
- Single parents
- Childless couples

The twentieth century is remarkable for both its scientific and techno-logical advances and its repeated breaks from tradition. The lifestyles of ever-larger numbers of the elderly, single parents, and same-sex couples continue to bend, stretch, and confront laws and regulations unques-tionably favoring the "traditional" family. Even for married couples, what's-mine-is-yours is just an old-fashioned sentiment.

When it comes to estate planning, getting the practical aspects of these situations on the table is a good deal more constructive than the supposedly tolerant "don't ask, don't tell" philosophy. We can help our-selves, our families, and partners only if we take the time to understand and mutually respect the true meaning of "each to his own."

The special needs presented by both the predictable and unpredictable turns of life are addressed in this chapter. In presenting the relevant elements of each situation, the material is, with apologies, necessarily repetitious.

Divorce and Remarriage
Breaking Up Is Hard to Do

Statistics indicate that breaking up is *not* all that hard to do. One of two marriages ends in divorce, breaking hearts, hopes, families, and fortunes. Second marriages are more often followed by third and fourth marriages. As life grows longer, octogenarians are remarrying in remarkable numbers. The concept of lifetime commitment has given way to looking out for number one. And divorce puts at risk a great deal more than a broken heart.

Unless a married couple has made a written agreement—a contract—the courts could play a significant role in division of property resulting from divorce. When a couple splits, the law often dictates how property will be divided. States with community property laws generally divide property fifty-fifty. Others, even some with community property laws, divide property of short-term marriages according to a sliding scale based on the number of years the couple was married. Inherited property is generally considered individually owned unless mixed with other marital assets. Also, divorce normally cancels spousal rights under an existing will.

> *When one door closes, another door opens; but we often look so long*
> *and so regretfully upon the closed door that we do not see the*
> *ones which open for us.*
> —Alexander Graham Bell

Any change in marital status warrants a complete estate plan review. As with any other major life change, you will want to reconsider the beneficiaries you have named under your will, living trust, retirement plan, annuity, life insurance, and so forth. Any appointments, such as executor, power of attorney, trustee, guardian, or custodian, must be reexamined. A thorough review of every document and every financial interest is in order. If you have made a working inventory of your property, it will come in very handy now.

Your divorce lawyer and estate planning lawyer will need to put their heads together. You don't have to go all the way back to the drawing board, but any substantial change in property ownership warrants an equivalent revision of an estate plan. With an understanding of what is at risk, let's look at the solutions.

Pre- and Postnuptial Agreements
Fifty Ways to Leave Your Lover

In an agreement made in writing either before or after marriage—*pre- or postnuptial*—a couple agrees in advance to a division of property in case of death or divorce. A prenuptial is also called an *antenuptial agreement*.

Like many legal devices, prenuptial agreements grew out of custom. Historically, a woman's property was automatically transferred to her husband upon marriage. Therefore, a woman with a large dowry was obviously a good catch.

The modern pre- or postnuptial agreement, an ironic fallback to the ancient marriage contract, has evolved to level the field for women and men. Now both can marry for (love and) money with no fear that divorce, untimely death, or a meddling mother-in-law will affect the distribution of wealth between them. The prenuptial agreement is a legally enforceable contract that supersedes state law. In some states, postnuptial agreements are restricted by statute.

Prenuptials are increasingly common, especially among couples with substantial differences in age or wealth. Couples might agree that property brought separately into the marriage will remain separate, in case of divorce or death. Or that separate career paths, particularly where significant income is involved, be kept separate. A couple might have a joint bank account, but agree that each may keep an individual, separate account as well. In other words, what's mine is *not* yours.

The agreement can also include a contract to make a will, which

" . . . for richer, for poorer, in sickness and in health,
until death or litigation do you part?"

guarantees a predetermined division of property. Husband and wife are thus legally obligated to draft contracts with specific distribution provisions. However, a contract to make a will, whether in a nuptial agreement or not, eliminates the benefit of the Unlimited Marital Deduction. Separate wills with mutual terms are a better alternative, though neither spouse is prohibited from changing his or her will.

In making a pre- or postnuptial agreement, each individual needs a separate lawyer to protect his or her individual interests. On the theory that you can't give up your right to something you don't know about, an agreement is not enforceable unless all assets and income are disclosed, each spouse understands all the terms of the agreement, and the agreement is consistent with state law.

Second Marriage and Grown Children

Almost without exception, grown children have difficulty adjusting to the remarriage of a parent. If an elderly widower marries a woman half his age, he may wish only to look after his new bride and let his grown children look out for themselves. His children will worry, for good reason, what might become of their family home and heirlooms.

Fears and emotions cloud our better judgment, and sometimes even our love for a parent. Where substantial wealth is involved, the concern intensifies. A widow might easily fall for a younger suitor more interested in her wealth than her well-being. Generally, people of wealth are all too aware of their vulnerability. For many, it is advisable not to marry without a prenuptial agreement. For most, it is smart to at least consider the possibility.

Counting on an inheritance is flirting with temptation. You know you might get something for nothing, and that you have no real right to it, but can't help coveting it, feeling possessive and defensive about it. If the couple divorces, the bride will probably get a big chunk. If he dies, she could get everything. Wonder all you like, but if you do not take courage and pose the question, and Dad takes the trophy wife, you could lose your family inheritance.

Perhaps this is a good time to work on the boat or play some golf with Dad. If the subject is approached with respect, he will listen, especially to constructive, unselfish concerns. The truth is, the property belongs to Dad and he has the right to make up his own mind, even if you can't get "No" satisfaction.

If you are the parent, being approached by the child who is nervous about getting his share, listen well, and then explain your plan, if you are so inclined. Tell the kids what you're doing, why you're doing it, and that it's your call. Like any productive family discussion, it takes judgment, brains, and maturity. These are sensitive issues for everybody involved. Give both the issues and the children your time and attention.

If spouses and children of different marriages are involved, a great deal more than inheritance and pride are at stake. Responsibilities and needs, if not addressed, turn to grudges and jealousies. Families stop speaking over perceived injustices between parents, stepparents, children, stepchildren, and so forth. Be careful that your personal life choices do not come at the expense of your family. A variety of estate planning tools tailored to your specific situation—even a complicated situation—are available to protect every part of a modern "extended" family.

Protecting the Family Estate
Show Me the Way to Go Home

Trusts. Try to eliminate or reduce the financial connection between spouses and children of different marriages. Either as part of a divorce settlement, a nuptial agreement, or entirely separately, an irrevocable family trust could provide for children of a prior marriage. With approval of the divorce court, alimony and/or child support can be paid directly to the trust. The trustee keeps child support monies from being misspent by ex-spouses.

Trust income distributions can be restricted to a certain purpose (such as education), to an established period of time, or according to age. And trust assets could, at a specific point, be distributed outright to the children. Presto! They have their inheritance. A family trust could also be divided into a number of different trusts, each operating to the benefit of different family members or children of different marriages. The right trustee can prevent mistrust and quarrels over investment policies, and challenges such as who-is-spending-whose-inheritance, or I'd-like-my-money-now, thank you.

A QTIP—Qualified Terminable Interest Property—trust is ideal for providing benefits to a second spouse for life, but leaving family property to your children.

Assets go into an irrevocable trust free of gift and estate tax under the Unlimited Marital Deduction and are distributed to the remaindermen (who get what remains in the trust, in this case the children) outside of probate. Under a QTIP, you could let your wife live in your family home for the rest of her life, but ultimately leave the house to your daughter.

Because the QTIP is subject to estate taxes when the surviving spouse dies, it is not as advantageous as other forms of irrevocable trust. A second spouse should probably not serve as single trustee of a trust for the whole family, but possibly as a co-trustee. The trustees must, in their hopefully infinite wisdom, choose among income for the spouse, asset growth for the kids, life insurance, and so forth, to balance the benefits to spouse and children.

"So, are you still with the same parents?"

A trust is very effective in creating lifetime benefits for a spouse or children, a desired chain of inheritance, as well as enforceable conditions and obligations. Draft a trust to suit your particular family situation.

Life estate. Much less streamlined than a trust, a life estate, usually created under a will, also provides benefits to a person for life, after which full ownership rights go to named heirs. A life estate has restrictions designed to preserve the property for the final heirs. The property may not be abused or diminished in value, and sale of the property, which could result in spending its value, is usually not permitted. In many cases, a life estate is conveyed by deed stipulating the succession of ownership.

The family home provides a good example. When you die, you could leave your home to your new wife, for instance, for her to use, to maintain, and enjoy for her lifetime. When she dies, your children (not her children) receive full ownership of the property. A cherished family

---

Shady Brady

In their wills, Mike and Carol Brady each have a QTIP trust in place to provide for each other and to protect their respective children in the Brady Bunch. When Carol died, a QTIP was created from her estate, tax free under the Unlimited Marital Deduction, to provide income to Mike for life, but preserve the trust assets for her girls, Cindy, Jan, and Marcia.

What no one had anticipated, but Carol had at least properly planned for, was Mike's subsequent marriage to the older, but mysteriously seductive, Alice!

---

heirloom or painting is also a likely candidate for a life estate. Estate tax, if any, is imposed when the life estate is created.

Henry the Eighth
Sure Had Trouble
Short-Term Wives
Long-Term Stubble
Burma-Shave

Life insurance. If you want to make sure all your heirs get theirs, life insurance, especially if held in trust, will make up for property that could splinter off because of remarriage. Protect your kids with a trust holding insurance on your life. Or leave the family property to your kids and make your third wife the beneficiary of the life insurance proceeds.

If a life insurance policy is owned by you, it will be considered part of your estate and taxed as such. It is therefore better if someone else, possibly a trust, owns the policy on your life.

You could make an annual gift to your daughter, for example, tax free under the annual $10,000 exclusion. She must have the so-called Crummey power to use the gift as she pleases, or it will not be considered a true gift. If she uses the gift—voluntarily—to pay premiums on a policy on your life, she will provide herself a generous inheritance. It's a bit like finding a million-dollar baby in a five-and-ten-cent store.

If you married several times and/or have children of more than one marriage, a life insurance trust—or a separate trust for each family of children—is a clean way to provide for everyone while holding on to your own property to impress your next spouse. With life insurance, you can please almost everybody, and if the policy is purchased early, it will be less expensive.

Property titles. Joint Tenancy with Right of Survivorship, as it is called, is the most common form of title for property owned by more than one person. No matter how many owners there are, all own the property equally. The last surviving co-owner, or joint tenant, is left owning the entire property. Husband and wife generally own their home as joint tenants.

If you and your wife own the family home, and she dies, you get it all. If you're the third husband, and it truly *is* the family home, your stepchildren will resent your rightful ownership of the house. If you've been married to your third wife for 20 years, it's one thing. If you have been married for 20 days, and you get the house that has been in the wife's family for three generations, heaven help you.

Many state laws, especially in community property states, entitle a surviving spouse to a statutory share of an estate, and the right to keep the marital home. A spouse may elect against a will to receive a statutory share instead of the share left in the will. However, a pre-nuptial agreement, unless inherently unfair, will prevail over state law.

Joint tenancy is not limited to real estate, but also applies to business property, bank accounts, and other investments. You will need an experienced lawyer to evaluate your property titles and make any necessary changes.

Qualified Domestic Relation Order—QDRO

Retirement plans require special consideration. Under some divorce settlements, spouses are entitled to all or a certain percentage of plan benefits. If distribution is made at the time of a divorce, ex-spouses receive their share, but a premature distribution triggers an income tax liability and a tax penalty, reducing the overall benefit.

Through a *Qualified Domestic Relation Order*—known as a *QDRO* (**quad**-row)—a divorce court can impose a new provision on a retirement plan. Benefits are preserved for the ex-spouse and children without incurring penalties and a tax liability. In this case, the ex gets the guaranteed benefits as originally intended, with no adverse tax consequences.

If an Heir Divorces

If making a lifetime gift or a bequest in a will to an adult child who might be headed for divorce, be sure to specify that the transfer is for your child and your child alone. If your intention is perfectly clear, the property will not be considered a marital asset in case of the divorce.

When a gift is substantial, rather than giving it outright, consider making a loan. If not repaid before you die, the loan could be forgiven as a bequest to the child under your will. More about gift loans in Chapter Four.

Families cannot be ignored or brushed off. They don't go away. Multiple marriages and stepfamilies come from new promises of fresh starts. Do what you can to honor those promises, no matter how distant they have become. No matter what personal lifestyle you choose, prepare yourself and your family for the long term, or prepare for the consequences.

Elderly and Disabled
Help!

Growing old is part of life. Some find their later years the best years, even as the physical plant starts to break down and it costs more than ever to keep it running. Responsible retirement planning and money management are essential to every estate plan. Making sure our resources will support us (in the style to which we have become accustomed) in our old age is a primary concern. Don't put money in trust

Elizabeth Greenway

for your grandchildren if you cannot spare it. Estate tax savings are not worth much if we have to do without when we are incapable of earning any more. We will all need help in one form or another in our sunset years.

Even the wealthy are vulnerable to personal setbacks and market swings. There is not an older person on the face of the earth who does not worry about having enough money to make it to the end. Our elders are stubborn and tightfisted for good reason. Many remember the hardships of depression and war. They respect and fear the value of a dollar.

We're all growing old, and as we do our outlooks, attitudes, and priorities change. These changes make it all the more important to make plans to secure our future now, while we can make sense of what we have, what we will need, and what our options are. Medical care costs more every day, and national health insurance remains an unsettled issue. We have to look out for ourselves.

Let's look at the numbers. Average life expectancy was 83 years in 1999. The baby boomers are facing long lives as senior citizens—and they're not the only ones who have to face facts.

Nearly one-third of those over 65 have a disability that limits mobility. The probability of Alzheimer's disease rises to 47 percent at age 85. One of two Americans over the age of 65 will require long-term care at one time or another. Past the age of 65, seven out of ten couples can expect at least one spouse to enter a nursing home. The average stay in a nursing home is two and a half years, and it's bound to grow longer as life expectancy increases. The average cost of nursing home care for a year is $40,000, versus at-home health care at $12,000 a year.

Q: What is the benefit of having Alzheimer's?
A: You get to make new friends everyday.

The medical cost of growing old is not entirely covered by Medicare, Medicap, or personal major medical health insurance. In fact, most people in nursing homes spend everything they have on their care before they die.

A hospital bed is a parked taxi with the meter running.
—Groucho Marx

Government Programs
High Hopes

If you are 62 or older, you and your spouse may be eligible for *Social Security* benefits. In fact, ex-spouses, children, and widows are also eligible for benefits to various extents. In a surprising gesture of kindness, Social Security makes a lump sum death payment of $255 to the surviving spouse or child of a covered worker to help with burial expenses. Never mind that the average cost of funeral and burial is several thousand.

Many of us will be just plain lucky if there's anything left of Social Security by the time we become eligible for benefits. Social Security will send a free statement of earnings covered and an estimate of future benefits upon written request. Either complete the appropriate form at your local Social Security office, or send a written request to the Department of Health and Human Services at the Social Security Administration.

If you're 65 or older, you are also a candidate for Medicare, Medigap, and Medicaid. Through these programs, the federal government provides health care assistance to individuals who "qualify."

Medicare consists of two parts. Part A provides hospital insurance at no cost, but is subject to time limits, a deductible, and co-payment by other health insurers. It provides limited coverage for care in a skilled nursing facility or hospice or for post-hospital, home health services.

Part B provides an option to pay premiums for coverage of physicians' services, again subject to a deductible and co-insurance.

If you do not automatically receive a Medicare card at age 65, apply for one through the Social Security office.

Medigap provides optional insurance, at additional premiums, to cover health costs not provided by Medicare.

Medicaid is designed to pay long-term medical expenses for those who cannot manage without professional care, and can demonstrate sufficient financial need. This federally funded, state-run program pays for 40 percent of patients in nursing homes.

Each applicant goes through a *means test*—an investigation of financial resources. To qualify, an applicant must own assets *below* a certain amount, be unemployed, or have low income.

Qualifying for Medicaid

Medicaid applicants are allowed to reserve for personal use only $3,000 cash, the home, car, personal jewelry, and limited funds for prepaid funeral expenses. Once in the nursing home, a Medicaid patient is permitted a monthly income of no more than $100. When they say "low income," they mean it.

The spouse of an applicant is permitted a monthly income allowance of $1,357. The spouse may also keep a maximum of $81,960 in marital assets. (These are 1999 figures, subject to annual adjustment.)

A residence may lawfully be transferred to a spouse, but also to a sibling who lives with the Medicaid candidate and shares ownership; a child of any age who has lived in and provided care in the home; or for the benefit of a disabled minor child.

All other assets are considered expendable for health care, and if above a certain value, could disqualify an individual from Medicaid coverage. It is easy to see that while an estate may be large enough to disqualify an individual from Medicaid, it may be too small to guarantee good medical care or a comfortable, secure old age.

> *Ask not what your country can do for you, but how much it's going to cost you for them to do it.*
> —Anonymous

Desperate times sometimes require desperate measures, and senior citizens have gone to extremes to circumvent the rules. Some older couples have divorced to separate assets in a way that allows one spouse to qualify for Medicaid. Some states permit a spouse to simply make the claim that "if we were divorced, I would get X amount; therefore, I am entitled to have that amount protected now."

To qualify, some people transfer their assets to others or into trust. Placing assets in a living trust does not escape the means test. Irrevocable trusts are generally inaccessible, though some trusts provide for invasion of the corpus in cases of dire necessity and could therefore be subject to the test.

Turning assets over to someone you think you can *trust*—rather than actually placing them in *a trust*—is a double-edged sword. Ideally, a loving daughter or son with some financial know-how might invest finances for an elderly parent, and arrange or personally provide care. Unfortunately, false affection too often wins a senior's trust and opens the door to financial abuse. We've all heard the horror stories. Rather than turning over assets outright—for any reason—sign a springing power of attorney that imposes a fiduciary duty on the person acting on your behalf.

Simply hiding assets is not uncommon, though it is unwise. It inevitably leads to a moral, if not legal, dilemma. Could you be happy "cheating" the government and having your nursing home expenses covered by Medicaid while your friend suffers with inadequate care at home because she does not qualify?

The rules for Medicaid qualification are strict. There is a *36-month lookback* at personal assets—60 months if you're setting up a trust. Your lawyer or accountant could get into big, criminal trouble for helping you skirt the regulations. And under the law, the Medicaid program has rightful claim to any assets owned by a patient at the time of death. If a person somehow qualifies, but dies owning a home, Medicaid can place a lien on the home.

Long-Term Care Insurance
You'll Never Walk Alone

As the elderly population has increased, health insurance, Medicare, and Medicaid have proven inadequate for long-term care. Nursing home, outpatient, and in-home nursing care and hospice expenses are not covered by most traditional health insurance policies. Even when covered by insurance, deductibles and co-payments remain the responsibility of the insured.

Long-term care insurance has evolved to fill the void. It provides reliable coverage of lingering illness and disability, and it preserves a bit of autonomy. *You* choose your long-term care facility, rather than having someone in the Medicaid office choose one for you. If desired, in-home health care may also be covered.

Defined premiums over the years are almost the same as saving money to cover long-term care expenses. The owner is free to spend down the rest of his estate, or leave it to heirs. Unused policy benefits, however, are lost.

Most of us insure our autos and homes to cover extraordinary expense. Just one person in 1,200 who owns fire insurance ever needs it; one in 240 uses auto insurance. But a remarkable 1 in 3 uses long-term-care insurance.

*   *   *

Follow the Golden Rule

The Golden Girls had worked out a pretty comfortable arrangement for themselves—they had a home and each other. Though not without financial worries (except perhaps for Blanche, who owned the house), they muddled along, side by side. They were anything but shrinking violets and continued to enjoy life to the fullest.

When Dorothy married she rewrote her will, springing power of attorney, health care power of attorney, and living will. Blanche, Rose, and Dorothy's mother, Sophia (who finally got the bed to herself), had to make only minor adjustments to their documents because their living arrangements stayed much the same. All had named the ever-responsible Dorothy executor and given her power of attorney, which they had discussed and agreed to leave as it was.

Blanche and Rose earned decent salaries and had retirement income to support them in later years, and Sophia lived on the life insurance proceeds she had received when her husband died.

But no one was prepared for what happened when Blanche became disabled and needed to move to a long-term care facility. Health insurance benefits and Medicare ended after a few months, and Dorothy had to apply for Medicaid on Blanche's behalf. Blanche's retirement plan and her home were worth enough to disqualify her for Medicaid benefits. These assets had to be sold to pay for her ongoing care until she was financially strapped to a point that Medicaid found acceptable. Blanche was then able to move into a state-run facility—not the one of her choice, since she had her eye on the "attending" physician at another nursing home.

Sophia moved in with Dorothy and her husband—this time she not only had her own bed, but her very own room.

Rose had unfortunately gone from airhead to Alzheimer's. But thankfully she had purchased long-term care insurance. Not entirely by chance, she ended up in the nursing home of her choice, where the apple of Blanche's wandering eye became the object of Rose's affection.

"Boy, I'm sure glad I got up here before Medicare started running low."

Qualifications. As with other health insurance, one must qualify for a long-term-care policy. Benefits vary slightly from policy to policy but generally are paid when a medical necessity arises, when the activities of daily living are compromised, or cognitive abilities are impaired, as with Alzheimer's and dementia. The daily living activities considered for qualification are quite basic: walking, bathing, and feeding ourselves, being continent and using the toilet, dressing, and transferring ourselves (moving from the chair to the bed).

Premiums vary with age at time of purchase, the length of time benefits are to be paid, and the chosen *daily benefit amount*. The policyholder also elects the length of time before the policy kicks in—the *elimination period*—which, naturally, affects the premium. Another option is an *annual inflation rider* that increases the daily benefit amount.

Most coverage takes effect 100 days after care begins. Medicare generally covers the first 20 days completely and pays a portion of the expense up to 100 days—though not in a facility of your choice. Medigap or private health insurance may also be used to supplement coverage of expenses during the elimination period.

Long-term care premiums usually qualify as income tax deductions. Like other health insurance, benefits are income-tax free. As with life insurance, the earlier the long-term care policy is purchased, the lower the premiums.

When choosing a long-term care insurance policy, check out the financial stability of the company selling it. Sign on only with an insurer who is certain to be in business when the time comes to collect your benefits. Several private firms and so-called rating agencies analyze the financial stability of insurance companies.

Viatical settlement. If an individual facing long-term or chronic illness has life insurance but no long-term care insurance, a *viatical settlement* could convert the life insurance into available cash. The name comes from the Latin word *viaticum*, the provisions ancient Roman families gave to soldiers going off to war.

Here's how it works: The settlement company purchases the life insurance policy from the individual for a percentage of its face value, usually 70 percent. The individual gets the money now, when it is most needed, and the company, which continues premium payments on the policy, gets paid later when it collects the life insurance proceeds. The Viatical Association of America can tell you more.

ALERT! Statistically, women outlive men and are therefore more likely to need long-term care. Yet how many women, particularly in the older generation, have actively participated in making an estate plan? Now is the time to find out if personal resources, government programs, and insurance are adequate for the long haul.

If you need long-term care insurance but cannot afford it, ask your children for help. They will probably prefer to help by contributing to premiums along the way, rather than face the unknown expense of your long-term care later.

If your parent or another for whom you are responsible is likely to need long-term care, you would be wise to discuss the issue with him or her, and offer to help pay premiums, if possible. You might not have room to take your mother into your own home, or might not be able

"I want you to have this. It belonged to my mother."

to, or want to; or she may need special medical care that cannot be provided at home. Though certainly not appropriate for everyone, in many cases, long-term care insurance provides peace of mind and protects an estate from prolonged, potentially ruinous health care expense.

Where resources and the family support system are completely reliable, long-term care insurance may not be necessary. For just about everyone else, it makes a lot of sense.

Incompetence
Still Crazy After All These Years

Sometimes life doesn't go as planned. A good estate plan not only provides for our own infirmity, but protects those close to us for whom we are responsible, or who cannot help themselves—a disabled or incompetent adult child, for example, or a dependent parent. It may be time for brothers and sisters to put their heads together and work out a contingency plan for Mom.

*   *   *

Protective trusts are most effective in providing for the disabled or incompetent, and protecting against unwanted or unnecessary invasion of privacy and assets. The more specialized your trust is, the more specialized your trustee must be.

Trusts designed to support a minor, senior, spendthrift, or incompetent are often called protective or support trusts. A *sprinkling trust* pays benefits to named beneficiaries as needed, paying medical bills as they arise or tuition, for example. A trust can also provide regular benefits for prescribed purposes, such as rent or food.

In a *spendthrift trust,* the trustee is obligated to take precautions to see that trust benefits are used as intended and protected from creditors. A wild and crazy guy who would rather buy his buddies drinks than feed himself may need a regular grocery delivery, charged to the trustee. The right trustee, with the right powers, can make the arrangements to satisfy your objectives.

An incompetent person could be protected through a *living trust,* with you as trustee until you die. Your successor trustee will continue paying benefits without interruption. Choose a successor who will put the care of the incompetent above the interests of the remaindermen. In extreme cases, if a legally incompetent person is denied government aid because of trust income, the trustee may have to withhold funds to help that person qualify for aid, while reserving assets and income for later benefit of the incompetent person.

Durable power of attorney. If you are providing for your own potential incompetence with a power of attorney, be sure to include a specific provision stating that the authority of your trustee or agent continues in case of your disability or incapacity. That provision makes the power "durable" and will generally stand up against a request for a conservatorship or property guardianship by a relative or business associate. Remember, a power of attorney ends at death when your will is executed.

*　　*　　*

Guardianship. Voluntarily, or at the request of another, a person may be deemed legally incompetent by a court and turned over to the care of a personal and/or property guardian. One guardian may do both jobs, or the court can appoint one for care of the incompetent person and one for management of the person's property.

The most immediate concern is that the guardian take custody of the incompetent person, to protect him and be responsible for him personally. Unless the personal guardian is not at all qualified to manage the property of the incompetent, the court generally appoints one person to serve as both personal and property guardian. Court-appointed guardians are required to make regular reports to the court.

Conservatorship. A conservator is basically a guardian, and like others appointed by the courts, is closely supervised through regular reporting to the court.

Mental illness and instability, progressive disease such as Alzheimer's, and permanent disability may lead to incompetence, but not all incompetence necessarily leads to a legal declaration. Nor should it. Many families care for their own with more devotion than any court could impose. There are occasions, however, when unstable health leads to a painful tug-of-war among family, hurting everyone involved.

If you have—or know of someone who has—a progressive, debilitating disease, or are quite sure *you* will need major help in the future, there are many estate planning tools available to provide for you, or that someone, and protect your property.

If you think someone close to you is legally incompetent, and you are willing to take full responsibility, consult a lawyer who has experience in these difficult matters. If you think someone would like to have you declared incompetent primarily to get his or her hands on your money and property, consult your lawyer immediately.

Singles and Widows
O Solo Mio

Sometimes solitude is treasured, sometimes feared. Whether single by choice, the surviving partner of a marriage, or between marriages, those who live alone have singular needs. The essential elements of an estate plan are the same for singles as for everyone else: a will, power of attorney for asset management, health care power of attorney or living will, and possibly long-term care insurance.

For the most part, singles have to look out for themselves, and they know how to do it. But who will look after them in an emergency? It's hard enough to arrange to have the car repaired when you're single. What if you end up in the hospital, laid up for weeks? Just because you're used to doing everything yourself (and you're good at it) doesn't mean you will never need help from others. We will *all* need help down the road.

Widows, widowers, and surviving partners face great uncertainty.

They have to grieve, must cope with loneliness and maybe children, and they're not used to doing it on their own. He doesn't know how the household works. She may not know where the insurance policy is, or what it's worth. There's a lot more to being single than getting used to being alone.

Financial security and health care are usually the biggest worries for singles. Take care of your personal needs first.

Begin with a review of assets and resources, possibly with your investment advisor or accountant. Check out your status regarding Social Security, Medicare, and Medicaid. Review health, disability, and long-term care insurance with a reliable insurance agent and your estate planning lawyer. You need to determine exactly what is covered, and more importantly, what is not covered.

Assess your long-term needs, and be practical. Think about what you'd like, ideally, and what you absolutely cannot do without. It's a mental closet cleaning. Keep what's important—pass along the rest. Whatever you do, be realistic. If you're truly on your own, you've got to make it all happen.

Health care is a particular concern for most singles. More than likely every single person has a relative or close friend who will come through in a crisis. Talk with this person, explain your concerns and fears, and ask her to be there for you. Bounce your thoughts off her, just as others would in larger family discussions. If you have an adult child who will look after you, be sure he knows your routine, your doctor, your personal needs. Assure yourself that someone will be there for you. No Man Is an Island.

Then: Getting out to a new, hip joint
Now: Getting a new hip joint

Will. You might think that, because you're single, a will is not very important. If you are truly alone and unconnected, this may be true. But it's hard to find a person who doesn't want particular people to have particular things—money, jewelry, porcelain figurines, the trophy elk, the lawn mower. Or what about your pet? Who will take care of little Pepe?

Remember, without a will, the state takes over under the laws of intestacy. The court appoints an executor, at the expense of the estate, and the state determines who gets what.

The will of a widow, written while her husband was alive, remains valid after his death, but ought to be reviewed and updated. If circumstances change, through remarriage or shifts in wealth or a change of heart, the will may be amended by codicil. If the changes are substantial, an entirely new will is recommended.

Some widows and widowers are beneficiaries of credit shelter trusts that provide income benefits for life. Though income received is subject to income tax, the property is not considered part of the widow(er)'s estate. At death, the trust is distributed to the remaindermen, outside of probate and free of estate tax.

The Unlimited Marital Deduction which applies to transfers between spouses is, of course, not available to singles or unmarried couples. However, the unified tax credit is available.

Living trust. A living trust accomplishes the same objective as a will, but without the interference of probate. If you are trustee, you control the trust while alive, paying all your bills, and so forth, from the trust. Trust assets are considered part of your estate for estate tax purposes, but probate is avoided.

And, in case of your disability or death, your successor trustee can take over and make the prescribed distributions without a big, legal fuss. Neat and complete.

Irrevocable trust. If your assets are sufficient to provide for your every possible need for the rest of your life, and you are comfortable turning over assets to a trustee now, an irrevocable trust will not only serve your needs, but also be passed along to your heirs outside of probate *and* free of estate tax. Assets placed in trust as well as any appreciation escape estate tax because they are out of your name and your control. The trustee looks after your needs while you are alive, and your remaindermen receive the benefit of untaxed assets.

An irrevocable trust usually contains a provision for invading principal to cover extraordinary medical or other expenses. If disaster strikes and you do become the primary beneficiary of the trust, the trust will be considered part of your estate for tax purposes. A small price to pay for a financial safety net.

A trust is also ideal for widows or widowers with plentiful assets, but neither the interest nor the experience to handle their own affairs. The old family retainer, your banker, investment advisor, or a qualified son or daughter could take over as trustee, or co-trustees. As mentioned, creating a trust for the benefit of another person could trigger a gift tax liability.

> *Nothing in life is to be feared, only understood.*
> —Mme. Curie

Charitable trust. If you have no heirs, or none you wish to name, consider leaving your estate to charity. A charitable remainder trust (CRT) will provide income benefits to you for life, and leave the remainder of the trust to charity. A charitable gift annuity, where the transfer is made in return for income payments for life, is similar in effect to a CRT, but is operated under a contract, not as a trust.

With either a trust or an annuity, you can have a source of reliable income and an income tax deduction, *and* the value of the charitable gift is out of your estate. Even Uncle Sam approves by permitting a calculated charitable deduction. Good work.

Power of attorney. If you do not create a trust, and in some cases even if you do, you still need somebody to look after "things" in case of disability or incompetence. It is important to sign a power of attorney giving the person of your choice the right to manage your affairs should you become incapacitated.

Even if you have a trust, other assets remaining in your name will need to be managed in a time of need. The power of attorney defines incapacity, such as debilitating illness, lengthy recovery from surgery, and mental impairment, and establishes how long the power lasts.

Health care power of attorney/living will. A health care power of attorney, directive, or proxy gives a person of your choice the authority to make health care decisions when you are unable to make them for yourself. A living will declares your end-of-life—resuscitate or do-not-resuscitate—wishes.

Be sure to ask the individuals named in your powers of attorney if they are willing and able to do the job. If so, tell them when the documents are complete, and where they are located. If no one knows about your living will or power of attorney, your life could be extended regardless of your intentions.

Looking out for yourself involves careful estate planning to be sure you'll have what you need, when you need it. You may want to look out for others as well. With a thorough estate plan, you can do it all.

Unmarried Partners
Sign of the Times

Most of the estate planning needs of singles are shared by unmarried partners, though joint ownership and shared assets often present additional concerns. Even operating as a unit, sharing income and property like a married couple, unmarried partners—including same-sex couples—face even greater peril than singles. Each partner generally has the interest of the other at heart, but the law does little or nothing to protect that interest.

Nontraditional does not mean uncommon. Free spirits made free love in the sixties, started living together, opening their marriages, living communally, and getting a kick out of nonconformity. Now more than ever, young—even middle-aged and older—couples live together before marrying. Many never marry, but happily continue the living arrangement.

Marriage is a great institution, but I'm not ready for an institution.
—Mae West

Couples who have experienced the division of property that follows divorce or death are often willing to "live in sin" to avoid a repeat performance. What they might not know is that their property remains at risk unless they have made a written agreement, created a trust, or otherwise protected their property rights.

Laws represent the values of society, but they often lag behind social change. Courts interpret and reinterpret our laws in an effort to balance the old and the new, often frustrating those caught in the middle.

Rallying to their cause, gay and lesbian groups have led efforts to improve employment benefits, health care, insurance, and public policy regarding AIDS and same-sex relationships, to the benefit of all unmarried partners. In some states, legal rights previously reserved for married partners have been extended to unmarried partners. Similarly, major corporations are increasingly providing "spousal benefits" for health care, including long-term care policies, to unmarried partners in a committed relationship.

Family Discussions

Perhaps the toughest part of an estate plan involving unmarried partners and same-sex couples is the family discussion. Bring your family into the loop, if at all possible. The best insurance against challenges to your will and other estate planning documents is an open, honest discussion with those who are interested, but left out of your plan.

If you choose your partner as your beneficiary, at least tell your brother and sister, or your children. Even judgmental relatives are usually responsive to calm, rational, straightforward conversation. If not, be sure your executor, agent, trustee, and their successors are up to the

Barbie Wears Basic Black

*K*en and Barbie have been devoted to each other for over 40 *years, though they never officially "tied the knot." Not only do they both have fabulous fashion flair, but behind those pretty faces are great financial minds.*

With Barbie's success as a nurse, doctor, lawyer, teacher, CEO, architect, engineer, senator, disco diva, and flight attendant, and Ken's unselfish willingness to keep the home fires burning, they built a substantial estate.

As an unmarried couple they knew they were not entitled to the same estate planning benefits enjoyed by married couples; therefore, it was very important to plan. They owned property in Joint Tenancy with Right of Survivorship, created trusts with each other as beneficiary, and wrote their wills naming each other as beneficiaries. Both gave each other durable and health care powers of attorney, and signed living wills to keep their families from interfering in health care decisions. And it's a good thing they did.

After a few months in her new job as a construction worker, Barbie was critically injured when a section of scaffolding collapsed. Mrs. Barbie (formerly Mrs. America), always the overprotective "stage mother," kept 24-hour vigil at the hospital. But she and Ken came to blows over Barbie's medical treatment. Thanks to prior planning, Ken had the legal authority to make health care decisions he knew Barbie would want.

Sadly, Barbie drifted into a coma. After five difficult years of renewed hope followed by frustrating setbacks, both Mrs. Barbie and Ken agreed that there was nothing more to be done. Ken exercised his right under the health care power of attorney and let Barbie go peacefully. She was, of course, dressed in basic black with a dramatic black hat with veil for the occasion.

task, and accept the responsibility with eyes wide open to meet your family head on.

If you are estranged from your family, or don't want anything to do with them, it is your responsibility to protect yourself and your part-

BARBIE: THE LOST YEARS

ner. Unmarried partners need to make their intentions and instructions perfectly clear in written, properly executed documents.

Will. A will is crucial. Without it, your family probably has the right to your property, including whatever you share with your partner, under the laws of intestacy. The courts have long assumed that family—not "friends"—are natural beneficiaries. A current, valid will clearly describing your instructions protects your partner. If you think your will might be challenged by your family or a previous partner, it would be smart to include the reasons for your instructions, as well as the reasons you have left out relatives or others whom the court might naturally consider your heirs. Do everything you can to clarify your intentions for the probate court.

An unmarried partner has no right to elect against a will like a spouse, but can challenge a will, though there is little if anything to be gained. A successful challenge only defeats a will, placing the estate under the laws of intestacy. The partner is cut out either way. The best defense is a good offense. Unmarried partners with current wills are off to a good start.

Health care power of attorney/living will. One of the most critical aspects of an estate plan for unmarried partners is a health care document. A living will states your wishes for end-of-life or emergency treatment. A health care power of attorney gives power to an agent you have named to make decisions regarding your health care.

You may prefer one or the other. If your partner knows your end-of-life choices, a health care power of attorney giving your partner the right to make decisions about your treatment may be all you need. Be sure to name at least one successor to the power. Some lawyers use a single document for the living will and the health care power of attorney.

Power of attorney. A durable, springing, or limited power of attorney gives the person you choose—your agent—the power to manage your affairs. *Everyone* needs a power of attorney in case of incapacity. If you've been out of touch with your family because of a lover or lifestyle, a power of attorney protects you and your partner from unwanted intervention. If you don't want your meddling sister taking over the business you and your partner have built, you both need mutual powers of attorney.

Property title is critical for unmarried partners. It establishes rights between co-owners and determines who gets what when one partner dies. Property co-owned in Joint Tenancy with Right of Survivorship goes entirely to the surviving owner regardless of what a will, or a disapproving family, says.

Joint tenants *without* Right of Survivorship and Tenants-in-Common own separate shares of property. When one owner dies, his

"Who said anything about marriage? What I'm offering is an array of mutual funds, variable annuities and life insurance."

share passes under his will or as otherwise prescribed. The surviving co-owner(s) has absolutely no right to a deceased co-owner's share.

Unmarried partners are wise to review all titled property—certainly all joint accounts and real estate—to be sure that title accurately reflects individual rights and rights of survivorship, as desired. Various types of property title are more fully explained in Chapter Four.

Contract. A written contract, similar to a pre- or postnuptial agreement, is the ideal solution for partners with substantial or complicated assets. It sounds harsh—especially when you're madly in love—but it's better than arriving at the end of the road with nothing to show for it. Properly executed, a contract between unmarried partners overcomes the legal inclination toward family, just as a pre- or postnuptial overcomes state law in case of divorce.

Write down who owns what (a working inventory), who receives what during the relationship, and what happens if the relationship ends. You might write one ending for breaking up and another in case one partner dies. You can agree to anything you like as long as it's legal and does not fly in the face of public policy. Needless to say, that leaves a lot of room for negotiation for two people committed to each other in love or lust.

Trust. If you are in a long-term, truly committed unmarried relationship, a trust should also be considered to protect your partner and preserve your property rights. Tailored to your particular situation, a trust is a very useful tool to share income and property while ensuring that the trust assets are passed along according to your wishes.

A living trust allows you and your partner to share certain benefits of trust property, but after both of you have died, distributes the property according to instructions. Remember that a living trust can be changed if you change partners, but an irrevocable trust is almost forever (at least for its term).

If you have minimal assets but want to provide for your partner or others, consider using life insurance to fund a trust, by creating an ILIT or having your partner purchase the policy on your life—or vice versa. You can make gifts under the annual gift exclusion to support payment of premiums which will bring a great reward to your surviving partner—or vice versa.

Estate tax implications differ with the trust type. See Chapter Three.

Protection of minor children. Unmarried and same-sex couples with children have a special obligation to provide for those children both personally and financially. The last thing any parent wants is for the child to fall into the cracks, or become the center of emotional family wrangling. Establish a guardianship, custodianship, and/or a trust, with successors, to protect the child should the need arise. Then make your hopes, plans, and dreams for the child known, to your family, or anyone who will be involved, or who might try to interfere.

Naturally, you want your partner to have what is rightfully hers or his. Perhaps more importantly, you want to hold on to what is rightfully yours, and pass it along as *you* choose. A will takes effect upon your death. But what if you break up with your partner, who is also a business partner? What if you both chipped in to buy and decorate the loft, but want to sell it when you split up? What if one partner paid for almost everything? Who gets what?

The infamous "palimony" suits arose from just such situations, where women became accustomed to the high life while living with wealthy partners. The couples were committed to each other, with no strings attached—until the relationship ended, and the woman wanted to maintain her lifestyle. Regardless of their commitment, she had no legal right to her partner's property.

Unmarried Parents (All Parents, For That Matter)
Parent Trap

It's the style of the moment. From movie stars to single women listening to the persistent tick of their biological clocks, to young couples with neither the interest nor the means to marry, parenthood without the commitment of marriage is all the rage. It sounds so simple. A love child, go with the flow . . .

Any parent knows, however, that parenting is not simple—the richest of experiences, yes, but not simple. Regardless of lifestyle, a parent is responsible for her or his children, legally, morally, completely. Those who are divorced or widowed with custody of their children are very familiar with the never-ending demands of single parenting. Even part-time parents know that the demands of raising a child are always full time and can be overwhelming emotionally, intellectually, and financially.

Whether or not the parents are married, both are legally responsible for their child. A single mother is totally responsible if the father is not known. In our society, the mother is sometimes totally responsible even if the father is known.

For estate planning purposes, let's assume that the parents have the means—no matter how modest—to provide for their children. Every parent wants to do his level best to ensure that, if something happens to the parent(s), the care and support of the children will continue uninterrupted. A few basic tools of estate planning can clearly express your wishes and protect and provide for the children.

Will. The first priority of a single parent—especially if the other parent is not present or is not known—is to protect the child with a provision for a guardianship, custodianship, and/or a trust in a will. If the parent dies while the child is a minor, the parent's wishes are made clear in the terms of the will.

Unmarried parents who are living together should have separate wills including guardianship provisions, just like married parents. A court is unlikely to interfere with a well-founded plan for a minor child's care and support.

Unclear or contradictory wills of unmarried parents, especially those not living together, could cause unnecessary confusion and difficulty for the child. The children of unmarried parents are too often subject to custody battles with grandparents and relatives of one parent or the other.

Guardianship is, therefore, the most important component in the will of every parent—and undoubtedly the strongest argument for making a will.

> *Parents can tell, but never teach,*
> *unless they practice what they preach.*
> —Arnold Glasow

Guardianship. Even if carefully chosen and named in a will, your choice of guardian is a recommendation, not an appointment, though the court generally looks to a parent's will first in determining the choice of guardian. Only the court can officially appoint a guardian and establish the terms of the guardianship. And the main concern of the court is the welfare of the child.

It is best if parents who are divorced, separated, or unmarried agree on the appointment of a guardian. Demonstrate in your wills that you also agree on the successor, financial arrangements, and so forth. When naming a property guardian, especially a spouse, it is usually advisable to waive any reporting requirement. Again, the court will consider your wishes but is not bound by them in any way.

Live as you wish, but do what you must to protect your children. See Chapter Two for more about guardianships.

Custodianship. Gifts of stock or cash or other property cannot be owned outright by a minor and are usually placed in a custodial account. Typically, one parent serves as custodian; the other parent, or a trusted relative, friend, investment advisor, or lawyer as successor. It is probably wise to name a second successor, especially if the child is very young or the parents very old or ill, or just as a precaution.

If the parent is custodian, he is considered to have complete control of the account; therefore, it will be considered part of his estate at his death. Custodial income over $1,400 is taxed at the parent's rate until the child reaches age 14. After that, the income falls into the tax bracket of the child.

As a child grows, so grows a custodial account. Modest assets are appropriate for custodianship, but at some point it might be a better idea to remove custodial funds to a trust for the benefit of the child. Otherwise, the child gains unlimited access to the funds when he comes of age.

Trust. A fail-safe way to provide financially for a child for the long haul is through an irrevocable trust. A parent creating a trust could

"Dad, I need to dip into my college fund."

Someone to Watch over Avery

Murphy Brown was actually humbled by the magnificent way in which her son Avery was growing up. He could boss around all his friends and most of his babysitters. He usually had the sandbox completely to himself to work on his masterpieces in his very own way. He won every race, hit every ball the farthest, and drove everyone—even his mother at times—crazy as he bullied his way through his small life. Murphy was busting her buttons with pride.

Avery's father had disappeared and took no responsibility for the boy. Murphy realized she could not count on him to take care of their son if anything happened to her. Avery's financial security did not concern Murphy—she had set up a trust for him and made contributions every year.

Avery needed a guardian who would look after his every need and raise him much as she would. A young boy needed a young, active guardian—one who would give him the necessary time and attention.

Eldin the painter would do anything for—and he meant

---

appoint himself or another person trustee. In any case, the trust puts property aside for the child and ensures that a successor trustee will take over if the parent/trustee dies or becomes incapacitated. In terms of property management, a trust is similar to property guardianship, but without any involvement of a court. Even with a trust, it is still necessary to name a personal guardian.

Consider putting gifts or property away for the long haul—for education, food, shelter, and clothing, or for the general financial security of your child. A small amount placed in trust for a young child will grow to provide a good education and perhaps a modest living for a young adult. The stock market has made millionaires of many trust fund babies.

Plan the trust to satisfy your objective. Income may be distributed for specific or general needs, in regular payments or as needed. As tuition costs skyrocket, creating a trust is a great way to ensure *everything to Avery, whom he had often cared for when Murphy fired a nanny a week. Frank would do all the guy things, and he was in the business, but what if he fell in love again, or again, or again? He was so distractible.*

Miles and Corky would be good parents, but would their marriage survive? Murph wouldn't want Avery to get attached and then experience another loss. Jim was way too stuffy and Dan Quayle was out of the question, though in an effort to make amends, he had offered.

Murphy decided that Corky was her first choice. When asked, the former Miss America burst into tears, hugged and thanked Murphy, and promised to honor her commitment, cross-her-heart-and-hope-to-die. Eldin was delighted to be successor guardian. Murphy knew he might not instill in Avery that cut-throat competitive edge, but Eldin would never let any harm come to the boy.

And the successor successor? Dan, of course. How could Murphy resist the poetic justice of such a decision? She walked out of her stunned lawyer's office with a smirk that didn't fade for days.

that your child will be able to afford the college of her choice. Some parents tie strings to trust benefits. Finish college and you get X amount. Don't smoke until age 30 and you get X amount. Some trusts distribute assets at certain ages: 50 percent at age 30, the balance at 40. Many trusts, especially those benefiting children or the elderly, provide for special distributions in case of extraordinary medical or personal need.

In another form of trust, an ILIT—irrevocable life insurance trust—the trust owns a policy on your life which will provide for your child upon your death. If you own the policy yourself, proceeds will be considered part of your estate. Consequently, life insurance benefits could be reduced by estate tax.

Childless Couples

Born Free

Married couples without children face fewer complications and conflicts in planning their estates. Their paramount concern is for each other. Couples without children often have significant assets because both spouses have full-time careers and the huge expense of raising children is eclipsed.

All married couples have the advantage of the Unlimited Marital Deduction, as well as the opportunity to preserve the unified tax credit for two generations. Couples without children are usually very dependent upon each other, sometimes to a fault. Most just want to leave everything to the other and are not concerned with potential tax consequences upon the death of the second spouse. Nevertheless, estate planning options are available.

Wills. The most important questions childless couples face are how to provide for each other, and who will be their final heirs. When the first spouse dies, everything usually goes to the surviving spouse. It is when the surviving spouse dies that the tax man rears his ugly head.

Without a will, or clearly identified heirs, the probate court will appoint an estate administrator who will search for descendants at the expense of the estate. If spouses die simultaneously, first-to-die clauses prevent double probate, but only named contingent beneficiaries prevent intestacy. Estate administration expenses are almost always higher for intestate property (passing through probate without a will). Even the simplest will and estate plan avoid unnecessary court costs and, possibly, estate taxes.

Many couples consider making one will between them, because they both want the same thing. However, a joint will is usually a bad idea, regardless of the simplicity of the estate. If both spouses make one will, whose intent is truly represented?

Separate wills with identical or similar instructions are less likely to be challenged because they clearly state the intentions of the individual making the will. Talk it over, think about it, and talk it over again.

Whether your heirs are nieces and nephews, siblings, or a favorite charity, make separate wills and name your beneficiaries.

Trusts. If a couple plans to provide completely for each other, and provide as much as possible for heirs, an irrevocable credit shelter trust, usually created under a will, preserves the unified tax credit of the first spouse to die. The amount of the unified tax exemption is put in trust, possibly with income benefits to the surviving spouse. The balance of the estate could go directly to the spouse. Your spouse receives all the benefits of the marital estate, the estate pays no taxes when you die, and the trust escapes estate taxes again when your spouse dies.

A QTIP trust, often established while both spouses are alive, takes advantage of the Unlimited Marital Deduction. Income benefits go to the surviving spouse for life. At her death, trust assets pass to the remainderman outside probate, though they are subject to estate tax.

A marital deduction trust, often funded under a pour-over provision in a will, takes advantage of the marital deduction and provides the surviving spouse unrestricted access to trust assets.

Charitable trust. Couples without children are often charitably inclined. A charitable remainder trust guarantees income to the grantor(s), qualifies for a tax deduction, *and* leaves the trust assets to charity.

In any trust, a trustee manages the assets and distributes benefits to the surviving spouse. If a surviving spouse serving as trustee becomes incapacitated, a successor trustee and terms for income and asset distribution are already in place.

Power of attorney. If marital assets are not in trust with a successor trustee in place, each spouse needs a power of attorney to take over responsible management of assets as needed. Spouses usually give each other power of attorney, but successor appointments are especially important for the surviving spouse of a couple whose relatives are few and far between.

Health care power of attorney/living will. Health care issues are also important for couples with no children and no parents or close (including nearby) relatives. The first spouse to die will have had the surviving spouse to make medical decisions. The surviving spouse, however, may be left with no one who knows his true wishes about medical and end-of-life treatment. Each spouse needs a living will and/or a health care power of attorney, and the surviving spouse may want to reconsider her emergency contacts and power of attorney.

It's Now or Never . . .

- When you get right down to it, *every* situation is special, requiring a tailor-made estate plan.

- With a large dose of reality and a little creativity, the unorthodox, unexpected, but not-so-uncommon situations of life can be very effectively protected with traditional estate planning tools.

- Look out for number one. Go to a pro, have your documents drafted, and do what is required to put them into effect.

- Then tell those involved (after you've asked them) the papers are in order and you are counting on them.

- After that it's time to rest easy knowing you have done everything you can for yourself and your nearest and dearest.

6

Qualified Retirement Plans
When I'm Sixty-Four

What's Goin' On . . .

- Elements of a qualified retirement plan
- Types of retirement plans
- Plan distributions and beneficiary designations

Retirement plans are the largest single asset owned by many Americans. The widely used 401(k) plan—named for the defining section of the tax code—is not only the favorite way Americans save for the future, but in most cases, the only way. As fewer Americans have faith in the Social Security system, personal retirement plans have gained popularity. The aggregate value of qualified retirement plans across the country is approaching $2 trillion, about two-thirds of which is invested in the stock market—and 20 percent of that is in employer stock.

Qualified retirement plans are a bit of a mystery to most of us. There is a plethora of options, though each serves a purpose. People dedicate entire careers to figuring out qualified plans. There's no need for each of us to try to become an expert on the subject.

"I don't mind working. It's the waiting
for a pension that gets me!"

Take it one step at a time. First, identify your current plan. Next determine its tax and distribution effects. Then play "What if?" Frankly, it's a bit of a puzzle to be solved. If your employer or investment advisor can't explain your options adequately, find an expert who can. And don't be afraid to ask. Your financial security is at stake.

Elements of a Qualified Retirement Plan
She Works Hard for the Money

Plans are "qualified" by specific provisions of the tax code that allow preferential tax treatment. In most plans, the *participant* and/or the employer (or both) makes pretax income contributions to a special account. Tax is due not when income is earned, but when distributions from the plan are received. The participant pays taxes not just later, but later in life, ideally in a lower income tax bracket.

When enrolling in a plan, the participant designates a *beneficiary* to receive funds in case the participant dies. The type of beneficiary—spouse, child, business associate, trust, estate, or charity—could dramatically affect the method of distribution and tax consequences. If things change, as they often do, and you wish to change the beneficiary of your plan, you may do so at any time. In yet another effort to preserve marital rights, a spouse may not be removed as beneficiary of an employer-sponsored plan without his or her permission.

Retirement plans offer a wide variety of *distribution* or *withdrawal* options, each with significantly different tax ramifications. A method of withdrawal can be designed to meet individual income and estate planning needs.

> *Just remember, once you're over the hill you begin to pick up speed.*
> —Charles Schulz

Ideally, distributions are intended to span the postretirement life expectancy of the plan participant. Distributions are generally subject to a 10 percent penalty if withdrawn prior to age 59½, and are mandatory at age 70½. The tax consequences of both distribution options and beneficiary designations are critical to an effective estate plan.

Some plans are *trusts* for the benefit of participating employees; others are *custodial accounts* safeguarding contributions under individual provisions. An employee's eligibility for an employer-sponsored plan is determined by age, years of service, and annual hours of employment. Depending on the type of plan, contributions are generally discretionary, but are limited by the participant's income. In certain cases, employees can borrow funds from their plans.

*   *   *

Types of Retirement Plans
I've Been Workin' on the Railroad

Whether sponsored by an employer or established by an individual, there is a retirement plan to fit the needs of every employer and every individual.

Basically, plans fall into two categories: *defined contribution* and *defined benefit*.

Defined Contribution Plans

In most defined contribution plans, employees contribute pretax dollars deducted from earnings. Employers can elect to make no contribution, match employee contributions, or make discretionary contributions.

Our overview of the plans goes from large to small:

The **401(k)**, the most popular retirement plan in America, is favored by larger corporations because it offers maximum flexibility to both employer and employee. Contributions of pretax income are made to an account at the election of the employee. Subject to antidiscrimination rules, employers have broad discretion to match employee contributions, or not. Total annual contributions are limited to the lesser of 15 percent of annual income or $10,000, adjustable for inflation. Distributions may be made in cash or securities.

A **Profit-Sharing** plan is a straightforward employee incentive plan sponsored entirely by the employer. Employees contribute nothing. The employer chooses the extent to which contributions—normally based on a percentage of profits—will be made. The more successful the year, the more likely the employer is to make a contribution. In less profitable years, the employer may not be obligated to contribute to the plan at all.

Contributions are limited to 15 percent of an employee's salary, to a maximum of $24,000, adjustable for inflation. Distributions are made in cash or securities. Profit-sharing plans generally favor long-term employees, but have been almost totally eclipsed by the 401(k).

403(b) is essentially a salary-deferral program for a not-for-profit organization such as a hospital, school, or museum.

A **money purchase plan** permits either a company or a self-employed individual to make contributions.

The maximum contribution is 25 percent of salary up to $30,000. But there's a catch. Once an annual contribution amount is declared, it must be made, or penalties will be imposed. Participants often combine a money purchase plan and a profit-sharing plan to achieve maximum flexibility.

An **Employee Stock Ownership Program (ESOP)** is a profit-sharing plan funded with company stock. The premise is that the good work of the employee will pay off in the form of a higher price on the stock. The employer holds the stock in a plan for the benefit of participating employees. Contributions are subject to the same restrictions as in a profit-sharing plan. Distributions may be made in either stock or cash.

Keogh Plan, Simplified Employee Pension (SEP) IRA, Savings Incentive Match Plan for Employees (SIMPLE) IRA, and SIMPLE 401(k). All are hybrid retirement plans for self-employed people and small businesses, affording employers and employees the advantages available under larger company plans. These plans are designed for ease of implementation and administration.

The **Individual Retirement Account (IRA)** is the most popular individual plan. A traditional IRA is generally established by self-employed individuals, or those not participating in or wishing to supplement an employer-sponsored plan.

Contributions are a bit of a good news–bad news situation. As much as (this is the good news) 100 percent of pretax, earned income may be contributed to the plan each year, to an annual maximum of (now the bad news) $2,000. In the not-such-bad-news-department, a nonworking spouse can also contribute $2,000 annually. If income of the plan participant exceeds a certain limit, contributions must be made with after-tax dollars.

IRA contributions are completely tax deductible if the individual is not participating in another qualified plan. If participating in another plan, deductibility of contributions is determined by income levels. Each IRA account is managed separately by the plan participant.

The Roth IRA
Retirement Stripes of a Different Color

The popular and distinctive Roth IRA, introduced under the Taxpayer Relief Act of 1997, is a defined contribution plan in a category of its own. The Roth IRA has two distinguishing features essentially the reverse of the traditional IRA. In a Roth, contributions are made with after-tax dollars. To compensate for the fact that *contributions are not deductible*, all *distributions are tax free*. The Roth provides a rare opportunity for tax-free appreciation of assets.

In order to qualify for tax-free distributions under a Roth, the participant must be at least 59½ years old and must have owned the Roth for at least five years. But there are no mandatory distributions, and contributions of $2,000 per year may, in fact, continue past the age of 70½.

The standard IRA 10 percent penalty for early withdrawal applies, but only to the earnings portion of distributions—not the contribution portion—taken before age 59½. Remember, in a Roth, you've already paid income tax on the contributions. If you have to make an early withdrawal, take the contribution portion first, free of the penalty.

There is a good deal of talk about "converting to a Roth." A participant may convert a traditional IRA to a Roth, provided adjusted gross income (single or joint) does not exceed $100,000 in the year of the conversion. The conversion, however, is treated as ordinary income, triggering an *immediate* income tax liability. Because the conversion spikes up income, and deductions are based on a percentage of income, the threshold for income tax deductions also rises. Thus, the conversion could diminish the effect of income tax deductions for the year.

An employer-sponsored 401(k) plan is eligible for conversion to a Roth only if it first rolls into a traditional IRA. And if the tax impact of a complete conversion is prohibitive, a partial conversion is permitted.

The tax-free retirement income of a Roth sounds almost irresistible, but conversion to a Roth is not a panacea. Weigh your options carefully before converting. The best candidates for conversion are generally younger participants who have plenty of time to make up the tax liability through tax-free appreciation of assets over the long haul.

Converting from a traditional IRA to a Roth requires taking a financial step backward by paying income taxes before moving ahead through tax-free appreciation. If converting requires using funds from the account to pay the taxes, it may be considerably less attractive and should be done only with great caution.

As an estate planning tool, the Roth can be used to secure retirement income or pass along appreciated assets as tax-free income to the grandkids or other beneficiaries. With a sound investment strategy, the longer the life of the Roth, the greater the benefit of tax-free appreciation. As with any qualified retirement plan, the options are many and the stakes are high. Discuss all the implications with your tax advisor and estate planning lawyer.

Defined Benefit Plans

In an effort to stabilize their workforces, employers have long made contributions to retirement plans as a fringe benefit to employees. A defined benefit plan, such as the old-fashioned pension plan, obligates employers to pay regular income to employees after their retirement.

"... and so, in appreciation of your twenty-five years
of faithful service, we present you this handsome watch,
appropriately engraved and bearing one of Walt Disney's
most beloved characters."

Under most defined benefit plans, monthly payments to participants are based on single or combined life expectancies of participant
and spouse. Wilma Flintstone would no doubt outlive that clumsy Fred;
therefore, she'd probably push for combining life expectancies to stretch
out payments and have something left for Pebbles and herself after Fred
is gone. IRA rollover and forward averaging of taxes on lump-sum payments are available under some plans.

Defined benefit plans can be costly for employers to fund and
administer. As lifelong employment has dwindled, large corporations
have almost universally discontinued traditional pensions. However, a
smaller company might find it advantageous to reward older or highly
compensated employees through a defined benefit plan.

Both employers and employees prefer the contribution and distribution flexibility of defined contribution plans to old-fashioned retirement benefits which sometimes amount to little more than the
proverbial gold watch.

Nonqualified Retirement Plans

A *deferred compensation plan* is generally offered to key employees as a supplement to other retirement plans.

The idea is simply to defer income, with interest, until retirement, when the employee presumably will be in a lower tax bracket. Though a deferred compensation plan is not "qualified" by distribution restrictions, it does require a beneficiary designation.

Plan Distributions
Know When to Hold 'Em, Know When to Fold 'Em

Choosing a distribution option most beneficial to your individual situation is a numbers game. Nearly all the options are defined by numbers taken right out of the tax code. On top of that, the numbers that define your age and life expectancy, tax rates, and potential penalties also figure into the equation.

....
Let Me Make Myself Perfectly Clear

If your bowling partner suggests taking a 72(t) distribution from your 401(k) before 59½, to avoid the 10 percent, make a quick getaway before you're completely bowled over.

The idea could be a good one, but who could tell? Get the help of a pro and ask for an explanation in plain English.
....

Most employer-sponsored plans offer two options for distribution: a lump sum payment or a rollover into an IRA. Income taxes on lump sum payments are eligible for ten-year forward averaging, creating an immediate income tax burden, but at a reduced rate. Rolling plans into an IRA triggers no immediate income tax liability and continues tax deferral under IRA rules.

Some plans also offer annuity payments, though it is usually not an attractive option in a low interest rate environment.

* * *

All plans, with the exception of the Roth, are subject to *age restrictions* and *mandatory distribution*. A 10 percent penalty is imposed on any distributions from an IRA or 401(k) taken prior to the participant's reaching age 59½. However, distributions *must* begin at age 70½. Most plans make allowances for disability, education, and first home purchase. As longevity increasingly delays retirement, both employers and employees who stay on the job past 70½ have the option to defer distributions from a company plan until the year following actual retirement.

There is also an exception to the penalty, that is particularly advantageous to those considering early retirement. Section 72(t) of the tax code permits distributions based on life expectancy calculation to begin *before* age 59½, as long as payments continue for five years or until 59½, whichever is longer. The 72(t) distributions escape the early-withdrawal penalty, though they are subject to income tax.

Plan participants have several options for withdrawal. Most attempt to minimize tax impact by maximizing income deferral. Consequently, a *lump sum* payment, resulting in an immediate income tax liability, is rarely chosen. The real beauty of these plans is in stretching out distributions over retirement years.

When mandatory distributions begin, the participant must choose a *method of withdrawal*. The options are many, the decisions irrevocable, and, frankly, the whole issue is pretty convoluted.

The period over which distributions are made is determined by *life expectancy tables*. One of three tables is used:

The *single* table is used if distribution is determined by the life expectancy of the plan participant only.

The *joint* table is used when a participant and beneficiary combine life expectancies to establish a distribution period. The combination results in smaller distributions—and smaller tax payments—over a longer period.

The *MDIB*—minimum distribution incidental benefits—table is used when withdrawal is based on joint life expectancies of the

*"I rolled my pension over and over and over,
and now I have no idea where the hell it is."*

participant and a nonspouse beneficiary who is more than ten years younger than the participant. (There they go, throwing in another number!) Even if distribution is based on combined life expectancies, payment is made only to the plan participant.

The method of withdrawal also includes two options for *calculation of the withdrawal period*. Once decided, the method of calculation cannot be changed. The options are affectionately known as:

Recalc. The withdrawal period is recalculated each year according to the chosen life expectancy table.

And *non-recalc.* The withdrawal period is calculated just once, at the time of the first distribution. It is not recalculated.

Yes, it's a double negative, but it's too late to change it. These terms are ingrained in the syntax of qualified plan *officionados*.

Tax Implications

Income tax. Distributions from qualified retirement plans are generally subject to ordinary income tax. If not rolled over directly into an IRA or other qualified plan, distributions are subject to 20 percent withholding tax.

Estate tax. If a plan participant dies before the plan is fully distributed, the estate is liable for estate taxes on undistributed assets in the plan. Estate taxes paid are deductible from income tax on future distributions to the beneficiary, legally known as "income in respect of a decedent."

Ten-year forward averaging. Some participants, especially those with larger estates, prefer to pay the income tax on a lump sum payment rather than expose their estates to both income and estate tax liability. A ten-year forward averaging method softens the blow of lump sum payments for qualified participants by imposing taxes at a lower rate. Baby boomers and those younger need not apply. To qualify for forward averaging, participants must have turned 50 before 1986 and must have participated in the plan for at least five years before distributions begin. Forward averaging is allowed once in a lifetime, literally.

When you come to the fork in the road—take it.
—Yogi Berra

Net unrealized appreciation—NUA. A very handy loophole allows an employee to convert appreciation of employer stock in a 401(k) plan to a long-term capital gain. When a distribution of stock is made, the participant is immediately liable for income tax only on the original cost (the cost basis) of the stock.

If and when the participant sells the stock, the appreciated value of the stock, or NUA, is treated as a capital gain. The 20 percent maximum tax rate on capital gains is almost always more favorable than ordinary income tax rates, providing a significant benefit to the participant.

If employer stock is distributed and still owned by a participant at death, the ultimate seller of the stock—whether the estate or the heir—is liable for capital gains tax on the NUA. Additional appreciation before date of death escapes taxation because the basis of the stock steps up, conveying a tax advantage to heirs.

Beneficiary Designations
B-I-N-G-O

For estate planning purposes, beneficiary designations are every bit as important as the method of withdrawal. When a plan participant dies, the value of a retirement plan is taxed as part of the estate, but distributions are made to designated beneficiaries outside of probate.

Just as with the appointment of an executor or custodian, naming a successor or contingent beneficiary for a retirement plan is crucial. If the primary beneficiary dies before the participant, and no contingent beneficiary is named, assets in the plan will be distributed to the estate of the participant at death.

Spouse as Beneficiary

As is the case with other laws, a married couple participating in a qualified plan is offered advantages unavailable to others. Once a spouse is named as beneficiary of an employer-sponsored plan, the designation may not be changed without consent of that spouse. In some states, spouses are entitled to a certain share of a retirement plan regardless of designation. In other words, I Got You, Babe.

If a plan participant dies, a surviving spouse may take a lump sum payment, but roll it over into the spouse's own IRA—called (it's a catchy name) a *spousal rollover IRA*. If distribution is deferred, the tax deferral continues until the spouse reaches the mandatory distribution age of 70½. When rolling over a plan, the spouse does not have to honor the participant's contingent beneficiaries, but may designate whomever he chooses as beneficiaries. If your second spouse is your plan beneficiary, he might not choose your successor beneficiaries, possibly your children from an earlier marriage.

She's Got Spunk

Mary *finally got her man. And yes, it was Mr. Grant, her boss. Try as he might, he could not resist her irrepressible spunk and that beautiful smile. The gruff old billy goat verily purred whenever Mary was around.*

Happy Homemaker Sue Ann, who had shamelessly chased Lou for years and even tried to bribe him with the income tax benefits of her new Roth IRA, gave up the fight begrudgingly. She simply turned tail and set her sights on Ted, who remained oblivious to her charms as he was obsessed with his own.

After working 40 years for WJM-TV, Mary retired with quite a nice nest egg in her 401(k). When she and Lou married, she had designated him as her plan beneficiary. If Mary died first, he would have the right to all benefits and could then name his own children beneficiaries. Because Lou's children were adolescents at the time, Mary's designation was as much a kindness to her husband as a practicality.

Now, with the mandatory distribution ages of 70½ fast approaching, Mary realized that Lou had plenty of income to live well and cover unexpected medical expenses. His middle-aged children had their own respectable income and had no real need for her retirement plan.

What she really wanted was to make sure Rhoda and her frail, elderly mother, Ida, would have what they needed to live comfortably. At age 69, Rhoda was still dressing windows at the local department store. Her modest income barely provided for her mother's care and her own living expenses, with nothing extra, and no cushion for emergencies.

With Lou's written permission gladly given, Mary changed her beneficiary designation from Lou to Rhoda. Even as Mary lives on to enjoy her own retirement, Rhoda takes comfort in the security net provided by her dear old friend.

Trust as Beneficiary

The advantage of naming an irrevocable trust as beneficiary is that the plan participant determines, in advance, how trust assets will be managed and distributed. The terms of the trust and the appointed trustee effectively keep the participant in control for a second round. Naming a trust as beneficiary is perfect for control freaks, but more likely, it is very useful in cases where the person receiving trust benefits would be ill-equipped to manage the assets outright.

The trust could be for the benefit of a spouse, a minor, any individual(s), or a charity. A charitable trust could pay benefits to a surviving spouse or another for life, with the remainder of the trust going to the charity at death.

A QTIP trust paying lifetime benefits to a surviving spouse has the unique additional advantage of qualifying for the Unlimited Marital Deduction. The IRA document must specifically declare that all income be distributed to the trust, and the trust document must ensure that all annual income will be distributed to the surviving spouse. If the language is correct, a lump sum payment of plan assets to the QTIP is permitted, and the tax deferral is continued. Upon the death of the surviving spouse, trust assets are distributed to the remaindermen, but trust assets are taxed as part of the surviving spouse's estate.

When enrolling in an IRA, ask a lawyer or a qualified plan expert to make sure the language serves your purposes.

Nonspouse and Multiple Beneficiaries

When a plan participant dies, a beneficiary who does not elect a lump sum payment may elect to receive distributions either within five years of the participant's death or over the course of his or her own life expectancy. If the life expectancy option is chosen, distributions must begin no later than the first calendar year following the participant's death. A beneficiary electing the five-year option is not required to take any distributions before the last day of the fifth year. In any case, a new account is created in the name of the beneficiary(ies). If there are multiple beneficiaries with a great age discrepancy, a participant could, before the age of 70½, choose to divide an IRA into separate IRAs, each subject to a separate method of withdrawal based on the life expectancy of the respective beneficiary. Otherwise, the IRA is divided *after* the participant's death, and distributions, though equal to all beneficiaries, are based only on the life expectancy of the oldest beneficiary.

A Minor as Beneficiary

If your intended beneficiary is a minor, distributions will be made only to a custodian or trust for the benefit of the child. Rather than naming a child beneficiary, you would designate, for example, Mr. Wilson, trustee (or custodian) for the benefit of Dennis "the Menace" Mitchell, as beneficiary of your plan. Distributions for the benefit of minors are not eligible for rollover.

Charity as Beneficiary

If a charitable organization is beneficiary of an IRA, the estate is liable for income taxes on the income in respect of decedent, but also eligible for a charitable deduction of that amount. The result is basically a wash for the estate, which, for all practical purposes, incurs no tax liability.

We make a living by what we get; we make a life by what we give.
—Winston Churchill

It's Now or Never . . .

- Enough with the numbers and the options and the loopholes. Let's just admit that qualified plans are highly technical.

- Carefully examine your personal retirement and tax situation before making the decision to roll over your plan or take any distributions.

- Even if you think you understand your qualified plan and all your options, seek the advice, or at least the blessing, of a tax or legal advisor to be sure the plan is in synch with other aspects of your retirement and estate plans.

7

Closely Held Businesses
Heigh-Ho, Heigh-Ho, It's Off to Work We Go

What's Goin' On . . .

- Planning for continuation of a business
- Types of closely held businesses
- Valuation and transfer of a business
- Special tax strategies

By failing to prepare you are preparing to fail.
—Benjamin Franklin

It must be true. More than 16 million American entrepreneurs own their own businesses. Yet less than one-third of these closely held businesses succeed to a second generation—not because the businesses aren't sound, but because of unexpected death, disability, and taxes. Only 4 percent stay in the family for a third generation.

If an owner dies or becomes incapacitated, and does not have a plan for continuing the business or selling it, the business will face un-necessary, often fatal losses. Many are forced to close their doors and sell just to pay estate taxes.

Those who own their businesses no doubt have pondered what would happen if they could no longer manage the business, or if they died. What if a spouse or child had to take over the business? . . . Or had to work with that incorrigible partner? . . . Or what if only one of your several children knows anything about the "family" business? What if your creative talent evaporated? . . . Or your partners tried to buy your share for less than its worth?

Closely held businesses come in many shapes and sizes. Many are the heart and soul of a family. Each decision about a family business affects the family as well as the business. Keep the family involved by asking for ideas and listening to concerns. And remember that only family can make a family business work.

Whether an owner is self-employed or holds a sole proprietorship, a partnership, limited-liability corporation, or small family corporation, the successful transfer or continuation of any business is contingent upon a well-executed plan, including a buy–sell agreement.

Continuing a Business
Jeopardy

One way or another, the death of an owner or partner triggers a transfer of the business. Whether a family member or partner takes over, or the business is sold or transferred to nonfamily members, often called "outsiders," the business changes hands. It is always best for a closely held business to avoid probate, where business operations are likely to be disrupted for a variety of reasons.

First, the executor takes over management of the estate's interest in the business. That's at least one good reason to choose your executor wisely.

Second, depending on the size and complexity of the estate, every aspect of the transfer or sale of a business could require approval of the court. Court scheduling involves inevitable delays. When a business goes through probate, the process is almost always a bit more cumbersome and costly than for a personal estate. And your private business—its ownership and value—becomes part of the public record.

· · ·

A *buy–sell agreement* or other contractual arrangement keeps your business out of probate. The contract supersedes a will, passing the business along as agreed and keeping everybody else's nose out of your business.

Many experts recommend that closely held businesses be placed in *living trust*. The terms of the trust can be essentially equivalent to a buy–sell agreement with the same effects. In most cases, the original business owner serves as trustee, retaining much of the authority of a business owner. As a trust asset, the business is transferred or distributed outside of probate. And, under the trust, a successor trustee is named to continue the business should the original trustee die, retire, or become incapacitated.

> *The method of the enterprising is to plan with audacity*
> *and execute with vigor.*
> —Christian Bovée

This chapter first describes various closely held businesses and related estate planning concerns. The elements and tax effects of a buy–sell agreement, including options for transfer of a business and methods for valuation, follow.

Types of Closely Held Businesses
Eight Days a Week

Sole Proprietor and Self-Employed
My Way

The buck stops here. You are the business. Nothing happens without you. These days more than ever, Americans operate independently rather than as regular employees. The self-indulgent boomers (and other free spirits) want the freedom to pick up and go wherever, whenever they like.

Corporations save money on employee benefits by hiring independent contractors. Telecommuting and the Internet have increased job flexibility and abbreviated many business practices. Working as a "company man" no longer means job security, so why bother?

The result is a skyrocketing number of freelancers in our midst. But without the "company" benefits and retirement plans associated with full-time employment, many of these nouveau independent operators overlook very important estate planning needs. If your livelihood, or that of your family, depends primarily upon your income, it is imperative that you take precautions—in case you can no longer bring home the bacon.

The man who is prepared has his battle half fought.
—Miguel de Cervantes

Insurance. Disability, life, health, and long-term care insurance are essential. Life insurance proceeds keep money coming in to support you and/or your family. Health and long-term care insurance pay the unpredictable expenses of extended medical care.

If you have borrowed money to get your business going, cover yourself with insurance to pay off the loans. If your equity in the business covers debts, consider whether your insurance is adequate to cover personal needs and replace lost income.

If the business is the bulk of an estate and funds are not available to pay estate taxes on it, the capital assets of the business, from real estate to office equipment, might have to be sold to pay the taxes. Under certain circumstances, tax payments may be deferred; otherwise, the estate—and the business—will stay in probate until all taxes are paid.

Power of attorney. To protect your business while you are alive, a power of attorney authorizes an agent of your choice to run your business in case you become incapacitated or under other prescribed circumstances. It could be a temporary, springing power, or a durable power that lasts from the time you sign it until you revoke it or die. Your agent has a fiduciary duty to manage, protect, and preserve your business interests according to the highest business standards.

Once the power takes effect, it is up to your agent whether to

"If I heard it once, I heard it a thousand times. 'Margie,'
he'd say, 'when I die, the business dies with me.'"

continue, liquidate, or close the doors of your business. The power of
attorney has far-reaching effects for a one-person business. If you are
running a business under your own steam, you need a power of attorney
in case something happens to you. Choose your agent very carefully.

A power of attorney is valid only while you are alive. If you have
no other agreements concerning the business, but have a will, the future
of the business will fall into the hands of your executor. Again, choose
wisely.

Contract. Another option for a one-person operation is to make
a contractual agreement with an associate or competitor in the same
business. You know your worth, as does the competition. Without you,
your business could fail, but your customer list might be valuable to
your competitor.

Whatever legal arrangement you choose, include a valuation

method for the business. The government does everything it can to tax a business at full value. Even if you leave it to a spouse tax free, when the spouse dies the government will tax the business. Unless value is clearly established, the government will impose its own standards. And you know what *that* means. Higher taxes.

Family-Owned Business
We Are Family

Estate planning concerns of family-owned businesses are much the same as for a sole proprietor. A family-owned business is generally started, owned, and managed by family members. It could be a bakery, a plumbing business, a website design business, a media marketing firm, a bed and breakfast, or a tattoo parlor.

As the business grows, it usually becomes an ever-greater portion of the owner's estate. Outsiders might come into the business as employees, especially if children of the owner develop other interests and careers. Families, as we know, often disagree, especially where business and money are concerned. Take all these factors into consideration when planning the future of your business. If a business that is your primary asset fails or is lost to creditors, your family could be in big trouble.

Insurance. A life insurance policy on key owners or partners, purchased and owned by someone else, provides funds to pay taxes or buy shares from family members of deceased or disabled partners.

Trust. A living trust could own the business and the life insurance. The trust form establishes income and asset distribution and guarantees succession.

Stock ownership. A good protection for a family-owned business is stock distribution combined with life insurance.

Here's how it works. Each family member owns stock—voting or nonvoting—in the business. Family members who are actively involved in the business usually own the voting stock; nonparticipating family

211

Three Cheers

After five years of running his bar, Cheers, Sam's tremendous success had gone to his head (what else is new), and he decided to modernize at the suggestion of his new girlfriend. No more free beers for Norm in exchange for accounting advice. No more friendly chit-chat with the customers for Carla. No more casual mail delivery stops by Cliff. And no more Diane, period.

He stopped serving draught beer and switched to designer martinis and expensive wines. The pool table in the back room was replaced with a sushi bar. There were lots of new faces, but none of the old gang found their old haunt cheerful anymore. And nobody knew anybody's name.

After a couple of years of wearing black shirts buttoned to the neck, Sam realized he had never liked fish, people who drank cosmopolitans were too-too, and he wanted out. He decided to sell, but couldn't find a buyer. Cheers had become just another piece of real estate, and the business was, it turned out, not worth much.

Sam's friends, the ones he had basically sold out, wanted in. They offered to buy out Sam and bring their old Cheers back. Sam, of course, said he had already planned to bring back the old bar, but would be happy to have a couple of partners. What they all wanted more than anything else was for Cheers to continue into the foreseeable future as the favorite neighborhood bar.

Sam, Diane, Norm, Cliff, Woody, Carla, even Frasier and Lilith formed a partnership. They all signed a written partnership agreement providing terms for cross-purchase and valuation of the business in case the business was sold or a partner wanted out or died. They bought life insurance to fund a potential buy-out, but because there were so many partners they chose a first-to-die life policy rather than owning individual policies on each other.

(To be continued . . .)

members usually have nonvoting stock. Each family member owns a piece of the business, but control is restricted to certain stockholders with the power to vote.

In a family corporate structure, voting stock is often called preferred stock; nonvoting is common stock.

Buy–sell. A buy–sell agreement formalizes the procedures for transfer and defines fair value. The government keeps a watchful eye on closely held businesses to prevent fraudulent transfers. Whatever agreement you reach, make it entirely above board.

Partnership
It Takes Two to Tango

A partnership is owned and operated by family members or outsiders under a written partnership agreement that includes all the terms of a buy–sell. Life insurance is used to fund a buy-out either through a *cross-purchase*, in which individual partners own insurance on each other, or an *entity purchase*, in which the partnership owns insurance to fund a buy-out.

Family Limited Partnership
It's a Family Affair

The title says it all. The idea is to limit liability of partners who have little or no say in the business. Control is often the most important issue in a family business. In a family limited partnership (FLP), the general partner who controls the business is also primarily liable for the obligations of the business—debts, taxes, and so forth. Limited partners are liable only for the value of their shares, and stand to lose only their original investment. The general partner takes any additional losses.

Often viewed as protection from creditors, family limited partnerships are widely used to shift income and appreciation to family members who are limited partners. Partial gifts of the business are made to

*"Bentley, I don't care if you <u>are</u> my heir apparent.
Stop peeking in here fifty times a day!"*

limited partners. But because no control is transferred, the value of the gift is discounted for lack of marketability. Therefore, significant business interests can be transferred without incurring a significant gift tax liability. The general partner thus maintains control of the property but effectively reduces his income tax while removing value from his estate.

When property in the partnership ultimately passes to heirs, estate taxes are saved because the business value is discounted by the divided ownership. The sum of the parts is worth less than the whole.

In some states, a slightly different form—the family limited *liability* partnership—limits the liability of general partners as well as limited partners.

Family Limited Liability Corporation

That's the Way I Like It

Once in a while you'll notice the letters LLC after the name of a business. It's the abbreviation for Limited Liability Corporation, a hybrid form of doing business with the liability limits of a corporation. Taxes are imposed as if the business was a sole proprietorship.

To qualify as an LLC, the business owner(s) must file articles of incorporation describing the business and its assets with the appropriate state agency. The articles of incorporation contain the elements of a buy–sell agreement, defining every aspect of a business transfer right down to dissolution of the corporation. The people who operate a family limited liability corporation are officially known as "managers"; the limited partners, as "members." An odd distinction of the law, but what's in a name?

Corporations

Risky Business

Incorporation of a closely held business makes sense when liability becomes a major concern, whether because of a growing number of employees or because the business has inherent risk. The corporate form protects owners from personal liability for business losses.

Some closely held corporations also offer tax advantages. If expansion results in major expenses, the corporate structure shifts responsibility for expenses, and possibly for income and capital gains taxes, from individual owners to the corporation.

Private corporate structures are defined in subchapters of the federal tax code. A subchapter C corporation pays income taxes as a separate entity. In a subchapter S corporation, income taxes are paid by the owner at the owner's tax rate. The tax ramifications of incorporation can be dramatic.

Corporation: an ingenious device for obtaining individual profit without individual responsibility.
—Ambrose Bierce

As with the LLC, articles of incorporation and other necessary papers are filed with the state, reporting requirements are imposed, and

(Now back to Cheers . . .)

Things would have been different if Sam had married Diane and they'd had a couple of kids. Cheers would be a family business and probably the major portion of Sam's estate. Let's say Sam is a responsible family man (pretend it could be so) and Diane continues to work as a waitress, but satisfies her academic urges by hosting a book club on Tuesdays, guest speakers on Thursdays, and poetry readings on Sunday afternoons. If Sam wants to keep the business in the family for the next generation, he could form a family corporation.

In a corporation, Sam and Diane own the voting stock and the kids own the nonvoting stock. Over the years, Sam and Diane's interest in the business, and the control, could be methodically transferred to the kids through annual gifts. The gifts are designed to keep the business in the family and reduce the size of Sam and Diane's estate, limiting the potential estate tax liability.

What if young Sammy has worked in the bar and hopes to continue the business, but daughter Fairchild has made it as a Major League catcher and has no interest in Cheers? As badly as Sammy wants the business, he could never afford to buy out the rest of the family.

Here's a plan: Sam and Diane make annual gifts to son and daughter. Young Sammy uses his gift to buy a life insurance policy on Sam's life. In his will, Sam should leave the voting stock to Sammy, keeping control in the hands of the person most likely to continue the business.

When Sam dies, Sammy uses life insurance proceeds to buy the balance of the stock from Diane and Fairchild. Sam and Sammy get what they want, and the others get fair value. Cheers!

the business keeps right on going—though as a corporation, it has a life of its own.

Incorporation is an estate planning option as well as a business option. Any transfer of corporate shares is subject to the articles of incorporation as well as the terms of a shareholder's will. Incorporation of a family business could jeopardize a valuable tax deferral opportunity available only to an individual estate. The structure could be good for business, but unintentionally limit your personal estate planning options.

Talk to your family, meet with the pros. You will almost certainly choose to have a lawyer who specializes in small corporations draft and file your articles of incorporation to conform to state regulations. Consider all the angles, objectives, and options—business and personal—before making any significant change to your closely held business.

Transfer or Sale of a Business

Taking Care of Business

Taking Care of Business was Elvis's motto. Souvenirs from solid gold tie clips to cocktail napkins featured the TCB logo over a lightning bolt. No one is quite sure just what care Elvis was taking, and of what business, but TCB was the standard of the loyal in-crowd at Graceland.

In fact, Elvis did not take his own advice to heart. His gross estate was worth more than $10 million when he died, but after taxes and settlement costs, less than $3 million was left. That's a 73 percent loss! No doubt about it, they were All Shook Up.

The circumstances and manner in which your closely held business is either continued or liquidated—and at what value—determines the fate of the business and your investment in it. A written *buy–sell agreement* between business owners or partners establishes the conditions, procedures, and a *method of valuation* for any and every transfer of your business. Valuation is a key element of a buy–sell agreement, but it is a double-edged sword. Too high and taxes take a toll. Too low and your family is robbed of full value.

For the sake of simplicity, we use the term *partners* for *owners* or *shareholders*, unless a differentiation is required for clarity.

A buy–sell is *essential* for any closely held business. The agreement

And how did each of you feel about signing the buy/sell agreement?

is legally binding, taking precedence over a will. Consequently, it has the distinct advantage of avoiding probate.

A buy–sell agreement also preempts the unpredictable family rivalries that could disrupt or even destroy a business. Not in your wildest nightmares could your daughter, the professor, take over your part of a construction business. And not in their wildest nightmares would your partners want her to. If you die, the buy-sell enables your partners to buy your share of the business from your estate. Your daughter gets the money; your partners keep the business. And your daughter keeps out.

> *The winds and the waves are always on*
> *the side of the ablest navigators.*
> —Edward Gibbon

The terms of a buy-sell establish the acceptable reasons for transfer consistent with the tax code. Many business owners attempt to make gifts of shares to reduce the value of their business interests and remove value from their estates.

Gifts and valuation of business interests are closely scrutinized by the IRS. For example, a gift of common stock, made by an owner who keeps all the preferred stock—and all the power and control—is likely to be considered a sham rather than a legitimate gift. The real value of the business remains with the owner of the controlling interest.

Buy–Sell Agreements
Hello, Goodbye

A buy–sell agreement establishes the procedure for sale of an interest in one of two ways at the partners' option. In a *cross-purchase*, the surviving partners buy out the deceased partner's share. In a *stock redemption*, the business buys out the share. In both cases, life insurance is generally used to fund the purchase.

Under the agreement, the business is obligated to buy, and the estate of the deceased partner is obligated to sell. Terms or installment payments may be permitted by agreement.

Cross-purchase. In a cross-purchase, each partner owns life insurance on the other partners. When a partner dies, the surviving partners use tax-free insurance proceeds to buy the deceased partner's share. If they eventually sell their stock, the higher cost basis resulting from the purchase reduces capital gains tax liability.

Ownership of insurance is an important consideration. If a business has several partners, the cost of premiums and administration of multiple individual insurance policies is prohibitive. Five partners would require twenty policies.

Thankfully, a recently developed insurance product, called a "first-to-die policy," will cover up to eight lives and will pay out when the first insured person dies. The policy then continues to cover surviving partners. The availability of the first-to-die policy makes cross-purchase a more attractive and less costly option if more than two or three partners are involved.

A life insurance trust could also own one policy on each partner, with all partners named as beneficiaries. Administration is minimal, and trust benefits would support a cross-purchase.

If the entire business is held in a living trust, the buy–sell is integrated into the terms of the trust, and the trust owns the insurance policies. Insurance proceeds go to the trust, and trust benefits payable to partners support the cross-purchase.

A distinct disadvantage of cross-purchase is that the individual partner, not the business, is responsible for the buy-out. Personally responsible. If a surviving partner fails to buy the deceased partner's share, the estate or family can go after the personal assets of the surviving partner. The potential liability of the surviving partner gives an advantage to the deceased partner's family.

Stock redemption. In a stock redemption, the corporation owns the life insurance and uses the proceeds to buy (redeem) stock. In a partnership, the same arrangement is called an *entity purchase*. We use the term *stock redemption* for both.

The advantage of a stock redemption plan is that the corporation or business, rather than individual partners, is obligated to buy.

If the business fails to buy, or simply fails, however, the estate or family of the deceased partner is at a distinct disadvantage. In such a case, the family will have to get in line with other creditors in bankruptcy court. The objective of the buy–sell agreement—to protect each partner's interest—could be entirely defeated. Not a good outcome, particularly for the partner's family. Perhaps your family.

Stock redemption also has tax disadvantages. Because the business pays for the redemption, there is generally no step-up in basis for surviving partners. Partial step-up in basis is possible in certain partnerships and corporations.

Furthermore, insurance proceeds are generally not taxable as income to either individuals or corporations. However, if a buy–sell allows purchase on the installment plan, interest is deductible to a tax-paying corporation, though not to individual partners.

Disability and the Uninsurable

Disability of a partner is also covered under the terms of a buy–sell agreement, and through insurance. A disabled partner is not usually forced to sell immediately, but becomes obligated to sell if unable to return to work within a certain amount of time, typically a year or two. Disability insurance proceeds then provide funds to buy out the share.

A partner who is uninsurable is usually required to contribute the equivalent of insurance premiums to a special fund to support the buy–out of his share. Some partners question the need for any insurance at all. They assume and hope and pray they'll have the means to buy a partner's share if necessary. Reality check. A business with an outstanding obligation to buy a partner's share, but without an insurance plan, seriously compromises its bottom line.

In solving—as in other activities—it is far
easier to start something than it is to finish it.
—Amelia Earhart

Private Annuity
There's a Kind of Hush

A private annuity agreement is like an installment sale except that it lasts a lifetime. By written agreement, a business is sold in return for periodic income payments from the buyer to the seller. The buyer gets the business; the seller gets regular income for life.

Income may be payable either to an individual or jointly to partners or co-owners, continuing through the life of the last to survive. The obligation to pay ends only when the last seller dies.

The benefits of a private annuity are numerous. Assets and appreciation are removed from the seller's estate, avoiding probate and escaping estate tax. In return, the seller (also called the "annuitant") receives a fixed income from the buyer (who is now the "obligor"). In effect, non-income-producing property is instantly converted to income.

The plan makes it possible for a buyer who might not be able to afford a lump-sum payment to purchase the business. And the seller gains a tax advantage. If the property has a low cost basis, periodic payments spread out the capital gains tax on the sale.

Through a private annuity, an owner can shift control to a chosen family member or key employee, ensuring continuation of the business. If the transferor keeps it in the family, but skips a generation in making the transfer, generation-skipping taxes do not apply because the transfer is considered a sale, not a gift.

Restrictions. Naturally, there are restrictions on an agreement with so many advantages. Unless the payment plan is unsecured, the sale is taxable in full, immediately upon transfer. In other words, if you sell the business to your son under a private annuity, but are holding the deed on your son's house as collateral, his obligation is secured. You will have to pay capital gains tax on the entire transfer at once.

A private annuity agreement with a trust or corporation owning very few assets is likely to be examined closely as a possible sham. Insurance companies are not permitted to participate in private annuity agreements at all. The watchdogs are out there.

The fair market value of a business property in a private annuity arrangement is reduced by the value of the income payments and any taxes due. Age factors, measured by actuarial tables, as well as cost basis and capital gains tax rates are used in calculating the value of the annuity and future tax obligations. Ask your accountant to do the numbers.

Installment Sale

You've Really Got a Hold on Me

An installment sale transfers property in return for a periodic payment. The distinguishing characteristic of the installment sale is that payments are completed within a certain number of years, not over the course of a lifetime as with an annuity. Property and appreciation are removed from the estate of the seller in return for income—and resulting taxes—spread out over the installment term.

The benefits of an installment sale are almost exactly like those of

"That's it. I'm taking the buyout."

a private annuity, but restrictions are a bit different. No payment is due in the year of the sale, but at least one payment must be made the following year.

If the buyer is a relative who sells out within two years of the agreement, the deal's off and the taxable gain to the seller is accelerated, unless—there's always an "unless"—the sale follows the death of either party. If buyer and seller are *not* related, and one dies before the installment period ends, the gain is accelerated, unless—there's another one—payments are forgiven by bequest under the will of the seller. Installment sale of depreciable property is usually not permitted.

Most families and business owners have a pretty good idea of how they'd like their businesses to continue. If you and your family or partners have answered the pertinent questions and know what you want to accomplish, it's time to go to the pros for legal, tax, and insurance advice.

Going through the motions of executing a buy–sell is simple compared to what your family and business partners will go through—financially and personally—without a written agreement covering all the important issues.

A verbal contract is not worth the paper it's written on.
—Louis B. Mayer

Valuation
The Price Is Right

Valuation is perhaps the most important consideration in transferring a business. When a business is sold, naturally the seller wants the highest price. You want to ensure that you or your heirs receive fair value for your business interests. However, for estate tax purposes, lower value is generally more desirable because it means estate taxes will also be lower.

When planning an estate that includes a family business, it is important to balance these concerns. In valuing a business, it is not easy to have your cake and eat it, too.

Valuation Methods
Let's Make a Deal

A written buy–sell agreement defines the method of valuation to be applied to your business. It may be fixed, based on a formula for capitalization, or determined by appraisal. If there is disagreement about valuation, a buy–sell agreement usually requires binding arbitration in which the parties involved negotiate and settle on a value. In the best of worlds, valuation represents the amount a willing buyer would pay to a willing seller.

Choose the method of valuation that most appropriately reflects the true value of your type of business. For liquid assets such as publicly traded stock, fair market value is the average of the high and low selling prices, or the bid and asked prices, on the day of valuation.

Many closely held businesses are worth a great deal more than they would bring on the open market. In an accurate method of valuation, tangible assets may be just one part of the formula. Earning capacity, goodwill, and other intangibles are also important components of the equation.

Buy–sell agreements and partnership agreements generally include one of the following accepted methods of valuation:

Book value is the bottom line or the net worth of a business. This black-and-white method works effectively for businesses operating strictly on equipment and inventory. Deduct liabilities from depreciated assets and that's what the business is worth.

But book value understates the true value of a business with intangible assets, such as goodwill, a customer list, or unique creative or management talent. Undervaluing may sound appealing from a tax standpoint, but it quickly loses appeal when you consider that your family could receive less than a fair value for your business.

For businesses based on capital assets and inventory, book value is a reliable method of valuation. However, businesses based on service require more flexible valuation.

Straight capitalization. Capitalization is the traditional method of valuation of a business that does not have significant tangible assets such as real estate, equipment, or inventory. A business is "capitalized" by determining how much capital (cash) it would take to match annual earnings. We're not talking about money in the bank at a standard interest rate here. A business is expected to bring a much higher return, especially if its future is unpredictable.

....

Monkee Business

Let's say the Monkees earn $100,000 a year taking their comedy/rock 'n roll routine on the road. Based on a 20 percent rate of return, it would take $500,000 of capital to duplicate those earnings each year. Under the straight capitalization *method, the Monkee business is worth $500,000.*

....

Capitalization of earnings is the more modern method of valuing a business with assets and intangibles. This formula attempts to measure the talent and skill that are part of the true value of a business.

Determining capitalization of earnings is just like a math problem on the final exam. First, current book value is determined. Second, book value is capitalized to determine capitalized earnings.

Third, the difference between the capitalized earnings figure and *actual* earnings—this is the amount attributed to special talent or goodwill—is capitalized at the same rate of return. Finally, the two capitalized earning figures are added to the book value to determine the value of the business.

Appraisal. Most businesses now turn to professional appraisers for valuation. In fact, valuation has itself become a business, with networks of appraisers specializing in various business sectors. An impartial business appraisal specialist provides a formal appraisal acceptable for most business transfers.

If you think these established valuation methods leave a good deal to be desired, you're not alone. As businesses take to the information highway, valuation is ever more difficult. The value of ".com" companies, for example, is more likely reflected in sales. For businesses like these, cash flow appears to be a better indicator of value than reported earnings.

Valuation is not an exact science. Nevertheless, the consequences of an inappropriate or inadequate method of valuation could place a business in jeopardy. You don't want anyone guessing the value of your business. Too high, and the taxes are punishing. Too low, and the business you have worked hard to build could be undervalued when bought from your heirs.

If a method of valuation is not provided by written agreement, or if it is ambiguous, the court or the IRS will choose its own formula. That usually means more for you-know-who and less for your heirs, at extra expense and hassle.

Odds Are, We Can Work It Out

Methods of valuation can be as different as Oscar and Felix, the quintessential Odd Couple. Oscar wouldn't care about which particular method was used. He'd be happy with a "ballpark" figure, taking into account the goodwill generated by whether or not the Dodgers won that year, or his horse won at the track last Friday. Bluster, contacts, creative talent, and all the intangibles (and unmentionables) stored in the old noggin were what counted, he'd say. That's what's fair. Yeah.

Felix, on the other hand, would choose the method of valuation that would allow him to figure it to the penny. He'd scour the books for facts and figures, list them in neat columns, total everything on his adding machine, divide ten ways, multiply by compounding interest rates, divide and multiply again, and triple-check his figures. It would all be there in black and white. Perfect, he'd say. No one could question it.

The truth is, in today's business world, Oscar's intangibles like talent, goodwill, and communication skills as well as Felix's cold calculations based on the bottom line are essential to accurate valuation. The trend away from traditional methods may seem odd to some, but valuation is a matter of dollars and sense.

Freezing Techniques

Time in a Bottle

In many cases, a good estate plan includes removing appreciating assets from a personal estate. Using an appropriate "freezing technique," lifetime transfer of a business interest can fix—or freeze—taxable value.

Freezing techniques are particularly advantageous when a business is growing rapidly or is swept up in a booming economy. The transferor reduces his estate and escapes tax on future appreciation of the property. The transferee gains a business asset and future appreciation.

Choosing a freezing technique that is right for your particular business depends upon the type of business, the size of the estate, and the people involved, whether family or key employees. Each technique has other estate planning benefits explained more fully elsewhere in this book. But all achieve the same result of establishing—or freezing—value when the transfer is made.

Gifts and gift-giving programs methodically remove property from the estate of the owner. The gift is received at the cost basis of the donor. Appreciation is thus passed along tax free. Gifts of re-capitalized stock in a rapidly growing business are very effective in removing future business appreciation from the estate of the owner.

In a *private annuity* or *installment sale,* an owner sells a business interest in return for income payments over a given period of time. Income and related taxes are thus spread out over the term of payment. Appreciation over the term accrues only to the buyer.

Grantor-retained interest trust. In this quite sophisticated form of trust, property is transferred into trust in return for established income payments to the grantor for a certain period of time. Income may be payable either as an annuity (GRAT) or at a fixed percentage of assets in a unitrust (GRUT). See Chapter Three.

Family limited partnership. The general partners, usually parents, with controlling interests, make partial gifts to limited partners, usually children, on a regular basis. Value is established when the gift is made. Business assets as well as appreciation and control are slowly shifted to the next generation.

Compare holding onto your business with transferring it using a freezing technique. A miscalculation could put you and your business on thin ice. Ask the pros for help.

Special-Use Valuation
Home on the Range

We've all heard that small farms and ranches are slowly disappearing. The pioneer spirit that built America is giving way to a population crunch and capitalist enterprise. In many families, mamas don't let their babies grow up to be cowboys, and the younger generation seeks the bounty of better-paying city jobs.

Many farmers and ranchers are offered huge sums to sell to commercial operations and real estate developers. And who could resist? It's a ready-made retirement package—instant security for people who have been self-reliant as long as they can remember. No doubt about it, the agrarian lifestyle is fading.

Urban sprawl and changing values are not entirely to blame, however. For decades, a poorly considered estate tax situation contributed to the decline of the small farm and ranch. The land was the farm, and the farm was the business.

Let's say Old MacDonald owned the farm and the farm equipment. It was all he needed. When Old MacDonald died and left the farm to his kids—no longer little, but big Macs—estate taxes came due. As the value of the land had increased over the years, the estate tax rate was high. So high that the farm had to be sold to raise the money to pay the taxes. Goodbye taxes, goodbye farm, goodbye to an all-American way of life.

When a person dies, his estate is generally expected to pay estate taxes within nine months. With a federal estate tax rate of 37–55 percent, farmers and ranchers across the country have been forced to sell to pay estate taxes. A working farm, once out in the country, may now be surrounded by suburban housing developments. Is it valued as a farm or at the sky-high value of potential real estate development? For years, the higher use value was imposed, resulting in higher taxes and forced sales.

Repeated loss of family businesses eventually led to revised tax regulations, giving owners a break in valuing their land. Farmers and others whose real estate represents a significant portion of their closely held businesses may now qualify for special-use valuation. (Though some use the abbreviation SUV, this has nothing to do with the other great American SUV, the sports utility vehicle.)

If working ranch or farm real estate meets certain qualifications, it is valued at "present use" rather than at "highest use" potential.

Qualifications
1. The business must represent 50 percent of the estate.
2. The business *real estate* must represent 25 percent of the estate.
3. The real estate must have been used in the business during five of the last eight years.
4. A qualified heir must manage the property after the owner's death.
5. And the property must be used as a farm or ranch for at least ten additional years.

If the real estate qualifies for special-use valuation, sale is restricted for 15 years. The land remains subject to a federal tax lien. Depending on the size of the owner's estate, qualified business real estate valuation can be reduced by as much as $760,000. Eee-i-eee-i-oh.

Tax Deferral and Exclusion
Take It to the Limit

Tax Deferral
In true American style, estate tax on a qualified closely held business may be paid on the installment plan. Tax payments may be deferred for 15 years, subject to remarkably low interest. The deferral allows one of our nation's most cherished resources—small businesses—to continue from generation to generation by eliminating forced sales to pay estate taxes.

For the first five years after date of death, the estate pays only the interest on the estate tax bill, at a low rate of 2 percent (on the first $1 million of the taxable estate, 4% after that). In years 6 through 15, the tax is payable in equal installments with continuing interest on the unpaid balance. If, at any time during the deferral period, a third or more of the qualified closely held business is sold, payment could be accelerated or demanded in full.

Qualifications

1. A closely held business is defined as a proprietorship, or a partner or stockholder with a 20 percent interest in a business.

2. The business must represent 35 percent or more of the *adjusted gross estate.*

   After Superman flies faster than a speeding bullet to his final reward, and his estate has paid all debts, claims, and expenses, what remains is his *adjusted gross estate.* If his telephone booth rental business accounts for 35 percent or more of it, the estate qualifies for the tax deferral.

3. Stock in two or more closely held businesses may be aggregated to meet the 35 percent requirement. Passive assets such as real estate or equipment not used in the business are not counted.

An estate whose major asset is a working farm or ranch property may qualify for special-use valuation *and* tax deferral. Business owners with gift-giving programs designed to reduce their taxable estates, beware. Despite good intentions, the gifts could reduce the value of the business to less than 35 percent of the estate, eliminating the possibility of tax deferral.

Pros and cons. The deferral has great appeal for families. Stretching tax payments over 15 years makes it possible to stay in business.

There is, however, a significant disadvantage to the deferral option. Until all estate taxes are paid, the estate remains in probate for up to 15 years—*15 years* is from age 5 to 20, or 35 to (agh!) 50. While in

**"Say, Dad—how about letting me
have the keys to the subsidiary."**

probate, the estate, including the business, is the responsibility of the executor. An executor may, in some cases, be relieved of liability, but the estate remains open, and the lawyers and courts continue to collect at least nominal administrative fees.

Qualified Family Business Deduction

A recent and astonishingly generous change in the tax code allows a $675,000 deduction to be taken from the gross estate of the owner of a qualified family-owned business. Combined with the individual unified tax credit to which every citizen is entitled, as much as $1.35 million could pass to heirs tax free.

Qualifications

1. The owner's family must own 50 percent of the business. If more than one family owns the business, the ownership requirement is 70 percent for two families, and 90 percent for three, but the decedent owner's family must own at least 30 percent.

2. The business must be left to "qualified heirs," meaning those who have worked in the business for at least ten years.

3. Those heirs must stay in the business at least five of every eight-year period.

4. And the heirs are allowed to transfer the business only to other "qualified heirs" or a charitable conservation easement.

A deceased owner's income from a personal holding company, or an heir taking the company public, could disqualify the business from taking the deduction. And if, for any reason, the business disqualifies down the road, the estate tax will be "recaptured" from the heirs.

Suffice it to say that an honest-to-goodness family business passing to the next generation, fair and square, is generally entitled to the deduction.

It's Now or Never . . .

- Remember, it's the *family* in family business that gives it real value.
- Plan for emotional and financial ease of transfer or continuation of your family business. Less than one-third of family businesses succeed to the second generation.
- Leave your heirs a business opportunity, not an ordeal.

8

Final Arrangements

Happy Trails

What's Goin' On . . .

- Funeral and burial arrangements
- Probate
- Settling the estate
- Moving on

It's not over 'til it's over. After we depart this world, there are tears to be shed, arrangements to be made, properties to be transferred, and taxes (hopefully none), to be paid. The tears are inevitable—a part of the healing process. Dying is part of life. But no matter how much we prepare ourselves, a loss is never easy.

The immediate task of making funeral and burial arrangements can be agonizing. Families, partners, and friends, particularly those unprepared for a loss, are often ill equipped to make immediate, important decisions. Their only concern is to properly honor and bury their loved ones. And you can help. A personal letter of instruction, in the right hands, will lift at least some of the burden from a grieving circle of friends and family.

Believe it or not, a thoughtful estate plan can also soften the blow. A carefully conceived and executed plan makes the work of managing an estate easier. If probate is avoided entirely through trusts, joint tenancy, buy–sell agreements, and so forth, all transfers will be quick and smooth.

If any or all of your estate goes through probate, your executor or lawyer takes your will to the court and "enters" it into probate, and The Paper Chase begins. Probate develops a life of its own, and in some cases could outlive its usefulness, such as when an estate remains open with no clear plan for continuation of a business by the heirs, or solely to distribute the odds and ends of a residual estate. If you and your lawyer have planned well, the court will allow the executor to move through the process quickly, without much supervision.

Funeral and Burial Arrangements
When the Saints Go Marching In

Customarily, a will includes instructions for an executor to pay all funeral and burial expenses along with other debts of the estate, but does not include specific instructions for a funeral and burial. Paying the bill is a simple matter of dollars and cents. Making the arrangements may be considerably more complicated.

Legally, a spouse or next of kin has the right and responsibility to make final decisions about funeral arrangements. If you prefer to have a certain individual, perhaps an unmarried partner, make arrangements, say so in your will and/or leave a letter of instruction known as a *precatory letter*. Make it as easy as possible for your partner to take the responsibility that legally belongs to your family.

Where absolutely no family or friend takes responsibility for burial, the state takes over, and there will be no one to sing "Amazing Grace" at the public cemetery.

As in other areas of estate planning, funeral and burial options present a host of personal questions. But when a death has oc-

"Maybe I should have gone with cremation."

curred, it is impossible to procrastinate. Who will decide whether to cremate or bury, have a private or an elaborate funeral? What kind of headstone, flowers, music, memorial cards? These are the hard, very personal decisions that those left behind will struggle to answer unless you let them know what arrangements you prefer. You may be lucky, and not be remotely concerned with these questions because of time-honored family or religious traditions. But if, on first thought, you sense any uncertainty, it is better to answer the questions yourself and leave a letter of instruction for your family and/or partner.

Anyone who has had to make funeral arrangements knows how difficult the job can be. Fear and anxiety run high in an effort to properly honor the dead, comfort the living, and stay within reason financially. Traditional funeral and burial cost anywhere from $4,000 to $15,000. If the will does not provide for funeral expenses out of the estate, the family or friends will have to pay all expenses out of pocket.

When the living disagree on how to honor the dead, as they often do, the universal stress level rises and the stars cross. Do you plan what you'd like, what your children would like, or what the deceased would like? Whose funeral is it, anyway?

Most of us have strong feelings, or at least inclinations, about how, where, and under what circumstances we want to be buried and remembered. We might not care what we wear, but we probably know if we want to be buried or cremated. We know if we'd like a religious service. We have some idea where we'd like to be buried, or have our ashes interred. If you'd like your ashes sprinkled over the pond at Giverney or the Grand Canyon, let somebody know, or you could forever spin in an urn on someone's mantlepiece. (No kidding.) The living want to honor the dead. They *want* to do the right thing.

Think about what you'd like; talk about it if you wish. Whether you are concerned for yourself, your spouse or partner, parent or friend, it's better to talk about it sooner rather than later. These are some of the questions that might be considered:

- What to do with your body—burial, cremation, or donation to science?
- What funeral home will provide the desired services?
- Your desired funeral plan. Elaborate or simple?
- Visitation of the family at a funeral home? At home?
- Open or closed casket?
- Religious service or not. If so, preferred clergy?
- Church and/or cemetery?
- Transportation for the body and the family?
- Who should speak? Will there be eulogies?
- Where will you be buried or interred?
- Or what will happen to your ashes?
- Music? Flowers? Tents, chairs?
- Reception after the service?
- Guest book and memorial cards?
- Who will write the obituary and notify newspapers and organizations?
- Is there a favorite charity to receive memorial contributions?

Don't be afraid to discuss funeral and burial plans with senior members of your family. The elderly have a better attitude about dying than younger people. They are usually perfectly willing to discuss their wishes. The questions are tough, and the issues delicate. Choose the best time and place for the discussion.

If you have planned the rest of your estate, you've already learned about the diplomacy required for fruitful family discussion. Your inquiry could prevent unnecessary financial losses and could open the door to a comforting exchange. Even if nothing is decided, the comfort of knowing someone cares is its own reward.

If, as many believe, funerals are for the living, the grieving process may be intended to include making funeral arrangements. Nevertheless, it doesn't hurt to think it over, and maybe talk it over with your spouse, partner, or family. And it might help to leave instructions at least about the larger issues, like service and burial, and let others tend to the details.

Older people do a lot of things that seem odd to younger generations. If you are—or might be—responsible, for the funeral and burial of a parent or older friend, for heaven's sake ask if she has any plans, or any wishes. A person could be dead and buried without your ever learning of a prepaid funeral plan, or that the new minister was *not* to speak at the funeral service.

The details of a funeral might be a blur to a widow, partner, child, or any person shocked by a sudden loss. Try to make everything as simple as possible. If you leave a letter, include all appropriate helpful information. Even if you do not leave a letter of instruction about your funeral, organize your papers and let your spouse, partner, or executor know where everything is located.

The business of managing the affairs of the deceased begins immediately after death. If you wish to have your will read after the funeral, be sure it is accessible. Hopefully, your executor is a close relative or friend and will be available to begin the process of administering your estate as soon as possible.

Precatory Letter

Gonna Sit Right Down and Write Myself a Letter

Leaving a personal letter of instruction—*a precatory letter*—expressing your funeral and burial wishes and explaining any arrangements you have made in advance is very helpful. The letter is not binding by any means, but it relieves your family and friends of a burden and potential source of conflict. A letter could spare your family the stress of worrying about details while they are grieving, or of confronting unexpected financial burdens. You might even have a little fun planning the whole affair.

"That being your mother's wish, I see no reason we can't arrange interment with all her old copies of 'Gourmet.' "

Some fun lovers set aside money under their wills for a round of drinks at their favorite bar, or a New Orleans funeral band for the memorial service. It is not necessary to be clever, just to be helpful. To let them down easy.

It is, of course, ideal to discuss your personal preferences with your family and let them know you have written the letter, particularly if you anticipate disagreement. If you own a burial plot for yourself or your family, tell someone. If you have a prepaid funeral and burial plan, let it be known. Tell your closest family members, partners, friends, doctors—whoever needs to know. You ought to have a contract or receipt indicating exactly what you have purchased. Include the paperwork with your letter or give it to a confidant.

Even if you do not write yourself a letter, take the time to make a list of the names of your executor and other key people who could be of assistance, and make a note of the location of your will. Include your most recent inventory of assets with updated notes on location of titles and other important documents. The names, phone numbers, and addresses of your lawyer, insurance agent, employer, business partner, and anyone who can be of special assistance are also very helpful. Get it all together, make a few copies, and tell the important people—the ones you can count on—about it.

The best place to keep a letter of instruction is *not* with your will, especially if your lawyer has the original will, or it is in a safety deposit box. If you have distributed copies of your will to those immediately concerned—a very good idea—give the letter of instruction to the same group of key people. Be sure the right people know where it is and what it says. If you wish to keep your instructions to yourself, seal an envelope with your instructions, and give it to a person you can trust to honor your wishes.

Funeral instructions from a woman who never married:
"I don't want any male pallbearers. They wouldn't take me out when I was alive; I don't want them to take me out when I'm dead!"

If you're not planning to write a letter, at least let those upon whom you rely know what you'd like in the way of funeral and burial. When people say they don't want to talk about it, they're generally speaking out of fear or superstition. It is not necessary to get into a deep conversation about the hereafter. Just speak your piece and let it go at that.

Prepaid Funeral Plans
Sounds of Silence

Funeral homes and cemeteries offer funeral "packages" sold in advance. Virtually every detail is included, from guest book to headstone. A prepaid plan, which might sound distasteful at first, offers relief, emotional and financial, to the grieving family. However, if you move to another city or state, such a plan is most likely not transferable. If you want to learn more about a prepaid funeral and burial, inquire of your local, trustworthy funeral director, or contact AARP (formerly known as the American Association of Retired Persons) for information and guidelines.

Remember that funeral directors are businesspeople. Most are perfectly decent, respectful, and good at what they do. But they earn a living doing what they do, and are as interested in the bottom line as the next guy. Some prepaid plans are shams. An elderly person is easy prey for a salesperson who promises an elaborate funeral and burial, but contracts only to deliver the most basic service.

Funeral directors also have been known to pressure the grief-stricken to purchase a finer (meaning more expensive) casket, or to hire extra limos for the drive to the cemetery. Even in those hushed tones, they are selling a product.

So Long, Farewell

When the Fonz died in his sleep at the ripe old age of 87, he was just as "cool" as when he had intimidated the guys and charmed the girls with his slick hair and his black leather jacket at Jefferson High. His wife, Muffy, a socialite from Chicago, and old pal Richie, retired CEO of a national chain of neighborhood hardware stores, knew Fonzie had left a precatory letter and went straight to it.

The letter included funeral and burial plans as well as instructions on distribution of a few precious personal items. Surviving members of Hell's Angels led the funeral procession, mostly in sidecars alongside motorcycles driven by grandchildren. An oldies band played Fonz's favorite slow dance songs as they rode through the streets on a float.

Thank heaven Fonzie's plan called for closing streets and police crowd control. No one else had anticipated the hordes of women of all ages who lined the streets as the funeral procession made its way to the service at Arnold's drive-in. Nearly a thousand women, some well into their nineties—but wearing black leather—carried signs expressing sentiments like "I'll Always Remember Smoke Gets in Your Eyes" and "Your Kisses Were Sweeter Than Wine." Some wore old prom dresses and dried-up wrist corsages saved for decades, and sobbed uncontrollably.

Traffic stopped; in fact, for a moment, everything stopped, as if the Fonz himself had walked into the crowd and said, "Hey-y-y-y."

As for the coveted personal items, the legendary leather jacket was left to grandson Arty Fonzarelli who had taken lessons on "cool" from granddad and was breaking hearts regularly. Richie, Potsie, and Ralph Malph got their pick of the motorcycle collection. The other bikes were to be contributed to the Smithsonian. And Fonz's little black book? It was buried with him.

(To be continued . . .)

Probate
It's Too Late

Most of us are totally unfamiliar with probate. In terms of personal priorities or intellectual curiosity, understanding probate is probably at the bottom of the list right above getting to know the IRS agent or having a root canal. Even those of us who have been peripherally involved in the probate of an estate may not understand the actual workings of the court procedure. The association between probate and death is an automatic turn-off.

Probate is like driving a car. You know what the car can do, and have some idea of how it's driven, but cannot fully appreciate it until you're in the driver's seat. There's no time for a learner's permit for probate. But if we understand how probate works, we will more fully appreciate the importance of an effective estate plan. In truth, it's not much of a mystery.

How Probate Works
The Long and Winding Road

Probate is the validation or "proving" of a will. The process includes the gathering of assets, payment of debts and taxes, and distribution of assets of an estate, under court supervision. Probate procedures are defined by state law, but probate usually takes place in county courts called—you guessed it—probate courts, with probate judges. Needless to say, the business of these courts is fairly regular. Once you're involved in the process, the "mystery" of probate quickly gives way to routine.

The purpose of probate is to protect the rights of the dead person (the deceased, or *decedent*), the rights of the heirs, and, of course, the interests of the state—in the form of taxes. Probate takes place in the state of domicile of the deceased person. Your domicile is that state in which you permanently or primarily reside, vote, register your car, and pay taxes.

The general functions of the probate process include:

■ Entering a will into probate.

■ Appointment of an executor, as named in the will. If none is named, the court appoints an estate administrator, or probate agent. *Letters Testamentary* issued by the court authorize the executor to act.

■ Identification and location of beneficiaries and heirs.

■ Resolution of conflicts among interested parties and any others making a claim against the estate.

■ Inventory of the estate, settlement of debts, payment of taxes, and distribution of assets, with court supervision as required.

■ Final approval by the court, and closing the estate.

In probate, distribution of property follows the specific instructions of the will. If there is no will, the estate is distributed according to "descendancy" under state laws of intestacy, which vary. In most cases, spouses, children, and parents share percentages of an estate, and the property of unmarried individuals reverts to parents first, then equally to brothers and sisters.

Escheat. If, after reasonable efforts are made to locate heirs, absolutely none come forward or can be found, an estate *escheats* (es-**cheets**) to the state. Reasonable effort to locate heirs must be exhausted before an estate will escheat.

An escheated estate actually becomes the property of the state. In the old days, the lord or king took the property. It's not much of a surprise that the modern word *cheat,* meaning swindle, stems from escheat, a fuedal term relating to disruption in the order of descendancy.

"After probate, family members will receive duplicate videos."

Types of Probate

Guess Things Happen That Way

Probate generally works in one of three ways, depending on state laws and the size and complexity of an estate.

Full supervision by the court is generally required for larger estates or in situations where an executor or the will itself is challenged. The court determines whether formal supervision is required. A complex estate, or one that owns real property in another state, is poorly organized, or involves parties destined for "battle," generally warrants full supervision.

If a will is invalid because it doesn't meet requirements, or fails as a result of a challenge, the court relies on either a previous will or the state laws of intestacy to distribute property and requires full supervision.

Unsupervised administration, permitted for smaller or uncomplicated estates, involves minimal court appearances. Usually, with an effective will and a qualified executor, the probate court will require only one appearance by the executor, at the time the will is entered into probate and the executor is appointed.

A well-organized inventory of assets valued below the Applicable Exclusion Amount ($675,000 in the year 2000), and just one named beneficiary, or very few, improves the likelihood of independent administration. Unless conflict or controversy arises, the court will be satisfied with a written report concluding the work of the estate.

If you believe this less complicated and less expensive administration is appropriate for your estate, say so in your will; otherwise, the consent of all beneficiaries may have to be obtained.

Small estates may sometimes conduct business by an *affidavit* declaring the value of the estate, and any debts, distributions, and taxes. The dollar figures defining a "small estate" vary from state to state.

The business of a qualified small estate is opened and closed upon filing a notarized affidavit with the court clerk, and no court appearances are required.

Some court clerks offer fill-in-the-blank affidavit forms, but it is probably a good idea to have a lawyer confirm that the work of the estate and the affidavit are complete. Real estate transfers are not permitted by affidavit. This type of probate is also called *summary administration.*

Through effective estate planning, even large estates can avoid probate or can qualify for smaller estate treatment. An estate that has largely been placed in trust or gifted away may be small enough to pass through probate unsupervised or with a simple affidavit proving satisfaction of obligations.

If everything is in a living trust, obligations and distributions are not handled by the probate court. Estate taxes may be figured, paid, and proven by the affidavit. If *almost* everything is owned by a trust, only the residual estate—the odds and ends, perhaps an auto, a personal checking account, and your golf clubs—will be subject to probate.

Your estate planning lawyer will know what level of supervision your estate is likely to require. You will want to refine your estate plan and appoint your executor accordingly.

Epitaph
Here lies Ann Mann
She lived an old maid
but died an old Mann

Who Assumes Responsibility for Probate?

Big Shot

When a person dies, the *executor* hopefully will know where the will is located and will be ready to spring to action.

A person who dies without a will is said to die intestate. In such case, the court appoints an executor or estate administrator and the estate is distributed according to state law. If a will is written but no executor is appointed, the court will appoint an executor.

When a will is filed and accepted by the probate court, the executor is empowered by Letters Testamentary, the official order of the court.

Point of information. A female executor may be called an executrix, but that title, like "chairman," is quickly going the way of nickel candy bars. In some states the title is personal representative. They all do the same work.

Is a Lawyer Necessary?

Depending on the size and complexity of the estate, the executor may want or need the help of a lawyer. The larger the estate, the more involved the court supervision, and the more likely the executor will need legal assistance. Full court supervision almost certainly requires the services of an experienced estate planning or probate lawyer. Unless, of course, the executor *is* the estate planning lawyer.

In many cases, particularly where estate planning is ongoing as property such as real estate and business interests is transferred or restructured over the years, a lawyer is involved on a continuing basis—

(Now back to the Fonz . . .)

Richie had been asked to be executor decades earlier. Fonz's estate
was well-organized and his will complete, but the estate was
large. Full supervision of the court would be required.

Not only was the Fonz part-owner of Arnold's, but his little
auto mechanic business had grown into a regional auto parts and
repair conglomerate. His will called for several charitable contributions
and creation of a credit shelter trust.

Richie was a businessman, but he did not know the ins and
outs of Fonzie's business or which particular assets were best suited
for the trust. He needed the help of a lawyer. The lawyer who had
helped Fonzie write the will had long retired. Richie was reluctant
to use his own estate planning lawyer—he was good, but had never
forgiven the Fonz for stealing his girlfriend. Richie chose another experienced
probate lawyer in the same firm who promptly got Fonzie's
will onto the probate court docket.

(To be continued . . .)

---

retained—to keep everything in order. This type of estate planning lawyer
is a natural candidate for executor because of his familiarity with
the estate.

If the executor hires a lawyer, the lawyer usually makes all arrangements
to get the will and the executor to probate court at the
earliest opportunity. If the estate is relatively simple, and little or no
court supervision is required, the executor can call the clerk of the probate
court directly to get on the docket. Let your fingers do the walking.
Local phone directories contain telephone numbers for courts and
clerks.

When making the court date, the executor should ask what documents
are required to enter the will into probate and move ahead with
settlement and distribution. The specific duties and powers of each executor
are included in the respective will.

If you are the executor, be sure you understand every requirement.
If you are missing just one item, the entire proceeding could be delayed.

If you don't fully understand what the court requires, it is best to seek the advice and possibly the assistance of a lawyer.

Probate Costs

Ain't That a Shame

The cost of probate includes probate court costs, legal fees, and executor's fees. All are deductible either from estate taxes, if any, or final income taxes of the estate.

Court costs generally entail only filing fees—the nominal, fixed fees associated with filing and presenting a will and estate to the probate court. When a will is entered into probate, the executor or lawyer goes to the office of the Clerk of Court, presents the will, pays the filing fee, and schedules an appointment on the court docket to make an initial appearance before the probate judge. Every time the executor or lawyer goes to court, files a paper, or obtains a copy of a court document, there will be a charge—a court cost.

Legal fees are usually the greatest expense of probate. Probate lawyers generally charge an hourly fee for their services, though a few offer a flat fee or charge a percentage. It is usually impossible for a lawyer to guarantee a fee for probate, as much of the work is determined by the pace of the executor, the court, and financial and governmental institutions.

Some lawyers—the ones who give lawyers a bad name—prolong probate, letting the wheels of justice turn slowly with the meter running. Thankfully, most state governments have stepped in to put a lid on lawyers' probate fees, allowing no more than 3–5 percent of the estate to be taken in fees. The restriction provides an incentive for the expeditious probate of even the most complex estates. Lawyers' fees are reviewed and approved as an expense of the estate.

In law nothing is certain except the expense.

—Anonymous

Executors' fees are established in the will. It is generally advisable to designate a fee even though executors who are also beneficiaries of the will often waive the fee. The executor bears a tremendous responsibility and is personally liable for losses to the estate during probate. Serving as executor is sometimes a thankless job. Compensate your executor accordingly.

The traditional combination works best—a close, trusted family member or partner serving as executor, working with an experienced probate lawyer. Combined knowledge and talent, plus a system of checks and balances.

If an executor and lawyer work together, the lawyer customarily prepares and files court forms and legal documents, prepares tax returns for the estate, and appears with the executor in court as required. It is usually best to have a lawyer register new titles to transferred property, especially real estate where title often involves intricate legalities.

An estate in probate remains open for a minimum period dictated by the court. The lawyer generally stays on the job for the duration. Every hour the lawyer works adds to the cost of administering an estate. With estate taxes due nine months from date of death, most of the work takes place early. Distributions usually follow payment of taxes, and the average estate closes within a year or so. If the executor is efficient, probate will conclude within a reasonable time at reasonable expense.

Probate is a predictable legal process. If you know what you own and how you would like it distributed, your lawyer can compare the potential cost of probate against the cost of creating and administering a trust or other estate planning vehicle. When it comes to probate, less is usually more. Less for the court, the pros, and Uncle Sam. More for your heirs.

(Now Back to the Fonz . . .)

Muffy *had transferred some of her great wealth into an irrevocable trust providing income to the Fonz for life. Creating the trust removed assets from Muffy's substantial estate, and now the trust assets would be distributed according to the terms of the trust— her terms. Even though the Fonz received income benefits, the trust would not go through probate with his estate.*

(To be continued . . .)

Is Probate All That Bad?

It Ain't Necessarily So

For many, avoiding probate is the object of the entire exercise. Estate plans that remove assets from your estate ensure the distribution you prescribe and achieve estate tax savings. Avoiding probate means saving probate costs and transferring property privately, off the public record.

However, not every estate benefits from avoiding probate. Examine your very own situation. Be sure your lifetime needs for financial security and health care are covered before removing assets from your estate. Your own well-being and that of your spouse, partner, children, as well as family assets depend upon the thoroughness and clarity of your thinking.

Probate is not as cumbersome or costly as it once was, mostly because the rules increasingly permit unsupervised probate for smaller estates, and limit lawyer's fees. In most cases, the process no longer involves court approval of administrative details. Less time spent presenting to the court means lower administrative and legal costs.

For most of us, publicity is not a major concern. Every will and estate in probate is part of the public record, accessible to anyone with an inquiring mind. But how many inquiring minds actually want to know? The contested cases reported in the papers usually concern celebrities already in the spotlight. Still, many people—of wealth or not—

value their privacy enough to do everything possible to keep their financial affairs out of the public record. In the information age, privacy has become very rare and precious.

With all the fuss about avoiding probate, it is important to recognize that all transfers triggered by death—even transfers outside of probate—*always* require some sort of proof. Generally, a death certificate and affidavit of domicile are the only requirements for transfer of authority or ownership of nonprobate assets such as a pay-on-death checking account, joint tenancy, trust, closely held business, or retirement plan.

The most effective way to facilitate probate of your estate is to ensure that everyone involved fully understands your intentions. If someone is likely to challenge your will, find out before it's too late—while there is still time to either assuage the concerns of the individual or change your will.

Honest, open family discussion, even late in life, after your will is signed, sealed, and delivered, is extremely effective in putting fears and jealousies to rest. If people know what to expect, they are less likely to be disappointed. Even unwelcome information is better than the unknown. Be firm. It's your estate.

Settling the Estate
After You've Gone

Details, details, details. Probate and the administration of your estate will be as simple or as difficult as you make it. There is no need for your family and executor to struggle with settlement.

Settling an estate in probate is a practical matter—organizational skills and attention to detail are required. A well-drafted will empowers a qualified executor to do everything necessary to gather, assess, and distribute assets as efficiently as possible. It is helpful if you understand the job description before filling the position.

"See if you can pass that car. He would have wanted it that way."

Death certificate. Nothing can be done to, for, or about the property of the deceased until the will is entered into probate. To start the probate process, the executor presents a certified copy of the death certificate, along with the original will, to the Clerk of Court. Death certificates are available from the County Clerk or Recorder.

Letters Testamentary. When an estate is officially entered into probate, the court issues Letters Testamentary authorizing the executor to act on behalf of the estate. If the estate is small, and an affidavit will suffice for administration, file the will with the clerk of the probate court to obtain authority to act on behalf of the estate. Letters Testamentary are available from the Clerk of Court.

When ordering certified documents, be sure to get originals, with the embossed seal—that little, bumpy insignia pressed into the paper. Request a sufficient number to get started on the work of the estate. It's usually a good idea to order no more than five Letters Testamentary at a time because they expire after 60 days.

Some executors require dozens of death certificates and Letters Testamentary to accomplish the task at hand. And like most things, certified documents are cheaper by the dozen. If you are certain that several documents will be required, or if you are administering an estate from afar, request a dozen—or an armful if appropriate—but keep the expiration date in mind.

The executor is obliged to present certified copies of *both* the Letters Testamentary and the death certificate to do almost anything on behalf of the estate. For example, both documents are required to open a bank account, transfer property, file an insurance claim, or do business in the name of the estate. Sometimes a bank or insurer will examine the certified copy but be satisfied with a duplicate for the file, returning the original to the executor. One never knows.

Keep the documents handy. You never know when you'll need to prove that the decedent is dead and you are authorized by the court to conduct the business of the estate. More than a few executors have walked around with Letters Testamentary and death certificates in their pockets or purses for years.

Estate checking account. Next the executor will usually open a checking account for the estate. The account will be titled something like "Estate of George Washington, Martha Washington, Executrix." Sign all endorsements exactly as the account is titled. Money to open the account could be paychecks or dividend checks, funds transferred from a closed account of the decedent, the sale of stocks or bonds, and so forth. Don't order too many checks for the account. You probably won't need the big box of 500 unless the estate is complex and is likely to languish in probate for a couple of years.

Death notices. Within a reasonable time, the executor must publish death notices to alert creditors and others with claims to the estate. Obituaries not only memorialize the dead, but serve as official death notices. Funeral homes usually make arrangements for obituaries and death notices based on information provided by the family. If a business is involved, death notices should appear in appropriate trade publications.

Asset inventory. The executor will gather and make an inventory of assets. Deeds, account statements, tax records, auto registration—*everything* belonging to the deceased now belongs to the estate. This is where a personal inventory of assets comes in very handy. It takes a long time for a stranger to locate all assets and related paperwork. An inventory saves time, trouble, and expense.

Personal and household items often have a more substantial value than realized at first glance. The executor could decide that an appraisal is required for tax purposes.

Property management. If a family business or real estate in the estate requires management or administration, the executor has the responsibility to manage the business or property in the estate. An executor's fiduciary duty imposes a personal liability for losses to the estate. If necessary and authorized to do so, the executor may hire staff with the requisite expertise and managerial skills.

An executor's responsibilities can be a burden to a person unprepared or ill-equipped for the job. Be sure to ask your intended executor if he or she is willing and able to assume the responsibility. And remember to provide an appropriate executor's fee under your will.

Pay debts. Throughout the probate process, the executor pays all "just" or "provable" debts of the estate. All bills attributed to the deceased, including those received after death, are obligations of the estate. Creditors' claims are considered, evaluated, and paid as required.

If a claim is questioned, the probate court may intervene to make a judgment about the validity of the claim. Under the Uniform Probate Code, expenses for the funeral, "last illness," and estate administration are paid before other creditors. Medical expenses may be deducted from income taxes charged to the estate, as on an individual return.

A will customarily includes instructions that the executor pay fu-

(Now back to the Fonz . . .)

Richie ordered a handful of certified copies of Fonzie's death certificate and appeared in court, with his lawyer, to enter the will into probate. The court issued Letters Testamentary appointing Richie executor and the business of the estate was under way. With both documents in hand, Richie opened a checking account.

Fonzie's will included instructions to pay just and provable debts, including funeral and burial expenses—lucky, because the security required to keep the burial private was a major expense. Richie paid recent bills and closed Fonzie's charge accounts.

Richie's immediate concern was keeping Fonzie's businesses up and running. Arnold's share of the business had passed to his son, who was to buy Fonzie's share from his estate at death. They had a buy–sell agreement that dictated the terms of the sale, and life insurance to fund the purchase.

The auto mechanic business was not as well-organized. The Fonz had never bothered to restructure his sole proprietorship in a way that made continuing the business easier. Each location had a manager to handle day-to-day operations, but Richie had to supervise all of them and keep tabs on the books. Richie hired his own trustworthy accountant to help, and together they developed a plan to value the business and sell it. Thankfully, one of the key employees stepped forward to purchase the business. He had limited resources and wanted to work with Richie to arrange an installment sale.

(To be continued . . .)

neral and burial expenses from the estate. Establishing a ceiling for expenses could help keep the decision makers within reason at a time when reason does not often prevail. This is the part of a will where people often express fantastic ideas and wishes. If the deceased instructs the executor to hire Jimmy Buffett to sing at the funeral, and the funds are available, the executor must do his best to follow the instruction. If Jimmy is in Margaritaville and can't make it, your executor will have given it his best shot.

Valuation of property. After six months, the executor, most likely with the advice of a tax advisor, will choose a valuation date for the estate. Property in the estate may be valued on either the *date of death* or the *alternate valuation date*, six months later. Only time will tell which option is best. Valuation determines tax basis, which, in turn, affects distribution.

Estate tax. When the valuation date is established, the executor, lawyer, and/or accountant calculate and pay estate taxes. As a rule, estate taxes are due nine months from date of death. Most executors pay taxes as close to the deadline as possible to obtain optimal interest on assets.

Each of us is entitled to a one-time credit against the Uniform Transfer Tax. Lifetime gifts in excess of the Annual Exclusion will have been reported via gift tax returns over the years. The value of any taxable gifts determines whether or not there is a tax credit remaining to the estate. The amount of the remaining credit reduces, in most cases eliminates, the tax liability of the estate. See Chapter Two for more about gift and estate tax and the unified tax credit.

If real estate, stocks, or other assets have to be sold to pay taxes, get cracking. Deferred tax payments are permitted for qualified farm or business property, but other payments are expected on time.

If the executor is unsure about the value of assets, or about which assets should be used to pay taxes, he or she should not hesitate to ask for legal, tax, *and* investment advice. This is about taxes, and *nothing* about taxes is easy. Furthermore, mistakes can be costly. Go to the pros.

Income taxes. Estates are responsible for the individual income taxes of the deceased. If an estate is open long enough to acquire income of its own, the estate is required to file an income tax return as well. Believe it or not, a surviving spouse can file a joint income tax return for two years after the death of a spouse.

Deductions. Administrative expenses and casualty losses (theft, loss, property damage) may be deducted from either estate or income tax of the estate, but not from both. If an income tax deduction is taken,

"His last request is to call up the Internal Revenue Service and
tell them to go to hell!"

the estate must also file a waiver of the estate tax deduction. If no estate
taxes are due, the deduction will, of course, be taken from income tax.

Transfer of title. Where real property and registered securities
(stocks and bonds) are involved, the executor will have to transfer title.
Lawyers normally do the real estate title work; financial institutions usually take care of the stocks and bonds. Transferring title to real estate
requires confirmation of precise legal descriptions of the property and
appropriate registration of deeds. Find a lawyer experienced in probate
and/or real estate transfers to do the work.

When transferring stocks held in the name of the deceased, the
stock transfer agent will require both Letters Testamentary and a death
certificate, plus an affidavit of domicile, for each security. If stocks are
held for an individual by a financial institution, in street name, just one
of each document—and the affidavit—is required. In either case, a writ-

(Now back to the Fonz . . .)

Richie's next concern was valuing all property in Fonzie's estate to figure what estate taxes, if any, would be due. Once he knew the figure for taxes, he could begin to fund the credit shelter trust for Muffy and distribute property as the will instructed, holding back the amount needed for taxes.

Fonzie and Muffy jointly owned a securities account and bank account with a pay-at-death provision. Those accounts were automatically transferred to Muffy, giving her immediate access to the accounts and avoiding a cash flow crisis.

Losing her beloved Fonzie and fending off all those women was more crisis than she could handle as it was. Thankfully, their daughters were middle-aged and very capable not only of protecting Muffy from the wild characters at the funeral, but also of giving their mother the TLC she needed in the following weeks.

The instructions from Fonzie's precatory letter, regarding his leather jacket and motorcycles, were also included in the will. The motorcycles not bequested to his friends were donated to the Smithsonian, and a modest contribution was made to the Riders Never Die Hell's Angels' Old Folks Home. Charitable deductions were taken on the estate tax return.

With the help of Muffy and the family, Richie divided everything else among them. The Fonz had left a few personal items to his girls. His championship bowling ball and Arnold's winning team shirt went to Faith. His '57 Chevy, with four-on-the-floor, the "shop car" lovingly restored by his students at Jefferson High, was for Hope. And Charity, still svelte at 44, was thrilled to get all the tight blue jeans and white t-shirts.

But negotiations over valuation of the auto mechanic business continued. Richie was well-suited to this part of his job as executor. He knew enough about business to negotiate effectively, and the court finally approved the deal. Richie paid estate taxes on time, nine months after Fonzie's death.

Richie and the probate lawyer made their final statement and an appearance before the probate judge, and the Fonz's estate was closed. But the legend lives forever.

ten letter of instruction stating how the transferred property is to be titled is also required.

Division of property is often a concern where a residual estate or other unspecified property is to be equally divided. Unless a will includes specific instructions, the executor will have to divide property using a method that is acceptable to the beneficiaries. Only an impartial method will defeat the rivalry, jealousy, and greed likely to surface when items of value, sentimental and otherwise, are divided.

Something as simple as following age succession, oldest to youngest, or drawing numbers out of a hat can establish the order for choosing items from the house. Number one chooses first, number two second, and so on. When the first round is completed, number one makes a second choice. The cycle continues until the heirs withdraw or everything has been selected. It's all very civilized.

Appraisal. If valuables are involved, the executor will probably request appraisal for estate tax purposes, and beneficiaries could make their selections from the appraisal list. The process preempts conflict and clearly establishes value, providing orderly and equal division.

Distributions. When creditors are satisfied and taxes paid, the executor can get on with the gratifying business of making distributions. Beneficiaries are notified earlier in the process of pending distributions and are asked to provide a signature accepting the bequest. Some distributions are used to create trusts. If created under a will, a trust is called testamentary and is by its nature irrevocable.

If assets have to be sold before distributions can be made, partial distributions or small bequests may be paid first. If there is no residuary clause, every asset must be divisible among named heirs as instructed in the will. Final distributions sometimes delay the closing of an estate. If a will provides for a residual estate, specific bequests are made before remaining property is distributed to residual beneficiaries. Distributions from the residual estate conclude the work of the executor.

This Magic Moment

Once upon a time, a charming bachelor uncle, beloved for his playfulness, left his rather substantial estate to 13 adult nieces and nephews. All had grown up in and around Uncle's beautiful home, being hopelessly teased and lovingly indulged by this clever gentleman.

Everyone had terribly mixed emotions about breaking up the household, but the executors worked out a wonderful plan, and invited the heirs (no spouses, please) to one last weekend "house party" to divide the estate. There was a long list of appraised items, and everything else had been pulled from cabinets, closets, and drawers to make sure each heir had the chance to consider his or her choices in advance.

With great anticipation, everyone drew a number from a hat, and selection of personal and household collectibles began. One through thirteen over and over again. Before long, subtle and not-so-subtle side comments, triggered by the selection of a particular item, gave way to colorful stories.

As the night grew dark, the nephew who had chosen Unc's wardrobe tossed an armful of old dressing gowns across the sofa and asked everyone to take the one he or she wanted. Business was concluded with everyone languishing in the robes, pondering the memories, and savoring the fantastic atmosphere of the soon-to-be-dismantled house.

It did not seem even slightly unnatural when these grown men and women decided to play a final round of Murder in the Dark, a favorite childhood game. The lights went out and everyone crept around the house, in the dark, in their silks, up and down the stairs, until all hours.

Uncle's true bequest was not the silk robes, or the magnificence of the estate, but the sense of play and precious memories of times happily spent.

Disclaimer. An inheritance may be disclaimed, in writing and within nine months of death. An individual intended to inherit property as a descendant or remainderman may not wish to increase the size of his estate. A disclaimed bequest is distributed according to the further instruction of the will. Typically, it either is shared by other heirs of the same class or reverts to the residual estate.

Disclaimer is allowed only before the intended heir receives any benefit from the property. A rental property, for example, might be left to your son the real estate agent. If he decides he wants to disclaim the property, but has received rent from the property, his disclaimer will not be allowed by the probate court.

Final statement. When all is said and done, a final statement proving settlement of the estate is presented to the court. If the count is satisfied that the report is accurate and the work of the executor is complete, the estate will be closed.

The Clerk of Court files the order, just as it filed the will to initiate probate. And it's over.

Thanks for the Memories
Twilight Time

It is important not to overlook the depths to which some people fall when grieving. People who are accustomed to companionship, or to being cared for, or being especially loved, are naturally frightened at the prospect of being left behind and alone. Sometimes grief hits people over the head; sometimes it sneaks up when least expected.

The frank family discussions that are essential to begin a meaningful estate plan ought to continue as circumstances change. Comfort and security mean everything to a person dealing with a loss. When you get right down to it, wealth is of little concern in time of personal crisis. Estate planning is all about looking after those who mean the most to us, keeping our balance, and doing what we can to ease *every* transition.

"Most of all, he'll be remembered for his irrepressible spirit."

As with any difficult situation, the best way through the grieving process is to take one day at a time. Just put one foot in front of the other. It is generally recommended to wait a year or more after losing a spouse or partner before making any major changes or decisions.

Once you've been through the funeral, the mail, and the dark period, you will go back to eating three meals a day, confident that you know what you're doing. But general wisdom informs us that after a significant loss, perspective and good judgment remain compromised for several months.

When your world stops spinning, it takes time to regain momentum. It's entirely natural. And the process takes time—it's not possible to rush it. Give or accept comfort, as the case may be, and take it easy.

When it's time to die, let us not discover that we have never lived.

—Henry David Thoreau

It's Now or Never . . .

- Explain funeral and burial instructions in a personal letter—a *precatory letter*—rather than in your will. Tell those who need to know about the letter or about your wishes directly.

- Probate and estate administration are predictable legal processes that follow an orderly progression. The better your estate plan, the simpler—shorter and less expensive—probate will be.

- If you're having trouble coping with a loss, don't be afraid to ask for help. And if you can, try to lend a hand, an ear, or a shoulder to those suffering the strain of a loss.

- You can make an estate plan to ease the burden. Only You.

Yesterday is history, tomorrow a mystery.
Today is a gift.
That's why they call it the present.
—Anonymous

Big, Scary Words
(and Other Mysteries of Estate Planning Explained)
The Name Game

Adjusted gross estate. The value of an estate after it has been "adjusted" by settlement of debts and expenses. Used as a tax basis.

Affidavit (aff-ih-**dave**-it). A personal, written statement of fact made voluntarily and sworn by oath, signed, and notarized. In some states, a small uncomplicated estate may be settled by affidavit.

Agent. A person legally authorized to act on behalf of another. If you create a power of attorney, you appoint an agent and convey "agency."

Alternate value. The value of an estate is determined either on date of death or six months later to the day on the "alternate valuation date." If the later date is chosen, the estate is given the alternate value. If property in an estate is sold before the alternate valuation date, the sale price becomes the taxable value.

Annual Exclusion. Every year, every person can make individual gifts of $10,000 tax free under the Annual Exclusion. Indexed for inflation, but increases only in $1,000 increments. Gifts above and beyond the exclusion are counted toward the Applicable Exclusion Amount of $675,000 (in the year 2000). Husband and wife are permitted to make combined gifts of $20,000 per individual under the exclusion. *Not to be confused with the Applicable Exclusion Amount.*

Applicable Credit Amount. Formerly the "unified tax credit." Dollar-for-dollar credit against the Unified Transfer Tax. One time, one per person.

Applicable Exclusion Amount. Formerly the "unified credit equivalent." The portion of an estate excluded, or sheltered, from the Unified Transfer Tax (formerly the "unified gift and estate tax"). In the year 2000 it is $675,000, on a sliding scale reaching $1 million in 2006. *Entirely separate from the Annual Exclusion.*

Beneficiary. One who receives benefits—of a trust, a will, insurance, retirement plan, or other legal arrangement.

Bequest. A gift of personal property made under a will. In legalese, "I hereby give, bequeath, and devise . . ."

Buy–sell agreement. Contract among business co-owners establishing terms for continuation, sale, or closure of the business. Supersedes the wills of individual co-owners.

Class. A group of beneficiaries with equal standing under a will, trust, or other legal entity. Not the kids who graduated with you.

Codicil (cod-uh-sill). A signed and witnessed addendum or addition to a will. If a codicil substantially changes a will or a significant clause in the will, it is advisable to make an entirely new will rather than leave the will and codicil open to challenge.

Community property. In the eight "community property" states, husband and wife own and are entitled to one-half of the marital estate—the property acquired during marriage. A spouse may therefore not dispose of more than one-half of the marital estate by will in Arizona,

California, Idaho, Louisiana, Nevada, New Mexico, Texas, and Washington.

Conservator. Property guardian, named by court to protect and preserve property or an estate.

Contemplation-of-death rule. In transferring ownership of a life insurance policy, the rule requires that three years pass before the gift is considered complete. Based on an old contemplation-of-death tenet that the gift would not have been made had death not been imminent.

Corpus. From Latin, meaning "body." The body or principal of a trust or estate, as distinguished from the income.

Cost basis. The value or cost of a property or stock when acquired. Also called *tax basis*, establishing taxable value. Other types of basis also serve as a tax basis in various situations. For example, *stepped-up basis* is the value of a property or stock in an estate, fixed either on date of death or the alternate valuation date, six months later. *Carry-over basis* is the value of a gift to the recipient, identical to the original cost basis of the person who made the gift. Beware: The word *basis* may also be used alone to mean any of these variations.

Credit equivalent. Or unified credit equivalent. See the new term *Applicable Exclusion Amount,* and don't confuse it with the *Annual Exclusion.*

Crummey power. Named for the family that instigated the ruling. A gift is not a gift unless the recipient, or donee, has a present interest—that is, the immediate power to determine how it will be used. Regarding life insurance, this usually refers to required written notice that a gift of cash is used to buy life insurance premiums, not as a set-up to fund insurance, tax free, at the donor's instruction.

Custodian. One who has custody of property for the benefit of another. Carrying a fiduciary duty. The job does not require a broom and a mop.

Descendancy. As in "laws of descendancy" or "order of descendancy." In estates, it generally indicates succession from one generation to the next.

Descendant. One who comes from, or descends from, another. Linear descendants include children, grandchildren, offspring, and issue. In recent law, descendants have included "collateral descendants" determined by going up a family lineage to a common ancestor and then following lineage down through various family lines to identify descendants for purposes of inheritance; and adopted children.

Decedent (de-**see**-dent). A big, scary word for one who has died, or is deceased.

Devise. Give by will. See *Bequest.*

Disinherit. The act of excluding a person from any rights under a will. Sometimes conditional.

Domicile. State in which one has established permanent residence. A valid will includes a statement of domicile and is subject to the laws of the state of domicile.

Donee. A person who receives a gift, or donation.

Donor. A person who makes a gift.

Estate administrator. Individual appointed by the probate court to manage and distribute an estate where there is no will. In some states called a *personal representative.*

Estate tax. Short for the federal Unified Transfer Tax, a single tax rate applicable to taxable lifetime and testamentary gifts and bequests. Formerly known as Unified Gift and Estate Tax. Sometimes called gift tax if related to lifetime gifts.

Execute. The legal completion of a document putting it into effect. Requirements vary for different types of documents. You execute your will when you make it. Not what happened to Louis XIV.

Executor (eggs-**eck**-you-tor). Individual appointed in a will to manage and distribute an estate according to instructions in the will. Known as a *personal representative* in some states.

Fiduciary (fih-**doo**-she-airy). Person who is entrusted with the legal responsibility for property for the benefit of another and is held to a high standard of conduct.

Gift. This is not a big, scary word, but it should be mentioned that for estate planning purposes, a gift is made while one is alive. A bequest of personal property is made under a will.

Gift tax. See *Unified Transfer Tax.*

Grantor. The creator of a trust. The person granting property and power to the trustee usually for the benefit of others. Also called a settlor.

Gross estate. The value of all property of the deceased, before payment of debts, expenses, and taxes.

Guardian. One who looks after a minor or other person unable to take care of himself. Like a guardian angel, only real, with legal responsibility.

Heir. Person who inherits or is intended to inherit property either by will or under the laws of intestacy. As in heir today, gone tomorrow.

Holographic will. Hand-written by the individual making the will. Valid in only a few states.

Inheritance tax. In some states, the tax charged against the adjusted gross estate less federal unified gift and estate taxes.

Inter vivos (inter **vie**-vose). Between or among the living. An *inter vivos* trust—commonly known as a living trust—is established while the grantor is alive; the trust is generally revocable or subject to change. An *inter vivos* gift is a gift made while the donor is alive, as opposed to a testamentary gift or bequest made under a will.

Intestate (in-**test**-ate). One who dies without a will is said to die intestate. Not to be confused with a superhighway. The laws of "intestacy" refer to succession established by state law, and apply to distribution of an estate when the decedent (dead person) did not have a will.

Irrevocable. That which cannot be changed, revised, or revoked. As in certain forms of trust which, once established, are set in stone.

Issue. Descendants; legitimate, natural-born children or offspring.

Joint and mutual wills. Separate but identical wills containing reciprocal provisions to mutual benefit, usually of husband and wife. Far superior to a single, joint will, but still confusing and not necessarily advantageous.

Joint Tenancy. Form of property title indicating joint ownership in which co-owners share equal, undivided interest in property. Generally expressed with *right of survivorship*, in which the surviving owner is entitled to the entire property. In some states, Tenancy by Entirety is the identical title for married couples.

Joint will. A single will signed by two or more persons, usually husband and wife. Not advisable in most circumstances. Compare *joint and mutual wills*.

Lapse. Failure of a bequest under a will. A bequest could lapse if an heir dies before the will is executed, but in most states anti-lapse statutes now preserve the deceased heir's bequest for his or her heirs. Little dogs have no place in this lapse.

Legalese. Slang for tried and true legal terms used in documents and discussions of law. Sometimes nothing more than big, scary words used by lawyers and others to impress or intimidate others. More often used because it is legally precise.

Letters Testamentary. Formal legal document issued by a probate court authorizing and empowering the executor, personal representative, or estate administrator to conduct the business of an estate. Required to buy, sell, transfer property or stock, open a checking account for the estate, and conduct any and all business of an estate. Executors are advised to have a supply of certified copies at hand.

Life estate. An heir or beneficiary who receives benefit, but not ownership, of a property for life.

Living will. Not a will at all, but a legally valid document containing end-of-life instructions for medical care. Gives your permission to pull the plug if all is lost.

Marital deduction. Allows 100 percent of an estate to be passed by will or transferred in any way to a spouse free of federal Unified Transfer Tax.

Marital estate. Property acquired by husband and wife during their marriage.

Per capita. Per head or per person. Method of distribution of an estate to heirs or a class of heirs. The share of a *per capita* heir who dies before inheriting traditionally reverts to the estate. Most states now have *anti-lapse statutes* under which the share of the named heir does "lapse," but passes to the intended heir's descendents.

Per stirpes (per **stir**-peas). Method of distribution along the line of descent. If an heir dies before distribution of an estate, his share is divided among his issue.

Personal representative. See *executor* and *estate administrator.*

Pour-over. Method of distribution from an estate in which property "pours over" to fund a trust. Efficient means to transfer either miscellaneous property or an entire estate.

Power of appointment. A property right conveying a level of control over property which could imply ownership. May be *general* or *limited.*

Power of attorney. Not a powerful man named Perry Mason. Legal authorization of an agent (another person) to act on your behalf under prescribed circumstances. May be *durable,* lasting from the time it is signed, sealed, and delivered until it is revoked—most common among business associates who heavily rely on each other; *springing* to arise on situations specified in the document, such as incapacity; or *limited* for a very specific purpose, such as signing closing documents on sale of real estate in your absence.

Precatory letter. Personal letter expressing desired funeral and burial arrangements, instructions for distribution of small, personal items in an estate, and other matters of a private nature. The letter has no legal standing and does not become part of the public record like a will, but such instructions are generally followed to the extent possible.

Present interest. The right to immediate use and possession of property. Required for completion of a gift.

Pretermitted child. Rightful heir or descendent who is born after or otherwise omitted from the execution of a will. May be called an "afterborn" child.

Probate. The legal process of proving a will and settling an estate in the probate court.

Qualified retirement plan. Special savings accounts usually based on individual earnings and structured according to the tax code to qualify for preferential tax treatment regarding accumulation or distribution of account assets. In the most common plans—the 401(k) and individual retirement accounts (IRAs)—income tax on plan assets may be deferred until distribution takes place, generally about the time of retirement. Each type of plan has strict participation and distribution rules.

Remainder. The remains or remnant—what's left—of an estate or trust after provisions of a will or terms of a trust have been met.

Remaindermen. Not little toys in military uniform. The remainder beneficiaries who receive what's left, what remains in an estate or trust.

Residual estate. The residuals, what's left at the bottom, the catch-all for everything not specifically bequested or otherwise distributed under a will.

Residuary clause. Clause in a will determining how the residuary estate is to be distributed—possibly to one for further distribution to all, or divided according to specific instructions.

Revocable. Subject to recall, change, or withdrawal. A revocable trust, such as a living trust, can be changed or revoked, and rendered void at any time.

Rule Against Perpetuities. There is really no way to simplify this strict legal definition of the principle establishing that a property interest is not valid unless it vests (conveys ownership) no more than 21 years after the death of a person who is living at the time the interest is created. If your grandson Johnny is a newborn when you create a trust, the trust must end and be distributed to the remaindermen, no later than 21 years after Johnny dies. The rule is precise and effectively brings all property within Uncle Sam's reach every couple of generations.

Settlement. Pertaining to an estate, the management and completion of the affairs of an estate according to instruction of the will. Including payment of debts and taxes, and distributions.

Special-use valuation. Formula permitting qualified business, farm, and ranch real estate to be taxed at the value of present use rather than at the value of its potential use. Could be the difference between Green Acres and green fairways at a high-priced real estate development. Rules for qualification are strict, but it's a meaningful step toward protecting the future of family farms and businesses from tax sale.

Stepped-up basis. Taxable value of property in an estate either on date of death or the alternate valuation date, six months later, at the option of the executor.

Successor. Named or appointed individual who takes over, or succeeds to, the responsibilities or position of another. It is critical to name successors to every position created in estate planning documents—executor, custodian, guardian, trustee—and to name successor successors as well, if deemed appropriate.

Tenancy by the Entirety. In some states, property title equivalent to Joint Tenancy with Right of Survivorship for husband and wife. Both own equal, undivided shares of the property, and the surviving spouse takes all.

Tenancy-in-Common. Property title in which co-owners each own a separate and divisible share in property. Each may sell or bequeath his share without permission or knowledge of other co-owners.

Testament. As in "last will and testament." Same as a will. Instruction for disposition of personal property upon the death of the *testator*, the person making the will.

Testamentary. Pertaining to a will. A *testamentary trust* is created by will; a *testamentary disposition* is a distribution or transfer made according to the instruction of a will; *Letters Testamentary* authorize and empower the executor to perform her responsibilities as instructed in the will.

Trust. A property right held by one for the benefit of another or others. The document creating the trust is the *trust instrument* containing the *terms of the trust,* or instructions, for management and distribution of trust assets and income. The "trust term," on the other hand, is the established length of time the trust lasts before assets are distributed to, or "vest" in, the remaindermen.

Trustee. Person appointed and entrusted to manage the trust according to the terms of the trust. More than one trustee may be appointed.

Unified tax credit. See the new term *Applicable Credit Amount.*

Unified Transfer Tax. Formerly unified gift and estate tax. Single tax rate applied to combined value of nonexcluded and nonexempt lifetime gifts and estate transfers.

Uniform Gifts to Minors Act (UGMA). Allows gifts of certain property to be held in the name of a custodian for the benefit of a minor. Now replaced by the more flexible UTMA in most states.

Uniform Transfers to Minors Act (UTMA). Allows gifts of *any* kind of property to be held by a custodian for the benefit of a minor.

Index

A Trust, 116
AARP, 241
Accountant, 19, 37, 41, 83, 171, 222, 257
  on team, 41, 42
Adjusted gross estate, 231
Adopted children, 62, 63
Adult(s)
  guardianship for, 59–60
Affidavit(s), 50, 74, 246, 253
  of domicile, 252, 258
Age restrictions (retirement plans), 198, 201
Agent, 34, 74, 75, 122, 178
  choosing, 76–77
  sole proprietor/self-employed, 209–10
  unmarried partners, 175
AIDS, 80, 175
Alimony, 154
Alternate valuation date, 135

Alzheimer's disease, 160, 165, 169
Annual Exclusion, 66, 96, 132, 133, 156, 257
  and gifts, 128, 129
  and lifetime gifts, 123–25, 127
Annual gift exclusion, 103, 180
  and lifetime gifts, 126
  noncitizen spouse, 134
Annual inflation rider, 165
Annuity(ies), 72, 150
  charitable gift annuity, 108, 128–29, 173
Annuity payments, 114–15, 197
Antenuptial agreement
  see Pre-/postnuptial agreement
Antiques, 21
Applicable Credit Amount, 61–62, 86, 95
Applicable Exclusion Amount, 86, 95, 96,
  96*t*, 97, 98, 102, 112, 246
  lifetime gifts, 125

Appointments (will), 56–60
Appraisals, 69, 226, 255
  in estate settlement, 260
Appreciation, 227, 228
Arizona, 141
Artworks, 21
Asset inventory
  in estate settlement, 255
  see also Inventory
Asset management, 187
  in time of need, 173–74
Assets
  gathering information about, 19, 20–27
  for grantor-retained trust, 112–13
  hiding, 162–63
  intangible, 225, 226
  list of, 21–24, 81–82, 83, 138
  nonprobate, 252
  protecting from creditors, 118, 143–46
  in qualifying for Medicaid, 161–63
  registered in name of trust, 89
  removing from estate, 227–28, 251
  of singles, 171
Attorney-in-fact, 74
Augmented estate, 62

B Trust, 116
Baby boomers, 4, 7–8, 47, 159
  parents of, 28
Bank account
  estate, 254
  joint, 151
  joint tenancy, 157
  see also Checking account
Banks, 37
  as trustee, 112
Beneficiaries, 56, 61, 67, 83, 147, 246
  defined, 41
  and division of property, 260
  identification and location of, 244
  ILIT, 105–6
  predeceasing, 64–65
  reconsidering, 150
  of trust, 88, 89
  unmarried partner as, 175, 177
Beneficiary designations, 13, 72
  retirement plans, 191, 197, 201–4
Bequests, 25, 65–66, 83, 121–22, 127, 260
  disclaimed, 262
  loan(s) as, 158
Bond(s), posting, 59
Book value, 225
Brokaw, Tom, 28
Business(es), 105

continuing, 207–8, 222, 223
  durable power of attorney, 75
  in estate, 52
  transfer or sale of, 207, 217–24
  see also Closely held businesses
Business interests, 22
Business property
  joint tenancy, 157
Buy-sell agreement, 207, 208, 213, 215, 217–
  19, 224, 225, 235
  disability in, 221
  options in, 219–20
Bypass trust, 116
  see also Credit shelter trust

Calculation of withdrawal period, 199
California, 141
Capital gains
  lifetime gifts and, 119
Capital gains liability, 219
Capital gains tax, 126, 135, 200, 201, 222
Capitalization, 224, 225
  of earnings, 226
Certified Financial Planners (CFPs), 38, 42
Change of circumstances, 34
  and codicil, 36
  and review of documents, 83
Charitable gift annuity, 108, 128–29, 173
Charitable gifts, 127–29
Charitable remainder annuity trust (CRAT),
  108
Charitable lead trust (CLT), 109–11
Charitable remainder trust (CRT), 105, 108,
  173
Charitable remainder unitrust (CRUT), 108
Charitable trusts, 107–11, 117, 203
  childless couples, 187
  for singles, 173
Charity
  as beneficiary of retirement plans, 204
Checking account, 82
  estate, 254
  joint, 138, 146, 147
  ownership and access to, 141–42
  properly titled, 146, 147
ChFP (Chartered Financial Planner), 38
Child support, 154
Childless couples, 186–88
Children
  of different marriages, 60, 100, 117, 154, 157
  distributions for, 62–64
  gifts to, 129
  illegitimate, 63
  as joint tenants, 139

Index

as limited partners, 144, 146
protection for: unmarried parents, 181–85
Social Security benefits, 160
see also Minor children
Children, grown
and second marriage, 152–53
Class of heirs, 63, 64, 68
and disinheritance, 71
and equal distribution, 69
Clerk of Court, 249, 253, 262
Closely held businesses, 206–33
defined, 231
incorporation, 215–17
types of, 208–17
CLU (certified life underwriter), 38
Codicil, 25, 36, 56, 83, 172
Community property, 51, 141–42
Community property laws, 22, 141–42, 150
Community property states, 141, 157
Competence, 71
Conservator(s), 59
Conservatorship, 60, 71, 168, 169
Contemplation-of-death rule, 104–5, 122
Contracts, 143–44
married couples, 150, 152
sole proprietor/self-employed, 210–11
unmarried partners, 179
Contract to make a will, 61
Control
in family business, 213, 214
Co-owners
contracts among, 144
Co-ownership, 138, 139
Corporations, 215–17
Corpus, 89
Cost basis, 126, 135, 222
Cost-of-living increases, 26
Co-trustees, 89
Court(s)
and guardianship, 59, 131
in transfer/sale of business, 207
see also Probate court
Credit equivalent, 95
Credit shelter trusts, 96–98, 116, 125, 172
cost of, 117
irrevocable, 187
Creditors, 107, 139, 142, 148, 220, 260
claims of, 255
protecting assets from, 118, 143–46
protection from, 168, 213
Cremation, 237
Cross-purchase, 219–20
Crummey power, 103, 156

Custodial account, 129, 130, 131–32, 183
retirement plans, 191
Custodian(s), 45, 65, 130, 150, 204
parent as, 183
Custodianship, 60, 130–32, 180
children of unmarried parents, 182, 183
tax effects of, 131–32
Custody battles, 182

Daily benefit amount, 165
Date of death, 135
Death, 235–36
transfers triggered by, 252
Death certificate, 147, 252, 253, 254, 258
Death notices, 254–55
Death tax, 85
Deathbed transfers, 105, 122
Deceased (decedent), 50
Declaration of Domicile, 51
Deductions
in estate settlement, 257–58
Deed(s), 68
Deferred compensation plan, 197
Defined benefit plans, 192, 195–96
Defined contribution plans, 192–93
Delivery of gift, 120
Dementia, 165
Descendancy, 244
Descendants, 62–63, 65, 262
transfers to, 115
Disability/disabled, 12, 158–67, 168, 169
of business partner(s), 221
and power of attorney, 173–74
and trusts, 68, 91
Disability insurance, 209, 221
Disclaimer, 262
Disinheritance, 33, 62, 70–71
Disney, Walt, 5
Distribution options
retirement plans, 191, 197
Distributions, 147
assets, 244
conditional, 68–69
in estate settlement, 260
method of, 13
retirement plans, 191, 192, 193, 194, 197–204
trusts, 22, 90, 91, 147, 154, 260
types of, 65–69
unequal, 33–34, 133
outside will, 72–73
under will, 62–70
Divorce, 13, 83, 150–58
of heir(s), 158
to qualify for Medicaid, 162

Index

Divorce settlements, retirement plans in, 157–58

Documents, 5, 8, 42, 188
  certified, 253–54
  essential, 73–82
  locating, 12, 24, 81–82, 87
  notes on location of, 240
  originals, 253–54
  review of, 12, 36, 151
  storage of, 45, 87
  validity of, 45–46

Domicile, 46, 51, 243
  affidavit of, 252, 258

Donee, 126, 127, 135

Donor, 123, 125–26, 128–29, 135

Donor's intention (in gift), 120

Durable power of attorney, 12, 74–75, 76, 77, 209
  in case of disability or incapacity, 168
  unmarried partners, 178

Dynasty trust, 111, 144

Educational gifts, 127–29

Elderly (the), 158–67
  senile, 57

Elect against the will, 62

Elimination period, 165

Emergency funds, 82, 146–48

Employee benefit packages, 26

Employee Stock Ownership Program (ESOP), 193

Entitlements, 137–42

Entity purchase, 220

Equal distribution, 68, 69–70, 72, 83, 133

Escheat, 244

Estate
  closing, 54, 244
  settling, 252–62

Estate administration, 13, 247, 264
  completed, 54
  expenses as deductions, 257–58
  key persons in, 45

Estate administrator, 186, 244

Estate checking account, 254

Estate plan, 12, 18, 45–46, 138, 167, 235, 264
  attention to detail, 148
  change in marital status and review of, 150–51
  lifetime gifts in, 119
  minimizing effect of estate taxes, 5
  necessity of, 1–2, 3, 8
  periodic review and update, 45, 83–84, 150–51

retirement planning and money management in, 158–59
  revision of, 151
  for singles, 170, 174
  tailor-made, 188
  unattended details and, 118–19
  women and, 166

Estate planning, 3, 6–7, 9–14, 149, 246, 262
  essentials, 44–87
  getting started, 15–43
  ongoing, 247–48
  surviving spouse, 98
  unmarried partners, 174–75

Estate planning devices, 143, 188

Estate tax rate, 229

Estate taxes, 12, 61–62, 72, 85, 87, 98, 246, 257, 258
  closely held businesses, 214, 221, 230–31
  due date, 147, 250
  escaping, 143, 172, 187, 221
  in estate settlement, 257
  life insurance proceeds, 103
  lifetime gifts and, 119–20
  and loss of farms and ranches, 229–30
  minimizing effect of, 5, 17
  paid through ILIT, 106
  probate costs deductible from, 249
  QTIP and, 154
  retirement plans and, 200
  trusts and, 91, 111, 144, 180

Estate transfers, 85–86
  stepped-up basis, 126

Executor, 34, 45, 52–55, 69, 135, 150, 172, 232, 235, 238
  appointment of, 244
  bank as, 37
  and business(es), 207, 210
  challenged, 245
  changing, 83
  choosing, 87
  and distributions, 69, 70
  fees, 54, 249, 250
  listing name of, 240
  and probate, 246, 247, 248–49, 250
  in settling estate, 254, 255–56, 257, 258, 260, 262
  unmarried partners, 175

Expenses, 26

Ex-spouses
  Social Security benefits, 160

Fair market value
  business property, 222, 224
  lifetime gifts, 125–26, 135

Index

Family(ies), 3, 9, 35–36, 43, 71, 158
  debilitating disease and, 169
  and estate planning, 16–18
  and family business, 207, 211
  jealousies and tensions, 7
  protecting, 153
Family business, 12, 22, 211–13, 233, 255
  loss of, 229–30
  qualified family business deduction, 232
Family discussion, 13, 27–36, 252, 262
  funeral and burial plans, 238, 240
  unmarried partners, 175–81
Family estate
  protecting, 154–58
Family home, 155–56
  ownership of, 157
Family Limited Liability Corporation, 214–
  15
Family limited liability partnership, 214
Family limited partnership (FLP), 144–46,
  213–14, 228
Family rivalries
  buy-sell agreement preempts, 218
Family trust, 116
Farms and ranches, 22, 105, 229–30, 231
Favoritism, 71
Fee Simple, 137, 138
Fiduciary duty, 209
  of custodian, 130
  of executor, 53, 255
  in power of attorney, 76
Final (will), 52
Final statement (estate settlement), 262
Financial advisor, 36
Financial institution
  as trustee, 112, 132
Financial planners, 37
Financial investments, listing, 22
First-to-die clause, 186
First-to-die policy, 61, 219–20
Foreign trusts, 144
401(k), 13, 192, 193, 198, 200
  conversion to Roth IRA, 195
403(b), 193
Fraud, 143
Freezing techniques, 227–28
Full court supervision, 245, 247
Funeral and burial arrangements, 13, 25,
  234, 235–42
  instructions regarding, 70, 264
  precatory letter regarding, 82
Funeral and burial expenses, 52
  paying for, 255–56
Funeral plans, prepaid, 240, 241

Future gift, 112
Future interests, 22–23, 103, 112, 121

General power of appointment, 122, 142
Generation-skipping trusts, 111–12, 116, 144
Gift loans, 133, 158
Gift tax, 85, 87, 112, 122, 123, 124, 132, 133
Gift tax liability, 92, 142, 173, 214
Gift tax returns, 96, 124, 126, 257
Gifts, 12, 13, 24, 96, 119–37, 141
  of business, 213–14, 219, 228, 231
  completion of, 120
  and estate tax, 257
  incomplete, 121–22, 129, 132
  to minors, 129, 183
  to noncitizen spouses, 134
  nonresidents, 133
  "power" to use, 103–4
  restricted, 133–35
  tax benefits of, 118
  tax-free, 66–67, 124
  used to pay life insurance premiums, 156–
    57
  see also Lifetime gifts
Gifts transfers, 85–86
Giving, pleasure of, 119, 127
Government programs for elderly, 160–61
Grandchildren, 111
Grandparents, 59, 128, 182
Grantor, 88, 91, 108, 109
Grantor-retained income trusts (GRITs), 115
Grantor-retained interest trust, 228
Grantor-retained trusts, 112–16
GRAT (grantor-retained annuity trust), 113–
  15, 116, 228
Greatest Generation (Brokaw), 28
Grief/grieving, 262–63
GRUT (grantor-retained unitrust), 113–15,
  116, 228
Guardian(s), 34, 45, 54, 87, 105, 150
  changing, 83
  choosing, 57–58
Guardianships, 56–59, 131, 180
  for adult(s), 59–60
  children of unmarried parents, 182
  for incompetent person, 169

Health care
  costs, 26
  for parents, 30
  for singles, 171
Health care directive/proxy, 73, 77, 87
Health care documents
  unmarried partners, 80–81

Index

Health care power of attorney, 12, 41, 77, 80
  childless couples, 188
  unmarried partners, 178
  singles, 170, 174
Health insurance, 159, 160, 165, 171, 209
Heirlooms, 21, 156
Heirs
  of childless couples, 186, 187
  divorce, 158
  identification and location of, 244
  see also Class of heirs
Holographic will, 25, 49
House
  parents, 30, 33
  QPRT and, 115–16

"I Love You" wills, 61
Idaho, 141
Illegitimate children, 63
Interrorem clause, 68–69
Incapacity
  and power of attorney, 174, 178
Income distribution rules
  grantor-retained trusts, 114
Income in respect of a decedent, 200
Income tax, 5, 103
  estate, 249, 257
  lifetime gifts and, 119–20
  retirement plans and, 197, 200
Income tax bracket, 131
Income tax deduction
  with charitable trusts, 109, 110
Income tax liability
  retirement plans, 158, 198, 204
  Roth IRA, 195
Incompetence, 56–57, 167–69
  and guardianship, 59–60
  and power of attorney, 173–74
  trust in, 68
Incorporation, 215–17
Independent contractors, 208–9
Inheritance, 141, 154
  chain of, 154
  counting on, 153
Installment sale
  closely held business, 222–23, 228
Instructions, 70–71, 87
  regarding equal distribution, 69
  see also Letter(s) of instruction
Insurance, 22, 26, 27
  family-owned business, 211
  for sole proprietor/self-employed, 209
  see also under specific type
Insurance agent, 19, 27, 37–38, 240

Insurance plan, 12
Intangibles, 225, 226
Intentions
  in living will, 77
  making clear, 158, 177, 178, 252
  in will, 186
Inter vivos trust
  see Living trust
Internet, 27, 36, 37
Intestacy, 48–49, 50, 186, 247
  laws of, 61, 63, 65, 139, 172, 177, 178,
   244, 245
Inventory, 25, 43, 151, 240, 246
  unmarried partners, 179
Inventory worksheet, 21–24, 23*t*, 81, 138
Investment advisor, 19, 41–42, 133, 171
Investment advisory firms, 37
IRAs, 13, 92, 193–94, 197, 198, 203–4
  spousal rollover, 201
Irrevocable credit shelter trust, 187
Irrevocable family trust, 154
Irrevocable life insurance trusts (ILIT), 103–
  7, 108, 144
  for children of unmarried parents, 185
  unmarried partners, 180
Irrevocable trusts, 90–94, 102, 144, 162, 180
  as beneficiary: retirement plans, 203
  for benefit of minors, 132
  charitable trusts, 107
  for children of unmarried parents, 183–85
  for singles, 172–73
IRS, 90, 101, 127, 219, 226
Issue, 62

Joint ownership
  unmarried partners, 174
Joint tenancy, 22, 72, 137, 235
Joint Tenancy with Right of Survivorship,
  55, 138–39, 157
  unmarried partners, 178
Joint tenant(s), 157
  unmarried partners, 178–79
Joint wills, 61–62, 186

Keogh Plans, 193

Lawyer(s), 8, 18–19, 36, 37, 40, 41, 51, 142,
  169
  divorce, 151
  estate planning, 22, 72–73, 133, 151, 171,
   247
  in estate settlement, 257, 258
  executor and, 53, 54
  and family, 34

help from, 60
with incorporation, 217
name, phone number, address, 240
and powers of attorney, 81
and pre-/postnuptial agreement, 152
and probate, 247–48, 249, 250
and property titles, 157
and team, 42
trusts and estates, 93
Legal age, 49
Legal fees, 5
probate, 249
Legally incompetent adult
guardianship for, 56–57, 59–60
Letter(s) of instruction
funeral and burial arrangements, 235, 236,
238, 239–41
transfer of title, 260
Letters Testamentary, 54, 244, 247, 253, 254,
258
Liabilities, 22–24
in buy-sell agreement(s), 220
of executor, 53, 250, 255
Life estate, 68, 155–56
Life expectancy, 159, 160
Life expectancy tables, 198–99
Life insurance, 36, 72, 150, 156–57
in buy-sell agreements, 219–20, 221
in family-owned business, 211
for sole proprietor/self-employed, 209
as tool for wealth replacement, 103
viatical settlement, 166
Life insurance policy, 107
ownership of, 103, 105, 156
transferring, 104–5, 117, 122
Life insurance proceeds, 144, 146
Life insurance trust, 117, 157
Lifestyle changes
and review of documents, 83
Lifetime gifts, 86, 119, 126–27, 135, 148,
158, 257
tax advantages of, 123–25
valuation of, 125–27
Limited Liability Corporation (LLC), 207,
214–15
Limited power of attorney, 76, 77
unmarried partners, 178
Limited/special power of appointment, 142–
43
Living trust, 36, 67, 90, 91, 144, 150, 152,
246
business held in, 220
for closely held businesses, 208
defined, 89

family-owned business, 211
for protection of incompetent person, 168
for singles, 172
unmarried partners, 180
Living will, 12, 36, 45, 73, 77–79, 81, 87
childless couples, 188
singles, 170, 174
unmarried partners, 178
Loan
forgiven as bequest, 133, 158
Long-term care, 27, 160
Long-term care insurance, 163–67, 170, 171,
209
Long-term needs, 26–27, 43, 73, 171, 251
Loss, 2
dealing with, 262–63, 264
Louisiana, 141
Lump-sum payment, 198, 200, 201, 203

Mandatory distribution (retirement plans),
198, 201
Marital deduction trust, 98–100, 116, 187
Marital estate, 117, 187
statutory share of, 62, 141, 157
Marital trusts, 98–102
Marriage(s), 83
multiple, 158
second, 28, 152–53
see also Remarriage
Married couples
contracts, 150, 152
GRATs/GRUTs, 114
laws favor, 35, 95
making wills, 60–62
second-to-die life insurance policies, 105
see also Unlimited Marital Deduction
Means test, 161, 162
Medicaid, 171
qualifying for, 161–63
Medical care costs, 159
Medical gifts, 127–29
Medical incapacitation
and power of attorney, 75–76
Medicare, 160, 161, 163, 165, 171
Medigap, 160, 161, 165
Mental illness, 57, 169
guardianship with, 60
Method of valuation, 210–11, 217, 224, 225–
27
Method of withdrawal, 198, 199, 204
Minor children, 17, 47, 56–59, 87
as beneficiaries: retirement plans, 204
gifts to, 129
guardian for, 57–58

protection of: unmarried partners, 180
protected by ILIT, 105
trusts for benefit of, 105, 132
Money management, 158
Money purchase plan, 198
Multiple beneficiaries
retirement plans, 203–4
Mutual wills, 61–62

National Charities Information Bureau, 111
Net distributable income, 108
Net unrealized appreciation (NUA), 200–1
Nevada, 141
New Mexico, 141
NIM-CRUT, 108
Non compos mentis, 122
Non-recalc, 199
Nonqualified retirement plans, 197
Nonresidents' gifts, 133
Nonspouse beneficiaries
retirement plans, 203–4
Nursing homes, 160, 163

Obituaries, 254–55
Order of descendancy, 63
Organ donor, 70
Outsiders, 207, 211
Ownership, 137, 142
of life insurance policies, 219
succession of, 155

"Palimony" suits, 181
Parents, 4, 8
as custodians, 131, 183
discussions with, 27–28, 30–33
and long-term care, 166–67
personal loans to children, 69–70, 133
as trustees, 132, 184
unmarried, 181–85
Partial gifts, 127, 145
Participant (retirement plan), 190, 191
Partners, 35
Partnership, 207, 213
Partnership agreements, 225
Paying debts, 255–56
Payment-on-death, 141–42, 146
Penalties
distributions: retirement plans, 198
Pension plan, 195
Per capita distribution, 65
Per stirpes distribution, 65
Personal and household items, 24–25
value of, 255
Personal guardian, 57, 169

Personal investment advisor, 41–42
Personal representative, 52
see also Executor
Pets, 47
Planned giving, 127
Pooled Income Trusts (PITs), 108, 129
Possession of gift, 120
Pour-over will, 67
Power of appointment, 99, 100, 122, 142–43
Power of appointment trust, 99, 116
Powers of attorney, 12, 36, 45, 73, 74–77, 81, 87, 122, 150
childless couples, 187
defined, 74
singles, 170, 173–74
sole proprietor/self-employed, 209–10
unmarried partners, 178
Precatory letter, 24–25, 66, 67, 70, 82, 235, 239–41, 264
Premiums
long-term care insurance, 165–66
Pre-/postnuptial agreement, 61, 101, 143, 151–52, 153, 179
prevails over state law, 157
Present interest
gift is, 120
Pretermitted child, 63
Primary beneficiaries (income beneficiaries), 89
Privacy, 98, 207, 252
Private annuity
closely held business, 221–22, 228
restrictions on, 222
Probate, 13, 67, 235, 243–52, 264
avoiding, 102, 218, 235, 251, 252
avoiding: closely held business, 207, 208, 209, 221
bypassing, 72, 111, 138, 142, 147, 172, 187
costs, 98, 249–50, 251
double, 61
how it works, 243–44
life insurance proceeds avoid, 103
responsibility for, 247–49
trusts and, 90, 91
types of, 245–47
will entered into, 253
Probate court, 50, 51, 54, 62, 186, 243, 246, 248, 255
Professional help, 13, 22, 27, 43, 46, 223, 228, 257
calling, 39–41
finding, 36–41
team, 41–42
Profit-sharing plan, 192–93

Index

Property
  distribution of, 63–64
  how titled, 55
  out-of-state, 25, 51, 91
  selling to children for annuity payments,
    114–15
  value and location of, 20
Property division
  in divorce, 150, 151
  in estate settlement, 260
  predetermined, 152
Property guardian, 57, 59, 60, 65, 131, 142,
  169, 182
Property guardianship, 168
Property management
  in estate settlement, 255
  with trust, 184
Property rights, 118, 141–42
  unmarried partners, 175
Property titles, 13, 20, 22, 51, 118, 137–39,
  148, 157
  unmarried partners, 178–79
Protective trust, 116, 168
Public record, 25, 98, 207, 251–52

QPRT (qualified personal residence trust),
  115–16, 121
QTIP (Qualified Terminable Interest
  Property), 154–55
QTIP (Qualified Terminable Interest
  Property) trust, 100–1, 114, 116, 187,
  203
Qualified Domestic Relation Order (QDRO),
  157–58
Qualified domestic trust (QDOT), 102
Qualified family business deduction, 232–33
Qualified retirement plans, 13, 189–205
  elements of, 190–91
Qualify(ing)
  for long-term care insurance, 165
  for Medicaid, 161–63

Real estate, 255
  joint tenancy, 157
  location, 21–22
  transfer of title, 258
Recalc, 199
Remainder, 68
Remainder beneficiaries
  see Remaindermen
Remaindermen, 68, 89, 97, 100, 154, 172,
  173, 187, 203, 262
  trusts, 113, 114
Remarriage, 13, 17, 83, 150–58, 172

Residual estate, 246, 260
Residuary estate, 25, 67
Responsibility
  of executor, 53, 250, 255
  of guardian, 59
  with power of attorney, 74
  see also Fiduciary duty
Restricted gifts, 133–35
Retained interest, 112
Retained life interest, 121
Retirement, 27
Retirement planning, 158–59
Retirement plans, 22, 26, 72, 150, 157–58
  parents, 30
  types of, 192–97
  see also Qualified retirement plans
Revocable living trust
  cost of, 117
Revocable transfer, 122
Revocable trusts, 90–94
  defined, 89
Right of Survivorship, 72, 138, 139, 142,
  146, 178
Right-to-die laws, 78
Rockefeller, John D., Sr., 5
Roth IRA, 194–95
Rule against perpetuities, 91

Safe deposit boxes, 82, 240
Same-sex couples, 80, 138, 175, 180
Savings Incentive Match Plan for Employees
  (SIMPLE), 193
Second marriages, 28
  and grown children, 152–53
Second-to-die life insurance policies, 105
Securities account, 141, 148
Self-employment, 22, 207, 208–11
Signed voluntarily (will), 50
SIMPLE 401(k), 193
Simplified Employee Pension (SEP), 193
Simultaneous death clauses, 61
Single parents, 13, 181–85
Singles, 13, 170–74
Small business
  asset protection, 144
Small estates, 245, 246
Small family corporation, 207
Social Security, 160–61, 171, 189
Social Security Administration
  Department of Health and Human
    Services, 161
Sole proprietorship, 207, 208–11
Sound mind, 49
  proof of, 71

Index

Special situations, 149–88
Spendthrift trust, 117, 168
Spousal rollover IRA, 201
Spousal trust, 116
Spouse(s), 35
    as beneficiary: retirement plans, 201
    of different marriages, 154
    noncitizen, 102, 134
    see also Surviving spouse
Springing power of attorney, 12, 75–76, 77, 209
    unmarried partners, 178
Sprinkling trust, 117, 168
Standard forms, 40–41
State inheritance tax, 85
State laws, 25, 45–46
    regarding executors, 55
    intestacy, 48–49, 139
    property laws, 130
    statutory share of estate, 157
State taxes, 5
Statutory forms, 78
Statutory spousal shares, 62, 141, 157
Statutory wills, 55–56
Stepchildren, 28, 62, 157
Stepfamilies, 158
Stepped-up basis, 126, 135
Step-up at death, 135
Stock ownership
    family-owned business, 211–13
Stock redemption, 219, 220
Stockbrokers, 37, 41
Stocks and bonds
    transfer of title, 258–59
Straight capitalization, 225
Successor(s), 74, 81, 83
Successor beneficiary, 72, 201
Successor custodian, 60, 130, 131, 183
Successor executor, 54
Successor guardian, 59
Successor trustees, 89, 91, 99, 112, 168, 172, 187, 208
Summary administration, 246
Support trusts, 168
Surety bond, 55
Surviving spouse, 48, 95
    and credit shelter trust, 97
    death of, 62, 98, 125, 154, 186, 187, 203
    joint income tax return, 257
    marital deduction trust, 116
    marital trusts, 98–99
    and retirement plans, 201
    statutory share, 141, 157

in Tenancy-by-Entirety, 139
trusts, 101, 102

Tax advantages
    of lifetime gifts, 123–25
Tax basis
    lifetime gift, 135
Tax deduction, charitable, 111
Tax deferral, 257
    closely held businesses, 230–33
Tax effects
    of custodianship, 131–32
    of trusts, 92–93
Tax implications
    of incorporation, 215, 216–17
    of private annuity: closely held businesses, 222
    of stock redemption, 220
    type of beneficiary: retirement plans, 191, 198, 200–1, 204
Tax loopholes, 86, 87, 94–96
Tax penalty
    retirement plans, 158
Tax rate
    unified tax, 85
Taxes, 27, 34–35
Temporary power of attorney, 209
Tenancy-by-Entirety, 139
Tenancy-in-Common, 137, 139
Tenants-in-Common 139
    unmarried partners, 178
Ten-year forward averaging, 200
Testament, 52
Testamentary gift, 121–22, 135
Testamentary trusts, 68, 260
    defined, 89
Texas, 141
Title, 13, 20, 22
    changed in gift delivery, 120
    custodial property, 130
    importance of, 55
    transferring, 137–38, 258–59
Totten Trust, 142
Transfer(s)
    automatic, 55
    of business, 207, 217–24
    deathbed, 105, 122
    to descendants, 115
    estate, 85–86, 126
    gifts, 85–86
    title, 137–38, 258–59
    triggered by death, 252
Trust fund babies, 89, 184
Trust document, 97

Index

Trust instrument, 89
Trust term, 91
Trustee, 34, 54, 67, 68, 88, 91, 99, 150, 168, 173, 187
  bank as, 37
  business owner as, 208
  changing, 83
  charitable trusts, 107, 108, 111
  choosing, 56–57, 97
  family trust, 154
  generation-skipping trusts, 112
  ILIT, 103, 105
  irrevocable trust, 132
  living trust, 172
  parent as, 184
  unmarried partners, 175
Trust(s), 12, 22, 56, 67, 68, 72, 86, 88–117, 142, 147, 235
  in asset protection, 144
  basics regarding, 88–94
  as beneficiary: retirement plans, 203
  for benefit of minors, 132
  childless couples, 187
  cost of, 91, 117
  distributions, 22, 90, 91, 147, 154, 260
  family-owned business, 211
  life insurance, 220
  names of, 116–17
  in protecting family estate, 154–55
  in protection of children of unmarried parents, 182, 183–85
  protective, 168
  retirement plans, 191
  strings attached to, 185
  tax effects of, 92–93
  types of, 89
  unmarried partners, 180

Undue influence, 7
Unified Gift and Estate Tax
  see Unified Transfer Tax
Unified tax credit, 61, 67, 86, 95–96, 102, 116, 128, 129, 133, 187, 246
  combined with qualified family business deduction, 232
  and lifetime gifts, 127
  preserving for two generations, 186
  for singles, 172
Unified Transfer Tax, 67, 85–86, 85t, 86, 94, 95
  lifetime gifts and estate transfers, 124–25
Uniform Transfer Tax
  one-time credit against, 257

Uniform Gifts to Minors Act (UGMA), 130
Uniform Probate Code, 46, 255
Uniform Transfers to Minors Act (UTMA), 130
Uninsurable (the), 221
Unlimited Marital Deduction, 61, 67, 86, 114, 152, 154, 186, 187, 203
  and marital trusts, 95, 98, 101, 102
  and lifetime gifts and estate transfers, 125
  not available to noncitizen spouses, 134
  not available to singles, 172
Unmarried parents, 181–85
Unmarried partners, 13, 28, 35, 76, 80–81, 138, 174–88
  contracts between, 143
  legal rights, 175
Unsupervised administration, 245–46
U.S. Constitution, 137

Valuation, 217, 219, 224–28
  farms and ranches, 229–30
  lifetime gifts, 125–27
  of property in estate settlement, 257
  special-use, 229–30, 231
Value, freezing, 227–28
Viatical Association of America, 166
Viatical settlement, 166

Washington, 141
Widows/widowers, 13, 65, 170–74
  Social Security benefits, 160
  trusts for, 173
  will, 172
Will(s), 5, 12, 25, 36, 45, 46–73, 150, 252
  bequests, 65–67
  challenge to, 3, 34, 62, 71, 177, 178, 245
  changing, 56
  childless couples, 186–87
  contested, 47, 63
  contract to make, 151
  copies, of, 240
  disinheritance in, 70–71
  distributions outside, 72–73
  distributions under, 62–70
  dying without, 48–49
  entering into probate, 244, 248
  importance of, 47
  instructions for executor in, 52
  instructions for paying funeral and burial expenses, 255–56
  instructions regarding funeral arrangements in, 235
  "international," 46
  invalid, 245

Index

joint, 61–62, 186
in lawyer's office, 40
life estate under, 155
married couples, 60–62
necessity of, 87
new, 83–84, 87
note of location of, 240
old, 52
pour-over, 67
and property titles, 138, 139
residuary clause, 25
singles, 170, 171–72
statements and instructions in, 55

superseded by buy-sell agreement, 208, 218
unmarried partners, 177–78, 180, 182
validation or "proving" of, 243
validity of, 46, 49–55
Withdrawal options
retirement plans 191, 198, 199, 204
Witnessed (will), 50
Witnesses
living will, 78
Women
and estate plan, 166
Written (will), 49